Pre-publication reader comments

"Remarkable." —K. C., Michigan;

"A compelling case; refreshing God-centered Gospel."
—G. C., Michigan;

"A great service to the Body of Christ and to unbelievers."
—G. D., Alabama;

"A personal blessing ... leading me to confession and adoration at the infinite value of the Name. Thank you for writing this." —Michigan.

"What a beautiful presentation of "the Story" from Genesis to Revelation highlighting the importance of God's name throughout. ... So much to take in and meditate upon. ... A masterful and theological treatise of God, a jealous God in all His glory." —M. B., Michigan

RESTORING the GLORY of the NAME

THE STORY'S ULTIMATE GOOD NEWS

Fredric A. Carlson

JohnTenTen Press
GRAND RAPIDS, MI USA

Restoring the Glory of the Name, the Story's Ultimate Good News

COPYRIGHT © 2019 BY FREDRIC A. CARLSON

ALL RIGHTS RESERVED.

All Scripture quotations, unless otherwise indicated, are taken from the Holy Bible, New International Version®, NIV®. Copyright © 1973, 1978, 1984, 2011 by Biblica, Inc.™ Used by permission of Zondervan. All rights reserved worldwide. www.zondervan.com. The "NIV" and "New International Version" are trademarks registered in the United States Patent and Trademark Office by Biblica, Inc.™

Scripture quotations marked *The Message* are quoted from *The Message*, Copyright 1993, 1994, 1995, 1996, 2000, 2001, 2002. Used by permission of NavPress Publishing Group.

Scripture quotations marked ESV are quoted from The ESV˚ Bible (The Holy Bible, English Standard Version˚), copyright © 2001 by Crossway, a publishing ministry of Good New Publishers. Used by permission. All rights reserved.

Scripture quotations marked NKJV are quoted from New King James Bible, copyright © 1979, 1980, 1982 by Thomas Nelson, Inc. Used by permission. All rights reserved.

PUBLISHED BY JOHNTENTEN PRESS, GRAND RAPIDS, MICHIGAN, USA.
www.JohnTenTenPress.com

ISBN: 978-1-7347238-0-9

ADULT, RELIGION, SPIRITUALITY, APPLIED BIBLE EXPOSITION

COVER PAINTING: Robert Zund, "Way To Emmaus"—1877

COVER DESIGN AND PRODUCTION: Jeff Carlson

INTERIOR DESIGN AND PRODUCTION: Catherine Williams, Chapter One Book Production, UK

Printed in the United States of America

Contents

INTRODUCTION	1
SECTION 1. FOUNDATIONS	
Prelude: How a name rescued me	11
Chapter 1. Why names matter	15
Chapter 2. The meaning of God's Name	21
Chapter 3. The glory of God's Name	35
Chapter 4. The intersection of name and glory	37
Chapter 5. Restoration	39
Chapter 6. The intersection of name, glory, and restoration	58
SECTION 2. THE STORY OF THE NAME	
Stage 1. The Name established in creation	81
Chapter 1. The Creator's name is Elohim	83
Chapter 2. The glory of the image	98
Chapter 3. I Am, Yahweh Elohim	106
Stage 2. The Name soiled in the fall	109
Chapter 4. The name distrusted	111
Stage 3. The Name enlarged in history	123
Chapter 5. The conflict for name continues	125

Chapter 6. God introduces more of his names	135
Chapter 7. An even higher view of I Am, Yahweh	138
Chapter 8. God rejected as wise guide	147
Chapter 9. God rejected as king	150
Chapter 10. The poetry exalts the Name	158
Chapter 11. The prophets plead for the Name	162
Chapter 12. Israel forfeits God's land	169
Chapter 13. Then heaven went silent	174
Stage 4. The Name restored in Christ and his people	**179**
Chapter 14. The promised Restorer arrives as the King	181
Chapter 15. The introducer prepared	187
Chapter 16. Jesus assumes royal kingship	190
Chapter 17. The King's royal conduct	198
Chapter 18. The King's royal teaching	205
Chapter 19. The new birth restores the God-exalting image	210
Chapter 20. Christ reunites mankind with God in himself	224
Chapter 21. The faith factor, and its Source	247
Chapter 22. Union with Christ develops the image	259
Chapter 23. The King's ultimate credentials	273
Chapter 24. Jesus' ambassadors build the church of his Name	291
Chapter 25. Jesus' messengers build on the Name	294
Stage 5. The restored Name exalted eternally	**301**
SECTION 3. EPILOGUE, ACKNOWLEDGMENTS, END NOTES	**307**
Epilogue	**309**
Acknowledgments	**313**
End Notes	**315**

Introduction

Purpose and objective

This book's objective is to help restore the focus of our lives and ministries onto what I have come to realize is the Bible's central emphasis and primary purpose, the glory of God's Name. I believe that in this age the Holy Spirit is calling every member of Christ's Church to see our primary calling, the scope and heart of the Good News we proclaim, the central purpose and meaning of our living, and our true and ultimate hope, to be the vindication, restoration, and exaltation of God's Name. Everything depends on it.

My purpose in writing this is to do my part in fulfilling God's purpose for giving humanity his Story. He stated that purpose in 2 Timothy 3:15–16 and 2 Peter 1:21. Knowing that he created mankind with the deep need to know and love him, God told his Story to make himself known to those who need so desperately to know him. The Story restores mankind's knowledge of God's Name in order to restore them to their designed place and character in that Story, as the creatures who consciously give God glory.

That Story is the Good News. Numerous parts of the Story include various kinds of good news, and parts, pieces, elements, and aspects of *the* Good News. I fear that at times some of us—perhaps out of concern to avoid Paul's proper curse on any substitute "gospel" (Galatians 1:8-9)—have camped on some element or elements of the Story's good news, as if those parts constituted the good news of salvation or the *whole* Good News. Examples of how the Story uses *good news* include: Jesus "went throughout Galilee proclaiming the gospel of the kingdom," (Matthew 4:23. He was announcing the good news that he, the King, had arrived). Philip preached "good news about the kingdom of God and the name of Jesus Christ," (Acts 8:12 ESV). Paul was unashamed of the Gospel, (Romans 1:16), including the good news of what Jesus *did* to save people (1 Corinthians 15:1–8), and "our gospel … the traditions that we taught you…," (2 Thessalonians 2:14). This book proposes to refute Satan's lies about God and his Name by restoring the foundation of the Story's *whole* Good News. All the pieces of good news find their proper places in the Story and its wrap-up. The living, gloriously *good* God will successfully restore the glory of his Name by restoring his creation—especially his *people*—to their original reflection of his own glory through his self-sacrificing union with fallen mankind, and his rebirthing work that restores mankind's union with himself in the Son, Jesus Christ.

Any "gospel" short of this not only fails to represent God properly, but ultimately will prove to be gravel in the stomachs of those who fall for it. I believe that the multiplied spiritual and moral failings of our nation will not find cures in any form of part gospel. In fact, I fear that several of today's truncated gospels—particularly those that appeal only to what the sinner gets out of "salvation"—contribute to human immorality by appealing mainly to lost mankind's greedy self-centeredness.

As Adam was in his created glory, and as restored human-kind will be in union with Christ, bearing the image and Name of God connects us with the Source and Force of life that is far larger and more powerful than any human desire, leader, or cause. Satan deceived original mankind into the rebellion that broke that connection, leaving us spiritually and morally dead. God's plan and action for restoring humanity unites individuals with the infinitely, radiantly righteous Christ, the Second Person of the Godhead. Only such union

INTRODUCTION

with Christ restores any person to their designed glory, to the praise of God's Name. The Story—the Good News—recounts how God defeats Satan, vindicating and restoring the glory of his Name by reuniting with mankind through the Son's incarnation and the Spirit's use of the Story's truth to rebirth mankind.

Throughout the Story, God revealed some of the life-restoring rays of his glory through the meanings of his names. That is, he made himself known to his beloved creatures through the gloriously rich meanings of his various names. Therefore, a reader gets to know God through comprehending his names.

In light of what we believe God wants to accomplish with his Story, this book's purpose is to exalt God by inspiring awareness and recognition of the centrality of his Name and glory in the storyline of his relationships with other characters as he developed it in his autobiographical Word, the Bible. I propose to show how those characters and events relate to the restoration of God's Name through the creation and subsequent restoration of humankind and nature.

The nobility of character for which right-valued people thirst is true, vigorous *goodness* of words and behaviors. Such worthy living grows from noble attitudes of the heart. Those attitudes are part of the likeness to our Creator that we lost in our first ancestor's fall, the failure that God's and man's mutual enemy blames on God. These pages include the ultimate good news of how, *in Christ,* God is restoring mankind's nobility in order to restore his own Name as the *good, right, and wise* Creator.

The book attempts to give real and practical answers to the questions, "What does God mean by his use of his *name* and his *glory* in his Story?" and "How are *name* and *glory* related to each other?" We will analyze a few of the Bible's intertwining subplots with a view toward recognizing its overarching plotline, the framework for all those interwoven subplots. As we recognize the Bible's subplots and their meanings for our relationships with God and each other, we will recognize the main plot more clearly. As the Story reveals the purpose of God's relationships with humanity, it puts meaningful and useful content to the biblical phrase "the glory of God" as it relates to his purpose for humankind and for us personally.

Plan

Section 1 analyzes and synthesizes ways in which God uses his own name and glory in the Bible's Story of his heroic relationship with his creatures. Based on those necessary foundations, Section 2 retells the Story of God's relationship with humankind as a continuing drama of how he intended to magnify his own Name and how he is restoring it. Our interests are in God's purposes for his Name, the conflicts that arise in the story's development, and the dénouement of that narrative.

Explanations

1. This book contains a summary of what informs my personal devotion to the only living God, the One to whom I owe my life. Only by comprehending the sweep of the Story can any of us understand our part in it, our reason for being alive. Because that is why he gave it to us. Along with all other thinking people, I have yearned to grasp and fulfill my particular role in life's purpose, God's purpose for my own birth and rebirth within his reason for creating human beings. This effort has involved a degree of complexity, for God's Story, simple as it is in the purity of its singular aim, truly is a multi-threaded and multi-featured tapestry.

2. God's truly epic Story actually encompasses not only the Bible's Story but all of history's dramas, many of which are but hinted at in the Story's text. God gave us the Bible's Story to make himself, the Creator and Superintendent of the cosmos, known to us, the people he created and cares about.

INTRODUCTION

3. The book asserts, attempts to prove, and works from the Bible's declaration that *the most basic and ultimate purpose for which God created all things was to give humanity their best gift, which is knowledge of his glorious Name—of himself.*

   That Good News incorporates and includes God's restoration, rescue, redemption, and preservation of mankind, with all the benefits, blessings, and consequences that his grace in and through Jesus Christ offers us. That is the gospel I learned in my youth and taught all my life. However, from the Story, I have learned that God has a higher purpose in restoring mankind. His *ultimate* objective is not man's benefit, but the restoration of his Name, that which makes possible all the other benefits of the Gospel.

4. With the loss of that which ultimately matters, the centrality of God's Name, our representation of him and his gospel has lost the footing for humanity's real hope, value, and meaning. For these can be realized only in the ultimate glory of God, as expressed in his Name—indeed, in the various nuances of his many names. Any faith is only as good as its object. God wants to be known in truth, as he really and fully is (John 17:3; Ephesians 1:17), so he can be fully trusted. He properly wants *himself*—not just what he can do for *us*—to be the full object of our faith and worship. Neither he nor we will be satisfied with our worship of only some of his gracious benefits.

5. The book's development considers three of the Bible's central themes: name, glory, and restoration. These three themes intersect, interweave, blend, and synthesize in God's purpose to restore humanity so that we fully and rightly *know* and represent him, in order to exalt his Name above all else.

   In this age, God's primary activity is *restoring* among men the *glory* of *the Name*. The essential sin that requires that restoration is humanity's insulting denial to God, or their equally insulting failure to render to God, the reverence and honor due to the glory of that Name. We sin in our concept of God, our attitude toward God, and our resulting immoral behavior. It is only the last—behavior—on which the part of the evangelical movement in which I was raised typically has focused our evangelistic attention. But foundational to God's redemption and restoration of all things, by restoring mankind in his likeness, God is restoring the glory of who *he* is, as represented by his own good Name.

6. You will notice that I still struggle to maintain language that is both appropriately gender neutral while at the same time grammatically smooth, correct, and syntactically acceptable. Where I don't succeed, please give me credit for trying.

The reader

This presentation is directed to the Christian evangelist/missionary who may wish to be certain that their message is fully accurate, because they know it will have an eternal effect on their hearers.

And it is for the pastor/teacher, discipler/mentor, seminary professor, and writer who likewise and from the largest perspective possible, wants their lessons to strengthen and benefit believers in various stages of growth and in various life situations.

Finally, I offer it to the biblical theologian, thinker, and philosopher who, with their historic understandings and perspectives, will clarify and correct these matters as necessary and make the truth found in them more intelligible to all.

Still, I hope that others will eavesdrop ...

INTRODUCTION

Guiding assumptions, understandings, and principles

1. God himself is the Author and Editor-in-Chief of that Story. It is his own account of real history as it relates to people. It is true that over a period of 1600 years 40 human writers from various occupations penned the Story's 66 books. Those books include hundreds of shorter stories couched in various kinds of literature—narrative, biography, history, theology, poetry, prophecy, and even prediction. Rather than refuting the single Story's authorship, the variety demonstrates God's super-genius mind and supernatural sovereignty over all arenas of human and spirit existence, personal, marital, family, social, community, governmental, economic, legal, military, agricultural, artistic, educational, religious, and every other aspect of life and time. In the final sentences of the last chapter of the Story's final book (Revelation 22), God reaffirmed both his authorship and the unity of the whole Story. One of the elements of that unity is that God appears either in or behind every scene of the Story, and in or between all its lines.

2. Only God *timelessly and immediately* comprehends everything about his Story, including its conflicts, resolutions, meanings, and wrap ups. The Story's human characters, along with its readers, live within time's dimensions, so experience those events as past, present, or future.

3. God desires to be known, and as a result to be revered, loved, trusted, and obeyed. To know God is to know him by name. To know God's glory is to know the glory of his Name. This is the heartbeat that moves the content of this book, and the primary theme that will be developed in it.

4. Only in the resolution of the Story's plot and subplots does the reader fully recognize the Author's intentions and discover the meanings of the hints he gives, both in the earlier parts and in the untangling resolutions of plot tensions.

Since God has revealed all that he has for us, he must expect us to read the completed Story in order to understand what participants in early events, or readers of only the records of those early events, could not have guessed would be the full meanings and outcomes of those events. At the same time, the reader who is aware of the Bible's larger content will recognize some of its later explanatory elements to be assumed and foreshadowed in the earlier scenes.

Thesis

The thesis of this book is that God's ultimate purpose and activity in this age is to restore humanity to our full, created image of him in a way that properly vindicates his own Name. In doing so God will prove himself to be the righteous and good Restorer of what he began in his good creation. This is the ultimate Good News. It's all about the Name.

SECTION 1

FOUNDATIONS

Prelude

How a name rescued me

Marshall and Vesta Reed, my wife's father and mother, had generously loaned us use of their nearly new Opel coupe. We had driven from Michigan to visit my mother in Denver so she could meet her new grandson, our first baby. While we were gone Dad and Mom Reed were using our aged and less reliable Nash. Now on our way home, six-month old Greg was sleeping peacefully in the coupe's makeshift back seat "bassinette." Our immediate destination, to exchange cars, was Maxine's parents' home at Kingsley, near Traverse City, Michigan.

Previous stops had brought us into central Wisconsin. As careful as we had been, the trip had cost more than we had expected, leaving us with barely enough money to get to Kingsley. Calculating between the cost of driving south around Lake Michigan through Chicago or north around it through Michigan's Upper Peninsula, we realized that either route would require more money for meals, gas, and an overnight motel room than we had. But if we were to ride the overnight car ferry across the middle of the lake from Manitowoc, Wisconsin, to Frankfort, Michigan, which was not far from Kingsley, we could eat on the boat and sleep free on the deck. Knowing how my father-in-law operated, I was pretty sure that our Nash, waiting for us at Kingsley, would have more than enough gas in its tank to get us to our home in Allegan. We headed for Manitowoc.

We arrived in time for our car to be the first loaded into the ferry's bottom deck. But since the boat's purser had not yet opened his booth to collect fares, Maxine and I, carrying Greg, climbed to the observation deck to wait. Dock workers loaded other cars, trucks, and railroad cars tightly behind and around our coupe. It would be the first driven out onto the Michigan pier in the morning.

Finally, the purser arrived and opened the ticket window. I was almost first in line.

When the purser told me the fare, I opened our checkbook and took out my pen.

He interrupted me with, "What do you think you're doing?"

"Writing a check for the fare," I replied.

"What do you take me for?"

"What do you mean?"

"Nobody in public transportation accepts anybody's personal check. Anyone can write a check on an empty account. I'd be a fool to take yours. I can accept only cash or a valid credit card."

"I'm about out of cash. That's why we're taking the ferry. And we don't have a credit card. But I promise you that we have enough in our account to cover this check."

"Yeah! You promise, all right!" he sighed sarcastically. I was imagining being put off the boat, leaving the immoveable car behind.

I tried that thought. "But our car was the first to be loaded. How can we get it out?"

"Now, that is a problem.... Where are you going in Michigan?"

"Kingsley, near Frankfort and Traverse City."

"I know where Kingsley is! Why are you going there?"

"We're exchanging cars with my wife's parents there."

"Who are they?"

"Marshall and Vesta Reed.'"

"Isn't Marshall Reed the pastor of the Kingsley Baptist Church?"

"Yes."

"He's your father-in-law?"

"Yes."

"Then I'll take your check," he said with his first smile. "Whenever my ferry is in Frankfort on a Sunday morning, while it's loading I drive to Kingsley to hear Pastor Reed preach. If your check bounces, I know he will cover it."

Those four words, "I'll take your check," welded into my memory three unforgettable messages: gratitude to have as my wife the daughter of parents of such known integrity; the value and power of a good name; and gratitude to God for his provision through the name of another, in this case that of Maxine's father.

Chapter 1

Why names matter; how the Bible uses names

In the Story, names matter in several ways, starting with:

Identity

A person's name is their primary means of identification. They are known by their name. Their name is the label to their person. It identifies them as an individual, distinct from all others.

But that name is much more than a simple label. If it were only a label, a number might do just as well. In fact, the practice of issuing identification numbers can cause distress. Why? Because over time one's name also comes to represent and communicate the major elements of its owner's history and character. No nameless person can really be known. The name represents the essence of one's being, the germinal core of their character, their brand.

The Bible includes stories of parents who recognized the prophetic power of suggestion-by-name. They gave to their newborns names related to character qualities they hoped they would acquire, or destinies they hoped they would fulfill. One's name is synonymous with their identity, both to themself and to others. It is their brand.

Relationship, Connections

In Scandinavia, a Johnson was a "son of John."

The connection with family that a name provides is essential in two ways: it gives the child a sense of belonging to something larger than their self; and society seems to require this connection in order to respect the child. In spiritual matters, the person who sins forsakes his relationship with God. For a sinner to be "saved" (restored) is to have their relationship, place, name, and honor restored with God and with the family and kingdom. It is only in view of relationships that names become necessary and meaningful.

Heritage and Perpetuity

At times the Story uses *name* to refer to both ancestral connection and one's future. Both are important to anyone's identity and sense of identity.

To give humans capacity to fulfill their mandate to populate earth with generations of God lovers, those who bear his likeness (Genesis 1:28), God created people as sexual beings. He put in their hearts and hormonal constitutions the deepest instincts and aspirations to produce successive generations, those who would carry the family name, the name that connects the individual with past generations and with those in the future. The hunger to perpetuate our name is among our strongest yearnings.

Kings Saul and David both knew that their families and they themselves were participants in the promise God had made to their ancestor Abraham—"I will make your name great"—partly by multiplying his descendants to a humanly uncountable number (Genesis 12:2) and partly by bringing the Messiah into the world as one of those descendants (Genesis 12:3; Galatians 3:16). Saul's family name connected him with God, his promises, and his future. So when he finally realized that God was transferring his crown to David, he begged David, "Now swear to me by the LORD that you will not kill off my descendants or wipe out my name from my father's family." (1 Samuel 24:21)

Reputation

Therefore, a person's name also is synonymous with their reputation. This is true in every culture, but most easily recognized among Asian peoples. When Asians refer to reputation as "face," they demonstrate respect for the person who carries that face and bears that name, and for their family. This is one way in which *name* and *glory* can overlap. A person's name, representing all that they are, is their glory and honor, their good reputation and that of their ancestral family and their offspring.

A great name is what is known of the sum of that person's sterling qualities and praiseworthy accomplishments.

This understanding of name is even truer of Bible names. Isaiah spoke of forming an identity, a name (Isaiah 52:6-7). In the Story, a good name is synonymous with glory and fame (Psalm 72:18; Isaiah 63:14).

Obviously, such use of name can be negative as well as positive, can connote shame and infamy. "The name of the wicked will rot" (Proverbs 10:7 ESV).

If this is true of humans, it is as true of God. During prayer, King David gave praise to Yahweh this way: "Now, O Lord, let the word that you have spoken concerning your servant and concerning his house be established forever, and do as you have spoken, and your name will be established and magnified forever, saying, 'The Lord of Hosts, the God of Israel, is Israel's God.'" (1 Chronicles 17:23-24 ESV).

Influence

Names influence behavior. All of us try to live up to our names, whether personal or corporate, given or chosen, noble or ignoble.

Opportunity

A person's name thus affects their opportunities. Historian Cody C. Delistraty wrote, "Names work hard: they can affect who gets into elite schools and who gets hired, and they can even influence what cities we live in and what products we buy, since we're attracted to things and places that share similarities to our name."[1]

"A stillborn baby … gets its start in a mist, and ends up in the dark—unnamed" (Ecclesiastes 6:4 MSG). The New Living Translation paraphrases this: "His birth would have been meaningless, and he would have ended in darkness. He wouldn't even have had a name."

For too many Americans of the seventeenth century, the practice of slavery included the conscious or unconscious belief that the African Negro was not fully human. Since the slave owner treated the slave as a mere object, a tool of commerce, they had to believe that the servant was subhuman, little more than an animal, a beast. It was this attitude that left slaves nameless.

One's name signifies their identity, connections, relationships, heritage, perpetuity, character, reputation, influence, and opportunity. Once established, a person's name and their identity are inseparable. Names matter. It's all about the name.

If a name expresses all this about a person, then having no name is the same as being nothing to anyone, and having the best name is tantamount to being everything to everybody.

Effects of understanding God's names

It is even more important to understand the connection between God and his many names. Why is his Name so important?

The first reason is that God created humankind to experience the joy of *knowing, loving,* and *enjoying* him. Not only academically, theologically, or theoretically, but *personally.* Since God's names define and describe his character qualities, an important way to *know* God is to know his names.

WHY NAMES MATTER; HOW THE BIBLE USES NAMES

The second reason is that God and his names matter most. Everyone and everything exists only by the good will of God. God is the weightiest being, bearing the most gravitas over all his creatures.

Another is that human creatures bear the image of their Creator. Our very being depends on his existence (Colossians 1:17; Hebrews 1:3). Our name depends on his. Our aspirations to be good persons not only derive from God's nature but depend on his ability to enable us to be good.

As the just-emancipated Israelite slaves were about to enter their long-promised land of milk and honey, Moses reminded them, "He [Yahweh] is your life" (Deuteronomy 30:20). If God is our life as much as he was Israel's life—and he is—then only if he is good can we be good. Only if he is right can we be right. Only if he lives can we live. Only if he rescues can anyone be saved. Only if he restores can anyone be restored. So, out of all the various gems of good news mentioned in the Bible, the most essential sparkle from Romans 3:23–26: God *is*, and God *is* righteous.

For those who live broken lives in a broken world, the essence of the Good News is that no matter what anyone says, no matter what happens, God is righteous in every characteristic, word, purpose, feeling, and action. He will vindicate his good Name. If he could not because he did not bear those qualities, then no person would have a sound basis for real hope. Hence, Paul wrote, "... Christ Jesus who is our hope" (1 Timothy 1:1). No other reliable basis for hope in life or eternity exists.

God's *big* gift to humankind is his name. In and along with Jesus Christ, he named us his sons and daughters! (John 1:12; Galatians 4:6). No born-again person is namelessly without a Father. We have a heavenly Father who seeded our rebirth with his Word. We are reborn in Christ to be able to fulfill that grand purpose. God is our heritage, as well as our inheritance.

The apostle James well understood this concept. In an encouragement to socially despised believers, he included the reference, "Aren't they the ones who slander Jesus Christ, whose noble name you bear?" (James 2:7 NLT).

> It is the noble name Jesus Christ
> that Christians bear.

The believer or church that accurately and joyfully bears God's name has both the honor and the responsibility of passing it on. Such evangelism is the essence of the discipleship of which Jesus spoke in his last commission to his disciples. That commission includes baptizing disciples in the *Name* of the Father, of the Son, and of the Holy Spirit (Matthew 28:19–20), thus identifying them with the triune God.

God's name is at stake in everything he has done and is doing. God's name is number One, and his devotees must recognize and exalt it as such.

Chapter 2

The meaning of God's name

One does not read very far into the Story before they realize that in it God gradually reveals more and more about who he is. Scholarly theologians describe this feature of the Bible's structure as "progressive revelation." God gradually revealed his nature by introducing more of his names.

We look on a person's name mainly as that simple label by which they distinguish themself from every other. With God's names, the fuller idea is that every one of his names identifies one of the almost countless features of his nature and qualities.

Thus, a mutual identification of character exists between God and his name. His name originates in his nature and character. The full Name of God is that description of him that encompasses and embraces all that he really is. The accuracy of that representation is what allows us to say that when we revere God's name, we revere God.

To revere God's name is to revere him.

Intersections of God's name with human names

The creature's character and behavior reflect those of its Creator

"You shall be a crown of glory in the hand of the Lord, and a royal diadem in the hand of your God" (Isaiah 62:3 NKJV). God said this to his chosen people, Israel. God created people to be his images on earth, moons to his sun, reflectors of his glorious character on earth (Genesis 1:26–27). God's name on earth rides at least partly on our nature, our conduct, our reputations. Recognizing his sinful failures, Israel's King David prayed, "Yahweh, you restore my soul; you lead me in the paths of righteousness *for your name's sake*" (Psalm 23:2–3, emphasis added).

Man's behavior and God's name

It is not just a figure of speech that human behavior affects God's reputation. Satan loves to accuse God of making mistakes in both creation and his care of his creation. When the biological evolutionist notices a genetic fault in an organism, such as one that causes a human disability like a missing limb, they automatically think *Another mistake in nature!* When the humanist notices such a flaw, they automatically think, *God made another mistake!* But God made it clear that it was *human* sin that resulted in genetic and ecological disruptions (see Genesis 3:17).

Ever since, and in every field of earthly life, *man* has been a toxic cloud hovering over creation, dripping death on everything he touches. Paul plainly explained that man's sinfulness, not God's carelessness, causes the faults, diseases, and violences of nature, and that man's restoration will result in nature's release: "The creation waits in eager expectation for the children of God to be revealed. For the creation was subjected to frustration, not by its own choice, but by the will of the one who subjected it, in hope that the creation itself will be liberated from its bondage to decay and brought into the glorious freedom of the children of God" (Romans 8:19–23).

Paul used this same reality to motivate believers to right living. In his first letter to Timothy, he urged a certain behavior "so that the name of God and the teaching may not be reviled" (1 Timothy 6:1 ESV).

Image and name

We need to take a moment to explain this book's use of the word *man* as the Story uses it. When God created the first human, he named him *Man*, Adam. The name means *mankind* or *humankind*. Adam contained all the genetic material and moral potential of all humanity, of all who would come after him to populate earth. Adam not only *was* man but represented all humans he and his descendants would beget. In his Story, God deals with both mankind and individual people. When God deals with humanity as a whole, he always respects, and never violates, the individuals who make up that whole.

For example, one reflection of God's glory in his image shines out of the creation account. The Holy Spirit's infinite *perfection* (the Hebrew root of *shalom*) in all his characteristics brought harmony and productive peace (shalom) out of the chaos, shining light into the darkness so as to produce everything he had planned for those he created. In the same way, man, God's image, was to bring God's perfection (shalom) to the chaos of the world. Much later, Jesus said that he was restoring humans to their original identity, enabling each of us thereby to "let your light shine before others, that they may see your good deeds and give glory to your Father in heaven" (Matthew 5:16 ESV). Our good works, especially our forgiveness of others in his Name, reveal and reflect the goodness and grace of God as he brings shalom out of the chaos of our damaged relationships.

God chose to have his name ride on man's reflection of himself. God wants his human creatures to delight in his radiant goodness in each other in the same way he delights in the reflections of that goodness he sees in them, because he created them in his own likeness. What more fundamental reason could God have had for endowing people with limited editions of some of his infinite qualities? God delights in the pleasure of our company, just as he wants us to enjoy the pleasure of his company.

God created man
capable of enjoying the pleasure of his company
while he enjoys the pleasure of ours.

The sixth commandment applies the concept of image to people's treatment of others. God based "You shall not murder" (Exodus 20:13) on the fact that every person bears his image or likeness: "Whoever sheds the blood of man, by man shall his blood be shed, for God made man in his own image" (Genesis 9:6 ESV). Just as all anger ends up blaming God, murder—anger's physical expression—aims at eliminating, or at least hurting, God's image in man.

On the same ground, the apostle James warned against human curses: "With the tongue we praise our Lord and Father, and with it we curse human beings, who have been made in God's likeness" (James 3:9). And Jesus used the same principle to urge care for the poor: "The King will reply, 'Truly I tell you, whatever you did for one of the least of these brothers and sisters of mine, you did for me'" (Matthew 25:40).

God loves his own name and likeness in all people and expects us to see and love it in all others as well. It is easier to see God's qualities in growing believers, those in some stage of restoration, but vestiges of those qualities remain in those yet to believe, and even in those who still refuse and reject God. Hence, everyone deserves the respect due to a reflector of something good in God.

In this connection of God's image in mankind and our connection with his own Name lies God's central and primary motive in the sacrifice of Christ on the cross. The only way for God to restore in sinful humanity the righteousness he forfeited in the fall was to substitute his own righteousness for human unrighteousness.

Self-respect, image, and God's Name

Another ramification of the connection of God's name with people's is that the value, worth, and weight we recognize in our Creator's Name—or fail to recognize—is the basis of the worth we attribute to our own name—or fail to give it. If we reverence our Creator's name in the way it deserves, we will understand the basis for our respect for our own dignity, our self-respect, that of being his creation, his reflected image. If we disrespect and dishonor the Creator, whose likeness we bear, we will be more likely to trash and shame ourselves and live that way. In this way, speaking of how the ungodly rich slander Christ's name, James wrote to believers that Christ's is the "noble name you bear" (James 2:7 NLT).

Face, honor, shame, and name

Most people expect others to recognize them by their names. The same is true of God. The Bible records hundreds of God's names. Each name puts into human language some quality, characteristic, attribute, faculty, or typical behavior of the God who is so immeasurably infinite that even that myriad of names is inadequate to describe him completely.

Asians and Africans, who have much more respect for the community among whom they live than do we "independent" Westerners, understand this. Their terms "honor," "face," and "shame" describe their most highly valued possession— their name, both personal and collective. A "shamed" person has brought disgrace on their own name and that of their ancestors, their family, their community, and their nation, and therefore is in danger of being ostracized from those groups. Such unbearable shame sometimes, according to this mindset, requires suicide, the act that to them atones for the shame. An "honored" person has brought respect to themselves and to the groups with which they are associated. The group embraces or includes them. Any slight to an Asian steals from them and their associates their most precious possession: their name—their face and their acceptance in the group.

Acting or speaking in God's name

Another intersection of man with God's name is that those who spoke or acted "in God's name" did so because they believed their words carried God's authority and power and that they performed their duties at God's command.

It doesn't take a professor to understand this. Even a little-educated farm boy did. King Saul's whole army cowered in terror when the Philistines' heroic giant, Goliath, boasted that he was stronger than the armies of Israel, the people whose God was Yahweh. When the sheepherder David, too young to join the army, heard that defiant boast, he asked, "Who is this uncircumcised Philistine, that he should defy the armies of the living God?" David knew what mattered to God—his Name. In the face of the giant, whose armor and weapons weighed more than David would have if he had soaked himself in the brook from whose bed he had selected his five stones, he shouted, "I come to you *in the name of* the LORD Almighty, the God of the armies of Israel, whom you have defied. Prepare to meet him, for you are about to die. And the whole world will know that there is a God in Israel" (slight paraphrase of 1 Samuel 17:45–47).

God stands behind his words that such messengers accurately speak on his behalf. Sometimes it is by miracles that God endorses the authority he grants them. The messenger speaks "in the name of" the Father, or of the Son, or of the Holy Spirit, as the case may be (Matthew 5:11; Acts 3:6, 16; 4:10; 9:15; 2 Corinthians 4:5; Acts 5:3–11). The messenger expects respectful hearing, not because they are intrinsically worthy of this but because the One who sent the message is.

Just as those who heard Jesus speak with the authority of heaven, those who read the Story with an open mind and heart hear its thunder and feel the irresistible force of the wind of the Holy Spirit (Luke 4:32; John 3:8).

THE MEANING OF GOD'S NAME

Another example is the activity of Jesus' appointed apostles as they established the Church. Acts 19:11–20 narrates how God humiliated pagan efforts to imitate his messengers' authentic work of freeing people from demonic possession. When seven pagan exorcists tried to copy Paul, and ended up running naked from the violent fury of the single evil spirit, "the name of the Lord Jesus was held in high honor … and the word of the Lord spread widely and grew in power." Evil spirits are subject to a believer's commands, not because a believer commands them but because Christ commands them through the believer. It's all about the Name.

Jesus recognized this principle when he told the men he was training to be his spokesmen, "Whoever listens to you listens to me; whoever rejects you rejects me; but whoever rejects me rejects him who sent me" (Luke 10:16). The human who knows they are God's messenger expects obedience to his Word, not just because he asks for it but because his authoritative Sender asks it. That is the reason one of God's appointed messengers, Peter, after being used by God to heal a lame man, declared, "Let it be known to all of you and to all the people of Israel that by the name of Jesus Christ the Nazarene, whom you crucified, whom God raised from the dead—by him this man is standing before you healed.… And there is salvation in no one else, for there is no other name under heaven given among men by which we must be saved" (Acts 4:10, 12 ESV). It's all about the Name.

Even the civil authority—knowingly or unknowingly—acts "in the name of" God (see Romans 13:1–7). The godly life of the messenger and of the authority helps authenticate the message and its sender, but it is that Sender who lends his authority to the servant. In the case of the one in Christ, this authority is the Lord's, delegated by him to the believer. It is that authority—not their own—by which the disciple works any miracles the Spirit directs, and that banishes any evil spirits the Spirit banishes (Acts 4:30).

"Hallowed be your Name"

The way we treat God's name is the way we treat him. Disrespectful, irreverent contempt for God is blasphemy. James lamented about the exploiting rich who persecute God's chosen and protected poor: "Are not they the ones who blaspheme the honorable name by which you were called?" (James 2:7 ESV).

Revelation conveys a striking affirmation about the rider of the white horse who is named Faithful and True: "He has a name written on him that no one knows but he himself.... His name is the Word of God" (Revelation 19:12b-13). The Son of God, the Word of God, the human expression of God, is so amazingly, so incredibly infinite that only he knows the full meaning, honor, and glory of his Name.

Yet this infinite God wants people to know him—by name. For in knowing some of his qualities by their descriptive names, we know something of what he is like. We can praise him for each character quality and attribute that his names reveal. And we can introduce him by name to those who don't yet know him. We know God by his names.

> For you who revere my name,
> the sun of righteousness will rise
> with healing in its rays.
> —Malachi 4:2

How humans "give glory" to the already glorious God

If God's greatness, knowledge, wisdom, goodness, power, and grace have no observable limits, his name must possess infinite glory. How then, can finite humans *give* God glory?

To rightly connect anything or any action with the name of the Lord—to do it in God's name so as to give God glory—is to do it with the full realization of what the name means, or to assert that it is being done as though God were doing it, by and under his authority, for his purposes, and in his prescribed way (John 14:10-14; Acts 3:6, 11-16; 4:12; etc.).

THE MEANING OF GOD'S NAME

This is the glory and honor the creature owes to the Name of his Creator and benevolent King, and that the redeemed owes to his Redeemer. Our failure to do so partly explains why Jesus taught us to pray, "Forgive us our debts, as we also have forgiven those of our debtors" (Matthew 6:12).

The debt we owe to God is the reverence, respect, love, belief, obedience, compliance, obeisance, and attention his great Name deserves. We owe him obedience to his expressly revealed principles and rules for the good life that constitute his perfect will and the fulfillment of his system and Story—the enhancement of the Name. We do this by multiplying and magnifying that Name, as he has purposed. Our failure to pay that debt—due to our moral-spiritual bankruptcy—is what led the Son of God to pay it for us, in his perfect life and voluntary sacrifice.

The fact and nature of sin also reveal the supreme value of God's name, as we will see.

The root and core of sin is to disrespect and disregard God, to view him as insignificant, unworthy of worshipful obedience, as less than what the Bible represents the Name to be. All sins grow out of this one.

Jesus' disciple John defined sin as "lawlessness" (1 John 3:4) or disregard for God's sovereignty and his law—and therefore of God himself.

We sinners demonstrate such irreverence to God by failing to see his image in other human creatures, by treating them as though they were animals. Perhaps this explains why God demonstrates his grace in granting to his elect the gift of repenting *faith*. For in its essence, faith is reverence for God, as revealed in his Name (see 2 Thessalonians 1:8–12). It's all about his Name.

The Bible Story's central conflict: competition for the Name

Every story's plot describes a conflict. The Bible Story—human history as a part of God's Story—has as its main conflict the battle over the value of God's name. What is at stake is the Name—God's reputation as right and good, his trustworthiness, his glory.

The Story is that of its Author, God, as he interacts with his creation, including humankind. The narrative's hero is God himself. The main supporting character, acting on God's cosmic stage, is man. He is God's originally good creation, designed in his own image to be the one through whom the glory of God's name and likeness would shine most brightly. The Story's villain is Satan.

The central conflict of the Story's plotline is Satan's competition for the honor, glory, and power of God's name. In an attempt to wrestle that name away from God for himself, Satan constantly challenges God's name, both directly and indirectly, raising the accusation, either overtly or by innuendo: *Is God really the only living, trustworthy, all-powerful, good, affectionate, and generous Sovereign he claims to be, infinitely different from all other so-called gods and beings? Or is he merely another manmade god, whittled and forged by man in his own image?* If he is the latter, *why can't people just be their own god?*

Satan's original God-given name, Lucifer, meant "bearer of light," with light meaning *glory*. God created Lucifer, one of his earlier and most beautiful angelic creations, as he would Adam later on, to reflect his glory. Satan became proud of his God-given beauty and power. He felt and acted as though he had created himself. He wanted the fame and power that only the true Creator deserves (Ezekiel 28:12–15). He renounced his own name (his place and identity as God's highest light-bearing angelic creation) to usurp his Creator's rightful name and place. But since he had in him only the life God had given him—derived life—he was incapable of creating anything out of nothing. So he attempted to take over God's position (Isaiah 14:12–14). Disturbing heaven's order and harmony, he led many other angels to rebel with him (2 Peter 2:4; Jude 6). God punished Lucifer by removing him from his leading position among the angels but permitted him to keep ruling over some realms, particularly including earth's "air" (Romans 8:38; Ephesians 2:2; 6:12; Colossians 2:15).

THE MEANING OF GOD'S NAME

Another of Lucifer's names is Satan, meaning *the adversary of God or enemy*, also translated as *the devil*. In other parts of the Story he is known also as *Accuser* (Revelation 12:10), *Deceiver* and *Liar* (Revelation 12:9), *Tempter* (Matthew 4:3), and *Murderer* (John 8:44). His competitive hatred for God is intense. In Section 2 we'll see the terrifying results of his rebellion in the development of the Story.

Satan wanted, and wants, the glory of God's Name without living up to that honor. He wants glory without giving, getting without sacrifice, reward without work, power without compassion. Apparently he did not understand that it is the very nature of God to give, to bless. Satan was and is blind to the fact that the essential drive and requirement of legitimate power is the desire to bless and benefit those under that authority. He conceived and devised his plot to capture man's worship because he coveted God's rule, throne, and Name as he mistakenly understood them.

By accusing God of the selfishness and lack of goodness that actually infected and filled only his own heart, Satan conned Adam and Eve into self-centered blindness. Satan did this in order to darken the glory of God's name among men, and as a result to separate God's highest creation, humankind, from him. Satan knew that God is the source and center of man's life (Deuteronomy 30:20) and that in the separation of mankind from God they would die. He succeeded. Self-barred from God's light, man died to God, died to true life, died in every aspect of their nature and personality, and began to die physically. Adam renounced his God-given destiny, instead letting Satan use him to hurt God by defacing and defaming his Name and place in human history. Satan filled Adam's heart with all his own moral corruption.

From then on, aided by his haplessly captive man slave, Satan has been strutting the stage he pretends to own. He has tried to make God into *his* and man's supporting character. Satan attempted to hurt and harm God and his creation with the idolatry he tricked men into committing. To usurp God's throne, Satan had to trash the glory of God's name. Ever since, he has been spewing his lies, darkening people's minds and perceptions, suffocating earth with aspersions about God.

But God said, "I am the LORD; that is my name! I will not give my glory to another, or my praise to idols" (Isaiah 42:8). So the war was on. The Bible's other supporting characters, from starlets to walk-ons, along with all its subplots, reveal Satan and his subject mankind in a succession of power struggles with God and his Name. All those conflicts, with all the miseries and suffering they have produced, are the Story's tensions, apparent setbacks, and suspense points as it moves inexorably toward its climax.

Over every page of the Story hangs the question "Can God restore his Name?"

Many have sought names of supremacy since Eden.

> Only one name
> will stand supreme in eternity,
> that of the King of all kings.

The bulk of the Story, Genesis 4 through Revelation 22, recounts how God patiently and continuously is rescuing, restoring, and repairing his creation and its myriad characters—and with it, his Name. Without irreverence, we might say that his Story portrays the Creator as earth's tireless maintenance and repair manager. Stretching more than seven thousand years so far, this part of the Story includes our twenty-first century A.D. Man destroys; God repairs. Man perverts, infects, and kills; God straightens, heals, and revives. Man disorganizes; God reorders. Man errs; God corrects and redirects. Man confuses; God clarifies. Man suffers the deadly consequences of independence and rebellion; God revives, forgives, and restores. God distributes among men gifts and talents for those restoring, repairing human services required to heal some of sin's effects.

This litany explains what has gone wrong with God's creation and details the depths of that evil. It chronicles what caused history's multiplied destructions, disorganizations, and deaths. The image of God is so damaged in fallen mankind that they have been rendered incapable of properly recognizing, knowing, or bearing God's name (Romans 1–3).

From before the beginning God planned to restore his Name and fulfill his created design in mankind by doing what man is incapable of doing for themself: using a new creation to restore his image. He would make that new creation by a demonstration of the glory of his Name, so powerful that no one ever again can malign it. By sacrificing himself in Jesus' death and resurrection, and in the gift of the new birth, he would take responsibility to forgive, redeem, and restore helpless humanity and to crush Satan's head at the same time (Genesis 3:15). To do so, God would unite with mankind in a relationship that both suffers the consequences of human sin and restores both God's Name and his image by beginning a final, new humankind with a new Adam (Matthew 17:11; John 3:1–8; Romans 5:12–21; Ephesians 2:15 in its context of chapters 1–3).

For there is one God
and one mediator between God and mankind,
the man Christ Jesus.
—1 Timothy 2:5

If God is going to restore his Name, he must defeat his accuser and restore his creation. *How* would God refute Satan's accusations, prove his name truly good, and outmaneuver the accuser for the throne? *How* would God reclaim rebel mankind and restore his divine resemblance? He would have to enter his creation's stage himself, dressed as man, the second Adam. He would have to start a new race of humanity. He would have to re-create humankind.

God's name, mankind's collective name, Satan's name, Israel's national name, the Church's name, every family name, and every individual's personal name are inseparably interconnected and interdependent. All human names are wrapped up in recognizing and perpetuating the Name—or in denigrating it. The primary conflict in the Bible's Story of God's relationship with mankind is Satan's continuing competition to secure for himself man's acclaim that only God deserves. It's all about the Name.

Chapter 3

The glory of God's Name

God is so vast, so immense, so infinitely monumental in the scope of his being, mind, character, and activities that no single name is adequate to describe the radiance of his various capacities and roles among his creatures. A few of his highly descriptive names come instantly to mind: Father, Son, and Holy Spirit identify his three Persons. Lord, King, Ruler, Lord of Heaven's armies, Judge, and Friend are just a few of the literally *hundreds* of God's other names the Story uses to begin to describe his incalculable dignity, the gravitas of his glory. It is no wonder the angelic seraphs proclaimed about God, "The whole earth is full of his glory!" (Isaiah 6:3). Full expression of God's glory would require the sum of all his descriptive names.

The name that possesses the highest, richest, densest gravitas is the Most High God, the triune Father, Son, and Holy Spirit. Since God is infinitely precious, his name has accumulated all the superlative virtues capable of expression. The name God carries the most precious connotations of any name known to mankind. It is so breathtakingly awesome that the effort to comprehend all that it contains, all that God is, leaves us limp. God is love personified, the essence of goodness, generosity, righteousness, justice, mercy, truth, authority, power, and so on *ad infinitum*. Only the Name Jesus Christ sums up all that weight.

Every biblical injunction and effort to make God known assumes that he must and may be known by at least one of his myriad names. The Bible mentions so many of his names because he possesses so many superlative qualities, each one expressed in yet another name. As one's name includes both his identity and his reputation, so in every case God's name is worthy of supreme value and glory.

The most godly Old Testament Jews so highly revered God and his name that they refused to pronounce it, feeling that the human tongue was unworthy of uttering so high a name. They identified God by the originally unpronounced letters YHWH, unpronounced because they so deeply reverenced the One who was so infinitely beyond description as to be *nameless*. Later Jews transliterated YHWH into *Yahweh*, from which the name Jesus is derived. Thus, the godhead's second person, Jesus, "became as much superior to the angels as the name he has inherited is superior to theirs" (Hebrews 1:1–4). Paul extolled Christ's name as the "name above every name, that at the name of Jesus every knee should bow, in heaven and on earth and under the earth, and every tongue acknowledge that Jesus Christ is Lord, to the glory of God the Father" (Philippians 2:9–10). Rightly to know God in Christ is to revere, love, trust, and obey him. The glory of the only name that truly matters will be restored when all the new earth and heavens, with all their redeemed inhabitants, exalt the Lamb of God who took away the sin of the world. It's all about the Name.

God's brilliance alone
requires countless words
just to *attempt* description!

Chapter 4

The intersection of name and glory: God reveals his glory in his names

God was in the midst of informing Moses that he was to tell enslaved Israel the good news that he was about to emancipate them.

Moses replied, "Suppose I go to the Israelites and say to them, 'The God of your fathers has sent me to you,' and they ask me, 'What is his name?'" Then what shall I tell them?"

God said to Moses, "I AM WHO I AM. This is what you are to say to the Israelites: 'I AM has sent me to you.... This is my name forever, the name you shall call me from generation to generation'" (Exodus 3:13–15).

Glen Davis writes, "If we ask anyone other than God to identify themselves, the response of 'I Am' would be incomplete. 'I am' for us requires a descriptive identifier to follow. With God, however, His I AM perfectly declares His essence. Of course, Scripture proceeds to add identifiers for our benefit: 'I am *the* LORD ... I am *your salvation* ... I am *your shield* ... He is *your life*,' etc. But God's essence is best titled by the simple expression of His being, I AM."[2]

Each of God's multiplied names reveals another ray of that radiance. "I AM compassionate; I AM gracious; I AM merciful; I AM truth; I AM Life; I AM the good Shepherd." Nothing about God is anything but radiantly, brilliantly glorious.

Moses thirsted to know God. He asked God, "Now show me your glory" (Exodus 33:18).

God loved to hear such a request from his friend. He responded, "I will cause all my goodness to pass in front of you, and I will proclaim my name, the Lord, in your presence. I will have mercy on whom I will have mercy, and I will have compassion on whom I will have compassion" (Exodus 33:18–19). He meant, "I will show you my glory, even though you don't deserve it."

Believers glory in God's Name

Kauchema is Greek for the object in which one glories, boasts, exults, or rejoices, either properly in that which is good, especially God, or in conceit, stealing glory from its rightful source. The *kauchema* are the grounds of the glorying, the reasons for praise. The most obvious such object and ground is God himself. The believer exults in God, and for *God's* sake.

One can glorify (give honor to, illuminate, exalt, render more radiant among men) God's name as righteous, faithful, kind, and loving, or just by trusting and loving him enough to obey him. Since all God's laws hang on the pegs of the first and second commands (see Matthew 22:37), to exalt God's name is the means of loving him, and the way to love him is to exalt his name.

God's glory shines partly through the light of his pure truth that exposes the corruptions of the human heart as it also generates true life therein. The Beatitudes, the constitutional principles and rules of God's kingdom life among his people on earth (Matthew 5–7), illustrate this. The radiant light of God's good truth dispels deadly error and disinfects the heart from Satan's evil deceptions.

It is difficult to imagine any word more appropriate to describe God's character qualities, or to represent his name, than *glory*, the Glory of Heaven, the Glory of his people, the Glory of Israel.

Chapter 5

Restoration

Another foundation stone is vital to understanding God's story and name. Beginning in this chapter, the reader will notice an increasing occurrence of the words *restore* and *restoration*.

Salvation is our common word for God's gift of rescuing people from their destiny in the Lake of Fire that gives them hope in heaven. It means that, and much more than that.

Salvation is a sound Bible word. It gathers up into one word all God's redeeming, justifying, forgiving, regenerating, rescuing, reconciling, and preserving work. Salvation's further component, *restoration*—another sound Bible word—is another vital part of that work. The Story pleads with us to recognize God's *restoring* work as a major part of his saving work. To *reconcile* means to *restore* man's broken relationship with God (Romans 5:9–11). Even the word *redeem*, signifying a purchase, means to buy *back, restore* from the power or domain of sin and Satan to the original owner and relationship. And New Testament *justification* is that work of God in Christ that *restores* the sinner's broken relationship with him. Justification sets a sinner right with God again. Thus, *restoration* or *renewal* are nearly synonymous with *salvation*.

> To justify humans of our sin,
> the Father respects and values the sacrifice of the eternal Son
> with whom the Holy Spirit unites us.

To use a current analogy, by restoring mankind as the chief part of creation's system in all its relationships and connections to fulfill their original purpose, God is *reconditioning* him and his system to original factory specifications. But that is too weak an analogy. Actual restoration requires a new creation.

Job, even though he lived perhaps sixteen hundred years before Christ came, understood this. As he suffered tragedy after tragedy, he declared in faith, "All the days of my hard service I will wait for my renewal to come" (Job 14:14).

Paul further spoke of how the Holy Spirit progressively restores the rebirthed mind (Romans 12:2) and of appropriating the new person that "is being renewed in knowledge in the image of its Creator." Here there is no false distinction based on nationality, race, religious background, or worldly status, whether economic or legal, but "Christ is all, and is in all" (excerpts from Colossians 3:10, 11).

Restoration conveys both salvation's place in the larger picture of God's Story and a vital aspect of his rescuing redemption of humanity. Starting immediately following man's fall, God has been at work *restoring* what Satan and man together ruined, polluted, killed, and damaged, beginning with defamation of God's name, and including every faculty and feature of earthly creation.

If this sounds new or even somewhat uncomfortable, discomfort is evidence that in one's education someone has overlooked the Bible's emphasis on God's restoring activity.

God's Story incorporates and includes his restoration, rescue, and redemption of man, with all the benefits, blessings, and consequences his grace gives us. But it seems to me that our twenty-first-century evangelistic message has become "God's *primary* purpose and intention in saving man is to benefit *man*." In our desire to make the Good News appealing to lost man's felt needs, including relieving their fear of eternal fire, we have allowed to slip from the center of our attention the *central and ultimate* theme of the Story—its narrative's wrap-up in *the glory of God's Name*. And along with our failure to represent that perspective, we have lost not only the Story's essential power but also the awareness that mankind's real meaning, value, and hope lie only in the certainty that God will fully restore the glory of his own Name, and that he will do so by restoring humans to their created glory as God's image-bearer.

This is not a plea to substitute "restoration" for "salvation" in every place the word appears in the Bible. It is a plea to incorporate the long-ignored restorative element into our understanding and our message, to weave the reality of restoration so thoroughly into our understanding of salvation that it no longer seems strange or even heretical.

The Story's use of restoration

Matthew reported a crucial but usually overlooked word of Christ. Peter had asked Jesus, "We have left everything to follow you! What then will there be for us?"

Jesus said to them, "Truly I tell you, at the *renewal of all things*, when the Son of Man sits on his glorious throne, you who have followed me will also sit on twelve thrones, judging the twelve tribes of Israel. And everyone who has left houses or brothers or sisters or father or mother or wife or children or fields for my sake will receive a hundred times as much and will inherit eternal life." (Matthew 19:27–28, emphasis added)

Jesus lifted Peter's eyes from the *what* to the *when*, and then from the immediate to the eternal, from the mundane to what the Creator originally designed. Jesus was foretelling, literally, the regeneration—the restoration of the earth and the heavens. In that future day when

God restores creation by first incinerating and then re-creating it, when the old is passed away, and heaven and earth are become new, every being will recognize Christ Jesus as the true King (Revelation 21:1).

Peter got the message. We know he did from Luke's report of the gist of Peter's later sermon to a crowd that gathered to see the crippled beggar whom the resurrected Jesus had just healed through Peter's agency: "Heaven must receive [Christ] until the time comes for God to restore everything, as he promised long ago through his holy prophets" (Acts 3:20–21).

Jesus' direct miracles, and those he later performed through his disciples, who acted in his name and power, not only verified his message and his Messianic person and Name but demonstrated his ability to keep his promise to restore all things. Each miracle Jesus did restored some element of sin-damaged life.

When Jesus declared himself to *be* life and its source ("I am the ... life" John 14:6), he laid the foundation for his essential work of restoring life, not only individually, in reversing disease and death at the time, but also historically, in reference to the death Adam had brought into the world through his fall.

Individual biblical resurrections were startling examples of Jesus' work of "making all things new" (Revelation 21:5), of restoring everything to what it had been when first created—"very good." *Renew* and *repair* are very close in meaning to *restore*. Jesus knew that his work required restoring life, giving new life, to everything sin had killed. While that certainly meant primarily replacing spiritual death with the spiritual life of God's image in man, it included physical life as a vivid reality and attention catcher.

All Jesus' miracles in both physical and spiritual realms demonstrated his ability to restore *all* things. Every converted sinner is a testimony to his Name—Savior, the Lamb of God who takes away the sin and resulting death of the world. Jesus, the Christ, could say rightly, "I have come that they may have life" (John 10:10).

In the new birth—*regeneration*—the Holy Spirit restores both spiritual life and the original image of God in man, with all its potential. Man's fall and resulting death changed people from being loving givers like God into grasping getters, takers. The new birth changes takers into receivers of Christ and his new life (John 1:12; 2 Corinthians 5:17). In that rebirth the Holy Spirit begins to grow the receivers of Christ back into complete image-bearers, loving givers (Romans 8:28–30; 1 Corinthians 13). The new birth restores even the definition of love, from its current misuse as a synonym for self-centered lust, to the giving that is concerned with the highest welfare of the one loved.

It must be this hope that moved the psalmist's heart to cry, "Restore our fortunes, O LORD" (Psalm 126:4). Isaiah's veiled prediction would be fulfilled in Christ: "You will be called Repairer of Broken Walls, Restorer of Streets with Dwellings" (Isaiah 58:12).

During the Jerusalem council that settled the controversy about circumcision (Acts 15), the Church's lead elder, James, quoted what Amos had predicted about God's plan for worldwide restoration: "'After this I will return and rebuild David's fallen tent. Its ruins I will rebuild, and I will restore it, that the rest of mankind may seek the Lord, even all the Gentiles who bear my name, says the Lord, who does these things'—things known from long ago" (Amos 9:11–12; Acts 15:16–18). Those words spoke volumes. At the same time they spoke of God's work of restoring the Jewish nation in faith, land, and influence; of his work redeeming and restoring humanity; and of how he will do so in the Jewish Jesus Christ for even the Gentiles who also bear his name.

Restoration and Israel, the new birth, resurrection, and Satan's defeat

Beginning with Deuteronomy 30:3 and continuing through at least Romans 11:12, God repeatedly promised that he will restore his kingdom in and through his chosen nation, Israel.

Thus, the restoration of *Israel* is part of God's ultimate restoration of all things. It was this restoration of God's kingdom for which all Israel looked when Christ came—and, because of their self-imposed blindness then, for which they still grope. While they missed the immediate expression of that kingdom in the King's arrival, at least they understood its eventual fact.

As one major feature of Christ's restoring work on earth, he inaugurated the new birth, human regeneration itself (John 3:1–15). Even the term "born again" implies restoration. The new birth granted to spiritually dead sinners restores the glorious Name of God as who he is, the *good* Creator of a *good* humankind living in and through his restored people who display in their holy lives the restored image of God.

Many of us appreciate today's emphasis on the *personal* application of regeneration, the new birth, a truth the New Testament certainly teaches. What we have not carefully or adequately considered, however, is the *corporate* level of regeneration God is accomplishing gradually through one-by-one regeneration. The larger picture is that God is restoring *humankind* in Christ. "God so loved the *world*" expresses God's saving work for mankind as a corporate whole, as well as for individuals. In the regenerating new birth of individuals, the Holy Spirit began the process that the Trinity will complete in the final regeneration/restoration "of all things" (Matthew 19:28).

Resurrection is a key part of God's restoring work, individual and corporate. When God puts flesh on the dead skeleton of Israel's national existence, he will be restoring the nation's spiritual life as well as its political existence. Both restorations will be historically miraculous.

Further, the Church is the microcosm and example of resurrected spiritual humankind. Just as only *God* creates life, only *God* resurrects life. In resurrection, it is the *dead* who are inert objects of God's re-enlivening, re-energizing work. The new birth, the "birth from above," *is* that spiritual resurrection! If the One who created life cannot counteract the death that is sin's effect, then sin's author wins. Hence, the Bible's Story is that life wins, for only the *living* God who created human life is able to bring back from the dead those gripped by sin and its inevitable consequence, death! It is the living God, the Creator of all other life, who said, "I AM ... the Life!" (John 1:3-4; 14:6).

When Jesus died on a cross, it appeared to many as though his name had died in both its purity and its perpetuity. The death sentence means guilt, not pristine goodness. Burial seemed to signify the end of Jesus' life and influence, not a slight pause. Dying as, and in place of, sinners required this degree of sacrifice. But it was only Friday; Sunday was coming. And it came.

Resurrection restores life. Herein lie the crucial centrality and climax of Jesus' resurrection. In that event, God demonstrated that he is the Source of life, the Creator of all life outside himself. By resurrecting himself from a human grave, Jesus revealed his glory as life's Restorer!

"The Son of God appeared ... to *destroy the devil's work*" (1 John 3:8b). All of Satan's divisive aims and activities are deadly and deadening. By reconnecting sinners with himself, Jesus Christ restores health and life at every level of mankind's diseased and dying existence—spiritual, moral, mental, physical, and consequently, also social and economic. Although Jesus' initial restoring work helped prove who he was, it was but a foretaste of the completed restoration that awaits God's entire creation. It is an evidence that God is fully capable of finishing what he began. Therefore, Hebrews 9:10 refers to "the new order," variously translated as "the time when things will be put right," "the time of setting things straight," and "the coming of the New Order." It is not clear whether the writer referred to the beginning of Christ's restorative work during his earthly sojourn or to the completed restoration he has yet to finish. Both are true.

What is God restoring?

Through all his work, God is restoring:
First of all, most of all, and last of all, the glory of his name.

Near the beginning of this book, we asked, "with whom was God establishing his name in the first place?" We answered that the witnesses included at least the angels, both good and evil, and the readers of the story.

The same question is fitting now: "Before whom, and with whom, is God restoring his good name?" Daniel 10:12-13, along with Ephesians 3:10 and 6:12, identify the same audiences that watched God establish his name through creation. They include even the "rulers and authorities in the heavenly realms." That means the angels. And they include, of course, all people who lived during every chapter of the story, including those who will be living when it ends. Yes, this includes everyone who lived as parts of the story, for all will be resurrected and assigned to their differing chosen destinies (Matthew 25:46) based on what they did with the Name. In that sense, the story has no end. This current era will turn out to have been only the first chapter, the one acted out in time.

The point is that both angels and humans will join in praise when God restores his name among men and angels. They will express that awe in the awareness of his Name, reverence for his Name, and trust in his Name. For they will recognize in that Name the expression of his nature, character, and will, as well as his reputation.

"When the Son of Man comes in his glory,
and all the angels with him,
then he will sit on his glorious throne.
And all the nations will be gathered before him; ..."
—Matthew. 25:31–32a

If restoration of the glory of the Name is such a central theme of the Bible, we could expect Paul, Peter, John, and the other apostles to emphasize it as the major theme in their epistles. More, we could expect Jesus to highlight it in his teaching, including in his letters to the seven churches of Asia Minor.

They did. Again, in our recent limited emphasis on "personal salvation," we have overlooked it. We need to recognize in *restoration* as much a synonym for *salvation* as we properly already recognize *rescue, liberation,* and *preservation* to be such. Our very lostness without Christ requires our being *restored* to his likeness and closeness. This is reconciliation. The guilt of our unrighteousness requires us to be justified, or set right again, with God, another expression of restoration, that of relationship. Even the term *born again* clearly implies starting life over—yet another expression of restoration.

We, being dead to God in our sins, have no way of giving ourselves life, of reconnecting with him. Only as God reconnects us with his own righteousness in Christ does he declare us to be right with him. Only as he restores and re-creates life in us through the new birth can we, and are we, restored to God's image in us. In that rebirth, God gives us faith to respond, to believe, to welcome his work of restoring us to himself and his righteousness, to say yes to God in Jesus Christ.

To restore his good Name, God must restore mankind to his original goodness, his original image of himself. And God must add the element of permanent righteousness. He provided these in the only source possible—the attributed and imparted righteousness of the Son. That is the clearly proclaimed theme of every New Testament writer.

God is restoring his truth. Especially his moral truth and its applications. Much of the Story's content corrects Satan's lies that have been believed about God, about mankind, and about life—lies that have destroyed so many lives. In Eden, Satan contradicted almost every truth God had established. Jesus used much of his time on earth correcting those lies.

The disciples were to hear in Jesus' words not a revolutionary new law but a correction to their misunderstanding of the constitution of their relationship with God through the ancient law. It was only their ignorance, misunderstanding, and contradiction of the law that needed correction, not the law itself. It was the successful deceit of Satan contradicting the Law of God, and believed by the whole world, that the Son came to correct. This is another instance revealing that Jesus came to *restore* what had been corrupted.

In his famous Sermon on the Mount (especially Matthew 5:17–19), Jesus made the point that the revolution he was instituting would not be based on a new law but would restore the existing law, the law he originally had given mankind, *as correctly understood and applied*, to its proper role. In government we recognize this as constitutional constructionism. The kingdom Jesus was bringing was the restored original one that had long been abandoned by both liberal and legalistic Judaism, as well as by most non-Jewish peoples. He was freeing people from moral bondage to the misunderstood and misapplied law so they could keep the truest meaning of the highest, royal law, that to love God and people. So these beatitudes were not new, but the original law, the laws of the eternal kingdom, properly understood and practiced. On them the church would be constituted as the model kingdom.

Jesus established himself as the chief restorer. As Matthew noted (5:17–18), Jesus repeatedly used the most powerful words in his vocabulary to thunder with the authority of eternity that his incarnate mission was not to destroy or abrogate the eternal law of God but to fulfill it. He was not changing or revising that original law, but as the second Person of the Trinity, as well as the last Adam, was rehearsing and completing it in the way God originally intended it for the first Adam and all his progeny. The descendants of the first Adam, during their entire history, have misunderstood, misinterpreted, twisted, denied, disbelieved, disobeyed, defied, and ignored God's law. The last Adam restored what the first Adam lost, corrupted, and ruined (Romans 5:12–21). Jesus was restoring the authority of that law and, along with it, the Lawgiver's name. Every healing and every other miracle Jesus performed, including every resurrection from the dead, and in every word of his teaching, Jesus shouted to the world, "My name is Savior-Restorer! I can restore truth, health, abundance, life, relationships." By resurrecting himself, he proved he could do what no mere man could do: restore his Name by justifying people forever.

It is that ability of the self-risen Christ that gives hope to believers, both those bereaved of loved ones and those still living. Jesus told the mourning Martha, "I am the resurrection and the life. The one who believes in me will live, even though they die; and whoever lives by believing in me will never die" (John 11:25–26). The restored life, the new life created by the birth from above, will never die.

God is restoring his system (Romans 8:18–25). God's system includes every bit of energy and matter he has created. Every subsystem, and all their relationships. Yes, his kingdom, his realm. And that realm includes everything.

As beautiful as it is, even in its present damaged state that is the result and consequence of man's fall, God's creation does not demonstrate the glory of its Creator as fully as it did when it was new. Mankind and their environment are inseparably linked. As Adam fell, he pulled his environment down with him. This damage to God's Name by damaging what he has made, is, of course, part of Satan's purpose. His desire for the throne included hatred for its rightful occupant and his creation. Thus, the Accuser can point with derision at God while he crows about having caused that damage himself—and simultaneously blame man for it. God's ability to restore his system along with and through mankind's rescue, in spite of Satan's deadening efforts, will restore his Name (Romans 8:19–21). Any "gospel" that does not focus on *God, and God as Creator and Restorer,* is part gospel, and consequently fake gospel, bad news gussied up to look good. Anyone who believes a false gospel has believed a false god.

Thus, as part of that system, God is restoring his people, a people for his name: "Where two or three gather in my name, there am I with them" (Matthew 18:20). Ancient Jews understood this concept. Predicting the return of his people from Babylonian and Persian captivity to the promised land (which return began in 538 B.C.), God said, "When I gather the people of Israel from the nations where they have been scattered, I will be proved holy through them in the sight of the nations" (Ezekiel 28:25).

Yes, as part of that system, that realm, God is restoring his people, the people of his name of every age. That "people" is a community, a family, a kingdom, a flock, a dynasty, a heritage. When Adam fell, he took with him all his descendants. Likewise, when Esau let his appetite blind him to his own future inheritance, he gave away to Jacob the inheritance of his descendants, along with his own. When he renounced his birthright, he forfeited the rights of the first born for all his descendants. When he later came to his senses, no wonder he pled "with tears" for its restoration. In Christ, the last Adam, God restored man's originally intended inheritance with all its eternal rights. Christ shares that inheritance with all those with whom he shares his resurrection life in the new birth.

Old Testament saints such as Abraham are part of that people, as are the true believers of Israel. The Church of Jesus Christ, made up of all true believers in Jesus Christ, is part of that people. To return to God is to return to his rule in his kingdom, whether it is his rule over the nation of Israel or his Church. In that sense, Jeremiah 24:7 seems to apply to both Israel and the Church: "I will give them a heart to know me, that I am the Lord. They will be my people, and I will be their God, for they will return to me with all their heart."

To restore his system fully, including restoring people to their original state, God must restore in them his likeness, his image that Adam lost in his fall into sin.

RESTORATION

The new birth restores the image in and by the Name

One of God's characteristics that he placed in newly created man, but which fallen man has all but obliterated, is righteousness. The universal hunger for goodness, the longing to be good—no matter how feeble, how strongly felt, or how poorly expressed—is evidence of the fact that everyone wants to be good, or at least to be thought of as good, or at least good enough. This is the basis of shame and the whole concept of guilt. The conscience—the sense of right and wrong—is the tool or instrument of this innate hunger. Before Adam fell, his only consciousness was of right—righteousness. Sin added his awareness of wrong.

Practically, the longing for lost righteousness and goodness that began in the Garden of Eden can be satisfied only in the new birth, for it is that regeneration of lost man's spirit that *imparts* the righteousness of God in Christ to him. The reborn is indwelt by the very One whose name is Righteousness (Psalm 89:16; Jeremiah 23:6; 33:16). Paul wrote to the struggling Corinthians that even they "were justified in the name of the Lord Jesus Christ" (1 Corinthians 6:11).

In attributing Christ's righteousness to sinners, and in rebirthing or regenerating them, God both *declares* sinners right and *makes* them right (see 2 Corinthians 5:17).

God has done in and through the Son what no one can do for themself. Just as no dead man can raise themself back to life, no one dead in sin can restore their own righteousness (Romans 7:14–25). But God invites us to enter into the righteousness of Christ by the faith in his Name that also is his gift (Romans 6:1–14; 8:1–11; Ephesians 2:1–10).

In the new birth, God is restoring our basic natures to be *givers* instead of getters (2 Corinthians 5:17, 21). Jesus crucified the greedy, self-centered taker—the old man—as he paid his penalty (Colossians 2:13–14). The new man's essential heart motive is to give God the honor his Name deserves, as the One who gave himself. Thus, the Holy Spirit generates a motive for the new birth that is far more than a desire for a fire escape from the unremitting pain of the Lake of Fire. He generates a new and endless desire: to *know* the infinite God. He implants what only God can satisfy, the thirst to be righteous enough to exalt God's name as the only purely righteous One.

Jesus did it all

That new man is renewed (restored and re-created) "in true righteousness and holiness" (Ephesians 4:24). The whole theme of Ephesians, typified in 4:24, is how God restores the glory of his Name by creating a new humanity in Christ, one so united with himself in and by Christ Jesus, that truly reflects God's likeness. God the Son would become Son of man, the God-man, himself the precise image of God, on behalf of those to be reborn into that image (see, e.g., Matthew 16:13, 16; John 1:1–14, 18; 14:9; Ephesians 1:3–4, 7; 2:1–10; Colossians 1:15–20; Hebrews 1:2). In that union, and to create that new humanity, God, through his special people, Israel, would become man, the second and last Adam (Romans 5:12—6:14; 1 Corinthians 15:20–22, 45–47; Philippians 3:21; Colossians 3:10). Jesus made clear what original true righteousness consisted in so that his disciples could live fully, restored to life as God had intended in the beginning. Such life, he said, characterized his kingdom, life under his righteous rule.

God legitimately can treat the new man as righteous because he himself, in the Second Person, has united himself with the reborn. The righteous person of Christ indwells his spirit. It is the indwelling righteous Christ whom God accepts. It is the indwelling Christ who makes it possible for the reborn to be "filled with the fruit of righteousness that comes through Jesus Christ" (Philippians 1:11), thereby restoring God's noble likeness in that person. Thus, the new birth exalts the Name.

The birth from above does not immediately annihilate or eradicate the person's old nature that wants to remain independent of God.

Yes, Jesus did crucify that old nature; legally, God wrote it off as dead (Galatians 2:19–20). But to *experience* the victory of that crucifixion, the believer must exercise their new man in Christ to treat the old nature as dead (Romans 6). In every believer, the new nature—the restored image of God he produces in the birth from above—battles with the fallen nature for supremacy. Perhaps God left the poison of the old nature in believers to remind us constantly of that from which he has rescued us, thus regularly pointing us to his grace in Jesus. To the glory of God, Jesus' gift, the indwelling Holy Spirit, gives the new nature power to prevail (Galatians 5:13–25; Ephesians 4:1–5:21; 2 Timothy 1:14).

The single most significant crisis of the Story: what God must do to restore his Name

As he has been doing from that terrible day in Eden—trying to usurp God's name and role—Satan has been attempting to block God at every step of his design to restore man in Christ. Satan did all he could to destroy Israel, but failed. He tried to prevent God from fulfilling his long-promised supernatural incarnation through Israel as Jesus, but he failed. Even though Israel abandoned God, God did not abandon his covenant to keep them in existence as a nation until they could produce the Messiah. Failing that attempt, Satan tried to have Jesus killed in his infancy (Matthew 2:1–18). Satan failed in his attempt to trick Jesus with the same temptations he had used successfully on Adam and Eve (Matthew 4:1–17). His final pre-cross onslaught in Gethsemane's garden failed to deter Jesus from the settled plan of the triune God (Matthew 26:36–46). Jesus refused the carnal self-centeredness that would have put self-preservation ahead of self-sacrifice. So Satan aroused Jewish and Roman hatred to kill Jesus (Matthew 26:1–5, 14–16; Acts 2:23, 36; 3:13–17; 7:51–52). As Jesus exhaled his final breath on the cross, Satan seemed to be winning (Matthew 27:44–50). But Jesus actually was triumphing through his voluntary, self-sacrificing death (Matthew 27:62—28:10; Acts 2:24-36; 3:15-17). Raising his face to the sky, Jesus used that last breath to shout to the world his victory cry: "It is finished!" (John 19:30). The evidence of that victory came three days later, Jesus' resurrection from his tomb (1 Corinthians 15:3-8, 12-24).

Thus, the birth from above restores God's name to man, and begins to restore his image in man, as it makes them capable of truly knowing God (Romans 8:28-30; 2 Corinthians 5:17-21; Ephesians 4:24; Colossians 3:10).

Although God certainly included man's benefit in his restoring work, he has a far higher objective than that benefit. The ultimate objective is the full restoration of God's name, the Name mankind has besmirched by his sin. To live for the glory of God's name puts meat on the bones of what Paul meant when he wrote to the Corinthian church, "Whatever you do, do it all for the glory of God (1 Corinthians 10:31)." Living for God's glory means properly to recognize, appreciate, revere, and adorn the glory of God's Name in the ways he truly deserves, and in so doing to join him in restoring and exalting his Name in all the earth. Since only the *living* God can accomplish such stupendous restoration, only he gains the resulting glory.

Whether in sinful failure or graciously redeemed new life, the creature's character and conduct affect the name of his Creator.

A close friend recently complimented his son about the effectiveness of his ministry in a church he had served as senior pastor. The son replied, "Dad, it was your name that opened the door to my ministry there." It's all about the name.

RESTORATION

> Every member of
> Christ's Church needs to repent
> of our casual sidetracks
> and weak grasp of our role in God's grand drama,
> and fully restore as our active passion
> the central issue of all of life,
> restoring and exalting the Name.
> For it's all about that Name.

For God to vindicate and restore his name as the good, just, righteous, wise, loving God he knows himself to be, and the best gift he can give to humankind, he has put himself in a place that he must be able to do two things:

First, God must defeat his enemy, who since the beginning has been accusing him of being everything *but* those things. Part of that defeat must be to rescue Satan's captives.

Second, God will have to do so by restoring creation to the goodness it exhibited originally. To restore creation, he must restore at least three aspects of the created order to their original goodness:

- ✧ God must restore all the originally right relationships that made up that system. Included in that fabric are God's relationships with mankind. He must reconcile rebel humanity and rebel individuals with himself, with the various sin-fragmented parts of human nature, with each other, and with creation. Not only must he restore individuals, but he must restore humankind. He need not restore every individual, but he must restore a people of God that represents humanity.

- ✧ God must do what spiritually dead man cannot do for himself: restore sin-damaged man in righteousness so as properly to represent God and fulfill God's plan.

❖ And God must accomplish that restoration of man in an unquestionably righteous way. That way requires both the attribution (imputation) of his own righteousness and the impartation of it—that is, through both justification and regeneration.

In justification, God *declares* the sinner righteous based on his union with the Christ who is and did all that righteousness requires. To be declared righteous is to be restored to relationship with God and legally declared to bear his restored image because of identity with Christ.

In the new birth, God *makes* the sinner righteous, restoring the image by uniting him with the living Christ so they can live up to what God has declared to be true. The new birth and its subsequent growth in righteousness vindicate what God declares in justification. To be made righteous in Christ is to be made right in character, to have the qualities of the image restored by the active working of the Holy Spirit applying Christ's virtues through that union.

Justification *qualifies* the sinner for heaven; new birth and growing purification *prepare him for God to enjoy him* there and for him *to enjoy sharing heaven's praise to the Name.*

God accomplishes both justification and restoration of the image only in and through the incarnation, perfect life, atoning death, resurrection, and ascension of Jesus Christ (John 3:3–21; Romans 3:21–26; 5:1–2, 6–11, 15–19) and the applying work of the Holy Spirit (John 3:3–8; Titus 3:5–6).

❖ God must restore the rest of sin-damaged creation, so that it properly represents the glory of its Creator (Romans 8:19–22; 2 Peter 3:10–13; Revelation 21–21:6).

The good news is that God already has done all of these.

According to 1 Corinthians 15:22–25, Colossians 2:13–15, and Hebrews 10:12–14, in the triumphant life, death, burial, resurrection, and glorification of the eternal Son, Jesus, the Christ, God has defeated Satan and all his evil spirits, and restored rebel mankind. Only the mop-up operations remain. That is why Paul could declare that our hope is in the glory of God (Romans 5:3) and why he wrote to his protégé, Timothy, that "Christ Jesus ... is our hope" (1 Timothy 1:6).

This is what demonstrates that the Story is mainly about God, not man, although it obviously includes human history. While man's happiness is involved, it is only because he is the main supporting actor in the story. Man's happiness is not God's main goal and end, despite what most philosophers assert. God's proper, primary goal for man is the glory of the Name. If it isn't, or if God cannot fully restore the Name, nothing that depends on it is of any value. Man can't fulfill their destiny any other way.

God is in the restoration business. The Bible's various declarations of that good news are parts of the whole and ultimate Good News the Story tells: God, the Creator, really exists and really is good. Those parts are so in the same way that the human benefits of God's saving work in Christ are parts of the whole restoring work of God.

Chapter 6

The intersection of name, glory, and restoration: making God known by his glorious names

The Good News is that from the moment of man's fall, God has been working out his eternal plan to fulfill his original purpose by restoring his name among men. His means of doing so is to restore man into his original image.

All the glory of God's multiple names coalesce in the name Savior. Redeemer. Regenerator. Reconciler. Restorer. Re-creator. The great Creator became mankind's Savior-Restorer. "I am making everything new" (Revelation 21:5).

> "Christ Jesus ... is our hope" (1 Timothy 1:1),
> for he is *the* representative Man,
> the One who restores mankind in the true righteousness and goodness
> that vindicate God's name
> as the righteous, good Creator.
> Hence, "we boast [or rejoice] in the hope of the glory of God."
> —Romans 5:2.

THE INTERSECTION OF NAME, GLORY AND RESTORATION

The biblical themes of name, glory, and restoration intersect, interweave, blend, and synthesize in God's purpose to restore humankind to its original glory *in Christ*, so that we fully and rightly *know* him, in order to exalt his Name above all. Knowing Jesus Christ is equivalent to having and enjoying the kind of right relationship with God that ultimately glorifies his Name.

It is that relationship with Jesus Christ—that *knowing* God—that infuses a person with life, the ability to live up to all of their original, God-created potential. This is what Jesus meant when he thanked the Father for having "given him authority over all people, to give eternal life to all whom you have given him. And this is eternal life: that they know you, the only true God, and Jesus Christ, whom you have sent" (John 17:2–3 ESV). Paul said the same thing when he penned his aspiration: "I want to know Christ—yes, to know the power of his resurrection and participation in his sufferings, becoming like him in his death" (Philippians 3:10).

Everything God does intends to exalt his good Name, and that name is Jesus Christ. This, the essential good for mankind, must be brought back into preeminence.

That objective is no less important now than it was in Moses' day. Many blame God for hardening the Egyptian pharaoh's heart against Moses' appeal in his name to free Israel. It was not bad but good that God confirmed the flintiness of Pharaoh's already hard heart (Romans 9:17), for the result was Israel's reverence of God, her Deliverer. And along with Israel, all surviving Egyptians and the surrounding nations learned to fear God's name. See Exodus 14:17–18, 31 and Isaiah 63:12, 14.

To know that God is sovereign, and that he will be exalted in all the earth, is the primary source of man's peace and the primary object of his hope (Psalm 46:10; Romans 5:2; Philippians 1:10; 2 Peter 3:13). That hope is going to be fulfilled because that home is God's home, and he is its righteous Head (Exodus 9:27; Isaiah 53: 11; Acts 3:14; 7:42; 22:14; James 5:6; 1 John 2:1).

It was good that God reestablished his trashed name among the nations by directing Nehemiah to rebuild Jerusalem's burned and demolished walls. Israel's capital needed to be known as God's rescued, rebuilt, restored citadel, "the place I have chosen as a dwelling for my Name" (Nehemiah 1:9).

In the same way, God restores man to relationship with himself, and to his original image, for the sake of his own Name, because he himself, represented by his name, is his best gift to humanity. According to Ephesians 2:10, from timeless past God planned these good works for his "masterpiece workmanship" to perform. Just as God revealed his creative genius and glory in the first pair, whom he crafted from dust, he reveals those attributes even more fully in his ability to rescue, revive, resurrect, and restore man from his self-inflicted deadness. He restores the glory of his Name by restoring, purifying, multiplying, and preserving believers' faith in himself.

Man's restoration begins and ends in knowing God rightly, fully, and intimately. In terrible contrast, God exalts his glory also to leave to their own consequences those who harden their hearts to remain dead in sin, to reject his grace in Christ.

> The Holy Spirit is reminding Christ's Church
> to see our primary calling,
> the heart of our message,
> the central purpose of our living,
> and our true and ultimate hope,
> to be the vindication, restoration,
> and exaltation of God's Name.
> Everything depends on it.

Paul explained to the Ephesian church that God's purpose in both the creation and the restoration of man is to produce an earthly and eternal family that has been rescued from Satan's control, one that knows and therefore loves God supremely, one that he knows and loves forever, one that cannot again be moved to unbelief.

God's love for people begins with his desire that we enjoy him. We can enjoy him only by knowing him. We know people in the qualities that their names express. Believers know God's qualities by his names. To love God is to exalt the glory of his Name. He himself is his best and most loving gift to people. Of all the good gifts God desires to give to mankind, the best is the privilege of knowing and enjoying him in Jesus Christ, thus exalting his Name.

To know and worship God rightly results in becoming like him. Jesus declared, "The first commandment is, 'Love God…,' and the second is 'love people….'" (Matthew 22:37). The opposite of what God means by the mutual knowing and loving he desires from men and women is the jaw-dropping expression, "I never knew you. Away from me, you evildoers!" (Matthew 7:23).

The Bible's story revolves around the justification of God, the restoration of his Name. Paul made this point in Romans 3:21–26, which couples man's justification in Christ with his own. That is the ultimate point of the whole story: by righteously justifying and purifying (restoring) man, God is able to restore his Name. The single, vital, all-encompassing element of the overarching Bible story requires us to recognize and know God's *self-justifying* work, the restoration among men of the glory of his Name. Satan began the trashing of that name in Eden's garden. Knowingly or unknowingly, all people have cooperated with him in that campaign ever since. but man has no independent capacity for rebuilding that name, partly because in cooperating with Satan we have become his dependent agent, his slave, a bond-slave to unrighteousness (John 8:34; Romans 7:23–25). Man cannot save even himself, let alone the name of their Creator. But in Christ they can be God's cooperating agent in his name-restoring process.

Only Jesus, God the Son, could restore the Name. And he is doing so. At the end of his short life, he could look the Father in the eye and say that he had glorified the Father and his name (John 12 and 17). He had respected it, devoted himself to making it known, submitted to its authority, conformed to it, and proclaimed it. He had enjoyed unbroken friendship with the Father. He had loved him supremely and constantly. Jesus fulfilled all that he, the Father, and the Spirit had started out to do in the beginning. Jesus was the model Man, the perfect image of God in man. In Jesus, God revealed his glory.

God's desire and intention to be *known* (not just to be known about), and thus loved and enjoyed, certainly is supreme among the Bible's major purposes and themes (2 Corinthians 4:6). This is another way of saying that the primary Bible theme is the establishment, restoration, reestablishment, and exaltation of God's Name in all the earth.

> By rescuing and restoring
> his originally perfect system, starting with man,
> Christ's work contradicts Satan's lying accusations,
> justifying God's name as the good and right Creator
> of his entire good system.

The foundation on which God is restoring his system is the Good News that in Christ he himself is righteous. Again, we have too narrowly understood biblical justification, seeing only its application to God's work in justifying the sinner. We have failed to see the foundation on which human justification rests, that by justifying man in Christ *God first justified his own Name* and is applying the effects of that work to the lives of sinners. In both respects, Christ's work restores: it demonstrates, vindicates, and restores God's righteous law and his righteous name through the perfect obedience of self-sacrificing love. And by rescuing and restoring his originally perfect system, starting with man, Christ's work contradicts Satan's lying accusations about God, justifying his Name as the good and right Creator of that system.

THE INTERSECTION OF NAME, GLORY AND RESTORATION

Why did God allow the conflict that required his self-justification? Why did he allow Satan to rebel and to take angels and man with him? We can only conjecture, for no one has found in Scripture an explicit statement of his reason. Could God receive more glory by demonstrating his ability to restore that system than he would have received only from creating it and preserving it from corruption? Maybe resurrection out of death reveals more of God's power than does creation out of nothing. If so, we can see why life and death are among the Bible's major themes—for resurrection is both necessary and possible only in the face of death.

If God had not allowed sin to enter his creation, he never would have been able to demonstrate his infinite mercy—his love to relieve distress—to humankind. This perspective gives us understanding of why all human history, sketched in the Story told in both Testaments, is the accumulation of subplots of everyone's miserable efforts to live without God, without knowing God. One of Jesus' most penetrating and all-encompassing analyses of human degradation was his word "Without me, you can do nothing" (John 15:5).

The glory of God
is restored in the knowledge
of the glory of his restored Name.

Even though the Creator is so infinitely other than man that no one ever can fully know him, still he wants his man-creature to know him as he has revealed himself in his names. The Unknowable wants to be known. "Will God really dwell on earth with humans? The heavens, even the highest heavens, cannot contain you" (2 Chronicles 6:18). Even though man cannot fully comprehend this, it is so. "Though it cost all you have, get understanding.... Knowledge of the Holy One is understanding" (Proverbs 4:7; 9:10). The foundation and heart of all true knowledge is knowing God himself as he reveals himself. To know God *is* understanding. All other truth, and all other understanding of truth, rise from our knowledge of him. And God is *known* by his names. The glory of God is known by the glory of his Name. The glory of God is restored in the knowledge of the glory of his restored Name.

In order to make himself knowable to man, God reveals himself. God describes himself with *names* by which we may know him. Since God is so vast, and has so many spectacularly brilliant qualities, he gives himself hundreds of names by which we may know him. As we address God with those names, and as we use those names to speak to others about God, we exalt the glory of who he is, of what he does, and of what he is like. By doing so we give or render glory to his Name. Ephesians 1:14 identifies the purpose of God's restoring work in Christ as "to the praise of his glory."

Isaiah 59:16–19 is one of the earliest revelations of the stupendous fact that God *initiates* human salvation. God's arrangement for rescuing and restoring man did not wait for or depend on man's plan or preparation to return to God. No, after lamenting man's perpetual failures to live right or even to seek God, the prophet declared, "So his own arm achieved salvation for him." In providing salvation or restoration in Christ for undeserving and helpless sinners, God vindicates his own Name as the One who does for dead men what no corpse can do for itself.

God is more than the initiator of salvation/restoration. He himself does what is necessary to accomplish it. The sinner's deadness in sin means that they are incapable of doing enough good or working hard enough to earn or deserve their forgiveness and reconciliation with God. The dead do nothing because the dead cannot do anything. In Jesus Christ, God did and does *everything*. He kept the law 100% in both behavior and attitude. He sacrificed himself, the just dying for the unjust. He rose from the dead. No sinner could do those things for himself or for others.

God's name not only rides passively in part on the reputations of his worshipers, but he actively puts his name on them. Jesus spoke of his disciples' relationship with him: "You will be hated by all nations because of My name" (Matthew 24:9 NASB). Jesus Christ is restoring a people *of* his Name, *for* his Name, and *to* his Name! And it is for his Name's sake that he is doing so. Everything about us and our salvation/restoration has to do with his Name. Everything we are and do affects his Name. The honor of God's name partly rides on ours. It's all about the Name.

So, man matters to God! You and I matter to God. His Name, his reputation, partly rides on ours. He is restoring his Name by restoring ours. That ought to be as much our first and last consideration as it is his.

And more, in his own resurrection Jesus triumphed over his crucifixion and demonstrated his possession of life. In those restorations of life that are termed resurrection (Matthew 22:30; Luke 14:14; John 5:29; 11:24; Acts 2:31; 1 Corinthians 15:13; Revelation 20:5), Jesus will fully demonstrate his authority and ability to restore life to all, and to maintain it forever.

John alludes to believers as God's children—those who bear the Father's family name (1 John 1:3)—and therefore as those that ought to act like God's *beloved* children. God is restoring in his children the likeness of the eternal Son (Romans 8:28–30). *God is restoring his Name by restoring his people in his likeness so that we bear his name properly.* The object of human salvation or restoration, personal and corporate, is restoring God's name among people through their restored relationship with the Father. That is the higher goal of God in our salvation, beyond just rescuing sinners from Hell. Only the work of the Son, sovereignly applied by the Holy Spirit, can perform that restoration (John 3:8). The sinner's repenting faith in Christ as Savior and Lord is the evidence of the Spirit's restoring work, the birth from above. James encouraged his believing readers that they were among those who bear "the honorable name by which they were called" (James 2:7). In Christ's restoring work, God is demonstrating to the world in and through his family, his children, and his Church what it means to bear his Name and reflect his image.

> To him who is able to keep you from stumbling
> and to present you before his glorious presence
> without fault and with great joy—
> to the only God our Savior be glory, majesty,
> power and authority
> through Jesus Christ our Lord,
> before all ages, now and forevermore!
> Amen.
>
> —Jude 24, 25

It is God's good name that is on the line in man's individual and corporate salvation/restoration. Surely, humans receive many benefits from God and from knowing God. However, the *first* reason for which God is rescuing sinners is to restore his own Name as the capable Creator and Restorer of a good world and cosmos—and a *very* good humanity.

> The *first* reason for which God is rescuing sinful man
> is the restoration of his own Name.

When he finished creation, God reviewed it and pronounced it "very good." That was when God's enemy, Satan, set out to prove God a failure and a liar. He would so damage God's creation as to make God look like a flop, unworthy of anyone's trust. His goal was to usurp God's Name and throne for himself. His strategy was first to gain control of mankind, to use man to destroy God's name (Ephesians 2:2-3). When God nears the end of restoring creation (Revelation 5:1-11), with whole-hearted song (with restored, freed heart and voice) restored man will praise the Son as The Lamb (note the name) exalted forever.

THE INTERSECTION OF NAME, GLORY AND RESTORATION

> The war between Satan and God
> always has been over whose name is supreme.

Since Satan, in envy, had renounced the good use of his own exalted name and role in order to usurp God's throne, the only way left for him to reign over God was to shove God beneath himself, as an apparent failure. *Satan's arrogantly self-centered struggle for final supremacy over God by his strategy to seduce God's proudest creation, man—who bears God's name and image—into his own sinful distrust, was doomed from the start. What doomed it is the triune God's unassailably pure goodness and righteousness that he demonstrated in Christ by his perfect human life and self-sacrificial love.* The war always has been over whose name is supreme.

Only Jesus Christ, the redeemer of lost things, the divine restorer of broken things, can repair us, to make us whole. He is the Cosmic Fixer, whom all the world's fixers emulate. Only he can continue the ongoing repair and redemption of any and all of us. Only he can preserve us: only he can finish what he has begun, the restoration of God's name.

Anticipating the work of Christ, the psalmist gave credit to the divine Shepherd for *restoring* his soul (Psalm 23:3), evidently to its right relationship with God, and thus to its health and true home with God.

> Jesus, name above all names
> Beautiful Savior, glorious Lord.
> Emmanuel, God is with us.
> Blessed Redeemer, Living Word.
> —Naida Hearn

Why is it so important to recognize the restoration of God's name as the most important element of the gospel? Because if God does not exist as his names describe him, and if he is not who he affirms himself to be, then it doesn't matter how much he is said to love you or any other person. And if God does not love his own Name enough to work toward restoring it, or proves incapable of restoring it, what difference does it make whether he loves you? The gospel is *God*! He is ultimate goodness, just as he is ultimate love. The good news is that God is who he represents himself to be in his names. God is who really matters, and he is who matters most. Everything else depends on him, and consequently depends on the restoration of his Name.

God's Name matters most because God *is* the Good News.

What God loves most is his own name.

The Story asks and answers, "Who and what is the *ultimate* object of God's love?" It asks us to lift our eyes above and beyond what benefits us, to the necessity that the supreme and final object of divine love must be his own Name. Why? Because if God is not worthy of his own love, he is not worthy of his creatures' love, and we have no ultimately perfect and reliable object of hope.

What justifies God's love for himself above all his creatures? God's love for himself needs no justification, other than in the mind of corrupt critics. The common objection is that self-love is selfishly corrupt, so if God loves himself, he is no better than selfish mankind. But that idea wrongly accuses God of man's corruption. It wrongly sees God in humanity's sinful image. Man's corruption warps his self-love into narcissism, damaging tyranny, and cruelly competitive power hunger. But God's love is pure; his settled determination is to do good for all his creatures, and thus to *be* the good man needs.

THE INTERSECTION OF NAME, GLORY AND RESTORATION

> It is not conceit for the sinless God
> to know that he is his own best gift
> to sinful mankind.
>
> —John Piper

As the Story reveals, God proved his purity in ultimate self-sacrifice. The most valuable being gave his most valuable possession, himself. God is *the* original and model Giver, the Mother of All givers. God never takes for selfish purposes (see, e.g., John 3:16). His self-respect is pure. He would be wrong if he did not love his Name. It is his best gift to mankind. And God is right to expect his creatures to love, reverence, and glory in his Name. It is their chief value. It is the source of their own value.

While the full restoration of God's Name is the legitimate and ultimate hope of truly redeemed people, our own completed restoration in his image is inseparable from it. Paul wrote, "That is why we labor and strive, because we have put our hope in the living God, who is the Savior of all people, and especially of those who believe" (1 Timothy 4:10). Our hope of being whole again—resolving the paradox of being separated from our old nature, the evil that divides, confuses, and dissipates our character—is wrapped in our hope of the revealed glory of God in the face of the returning Christ to rule his kingdom as he rules heaven. At the same time, our ultimate hope for the revelation of his glory is the basis for our secondary and resultant hope in our own freedom from our old nature (Philippians 3:20-21). Saving, rescuing, or restoring lost mankind is a vital part of God's restoration of the glory of his Name. And only a restored person, purified of all self-centeredness, can truly enjoy God.

Another way of saying this is in the arrestingly true words of Barbara Duguid, the author of *Extravagant Grace: God's Glory Displayed in Our Weakness*. In an interview with Marvin Olasky before Patrick Henry College students, Mrs. Duguid said, "Ultimately,

God has staked His reputation on Christ, not on us."³ That reality takes us back to Jesus' union with man and the union of man with him that God accomplishes. In that union, God attributes all Christ's virtues to them, and the guilt and consequences of all our failures to himself (2 Corinthians 5:17). Thus, Jesus Christ receives *all* the credit for the righteousness that becomes ours. It's his, and therefore his to give. To make this point even clearer, Mrs. Duguid went on to connect Jesus' perfection with our failures:

"(When we fail) God will discipline us…. But what gives you the courage to get up tomorrow when you have failed utterly again today, if it isn't the wonderful news that it's not your performance that earns God's favor? He is for you. Your past, present, and future sins are paid for. God chose to leave us significantly deformed and imperfect after our conversion because He values something more than our sinlessness. That something is His Son…. When we are shredded (by failure) there is nowhere to look but to this Savior. God loves His Son. He loves it when we love and cherish His Son. He loves that more than our sinlessness."⁴ It is the union with Christ that God the Spirit accomplishes in our new birth that makes this possible and real. God's unconditional love for all people grows out of his love for the Son with whom he has united us sinners. Ultimately, God's name rides on Jesus.

> My hope is built on nothing less
> than Jesus' blood and righteousness;
> I dare not trust the sweetest frame,
> But wholly lean on Jesus' name.
> On Christ, the solid Rock, I stand;
> all other ground is sinking sand.
> —Edward Mote

Why did Jesus Christ, God the Son, die for man? The typical twenty-first-century answer is, "Because he loved us." That statement *contains* Bible truth. It is true as far as it goes. But that answer often is tossed off as though it were God's *whole* reason for that sacrifice. As a complete reason for Jesus' self-sacrifice, it is too limited. So much more than God's love for man is at stake, something our generation seems to have overlooked. Yes, God does love us, because he *is* love, and because he *chose* to love us. Yes, God loves us because he sees vestiges of his own image in us, his image that even though defiled by our sin yet bears his name. What we have overlooked is that something exists that is more adorable to God than his image in humans. That something is the God whose likeness man reflects, personified in Jesus. The ultimate object of God's love is his perfectly lovely, loveable, adorable self in Christ.

One thing is more adorable to God
than his image in man.
That something is the God whose image man bears.

The supreme proof of Godhood

All the man-created gods demand the blood of their followers. But in Jesus' self-sacrifice, he proved finally that God truly had no self-seeking corruption in his motives. The cross proclaims, "Helpless sinners, perpetrators and victims alike, what you cannot do to rescue and restore yourselves from sin's power, guilt, and consequences, I, and only I, by pure grace and self-sacrifice, do for you and in your behalf!" The cross is the centerpiece of God's restoring work, the proof that his Name is trustworthy.

The cross is the centerpiece of God's restoring work,
the proof that his Name is trustworthy.

In all the idealism and positive promises of Jesus' proclamations about the nature of his kingdom, he never lost sight of the reality that the enemy constantly assails his realm from every direction, attempting to harm God's name by subverting and corrupting the realm's citizens. Jesus foresaw all the corruptions of false teaching and hypocritical performance his external church would endure throughout the ages. He well knew that in the end he would have to say to some, "I never knew you. Away from me, you evildoers!" (Matthew 7: 23). The God-proving factor is that his purifying work would preserve his real Church, his Bride! Just as giving and restoring life is the work only God can do, so preservation is the vindicating work of God. Preservation of true life vindicates and exalts *God's* Name (John 10:29). Jesus asked his Father to *keep* his new-birthed disciples in his name (John 17:6–26). Would the Father refuse anything his beloved Son asked?

In a pre-climactic encounter, Satan will put up his anti-Christ as his agent of rebellion against Christ. But Christ will put him down (Luke 17:24; Revelation 13; 19:19–21). In the end, God will put an end to all Satan's malicious designs and efforts. In a final battle, he will remove Satan from the scene forever (Revelation 20:1–10).

Then God will finish restoring his Name by restoring earth and the cosmos to its original perfection. He will do this by creating a new earth in new heavens (Isaiah 65:17) and place in that perfectly restored environment renewed humankind, his perfectly purified and restored people (Revelation 21:1—22:6). Imagine the glory: God will know man, and man will know, treasure, love, and serve God in the glory of all that his Name means (Revelation 22:16)—and in the glory of a perfected earth and heavens. All pollution, all earthquakes, all floods, all tragedies, all suffering, all the effects of sin—banished and ended forever!

THE INTERSECTION OF NAME, GLORY AND RESTORATION

> Yesterday, today, forever, Jesus is the same,
> All may change, but Jesus never—
> Glory to His name!
> Glory to His name! Glory to His name!
> All may change, but Jesus never—
> Glory to His name!
> —Elisha A. Hoffman

Those last two chapters of *Revelation* describe the fullness of that restoration. We will not here do so, but it will be of striking interest for the reader to compare each detail of these chapters with the first chapters of Genesis. Watch in both Genesis and Revelation 21 and 22 for the reflections of God's good Name that—because of our sinful cooperation with Satan—required the restoration described in Revelation.

Our ultimate hope

The believer's *ultimate* hope is not that someday they will get to heaven! Because the hope for a heavenly destination depends on something more basic than our faith. For even that faith is worthless if it is not anchored to something greater than itself. The ultimate object of the true faith and of hope that matters is *that God will forever reestablish the glory of his Name.* David prayed, "But now, Lord, what do I look for? My hope is in you" (Psalm 39:7). And Paul wrote, "We rejoice in the hope of *God's* glory!" (see Romans 2:7; 5:2; Ephesians 1:18, 21; Colossians 1:27; Titus 2:13; Hebrews 6:12–20 with 10:23 and 11:1; 1 Peter 1:21; 2 Peter 1:4; Jude 25.)

History shows that God, the *good* God, is not only mankind's ultimate hope, but his *only* hope.

It is entirely possible that hope for heaven can express nothing more than selfishness. How many look forward to heaven because

God is there, longing to be closer to him because they love him and want to know him to the fullest? For the true believer, the one with the new heart, his hope is far deeper than getting to heaven to finally find rest. His hope is that his God will be able to restore his good Name among men. Hope for God's Name expresses love for *him*. The fulfillment of all legitimate hopes depends on the fulfillment of the ultimate hope, the hope that God will vindicate his Name as the good Creator, Sustainer, Ruler, Judge, and Restorer of his good system.

Therefore, "May the God of hope fill you with all joy and peace as you trust him" (Romans 15:13). Trust whom? God. Believing what? That he will restore the glory of his Name by restoring fallen man and his corrupted world.

A Mundane Illustration

I wrote these notes in the spring of 2012:

"This week I had the satisfaction of completing a major home repair job. A wall carrying heavily loaded cupboards had begun to sink into our kitchen floor. Inspection revealed that a necessary joist beneath the wall was missing. Subsequent construction had filled the gap beneath the subfloor with electric cables and water pipes, so I could not simply add a joist. As I prayed and pondered the situation, an idea came to me. With gluing assistance from my amiable wife, piece by piece I assembled and laminated bendable plywood "boards" into a 4" x 6" beam in place above the cables and pipes beneath the drooping floor. When the glue cured, I jacked up the new beam, along with the wall above it, and bolted it securely to a 6" x 10" joist on one end and resting on the concrete foundation wall on the other. It feels good to see the wall solidly back in place."

Most people—whether they follow callings in jobs, trades, professions, family care, or whatever—work to repair, restore, or clean something that has broken down or gotten dirty. Objects break. Appliances wear out. Rooms collect dirt. Bodies sicken—and die.

Relationships fracture. Laws are violated. Marriages crack. Spirits get broken. Personalities self-destruct. Churches split. Communities divide. Wars break out. Cultures disintegrate. Consciences hurt. Much of life's work has to do with repair and restoration. Thank you, Adam and Eve—and your inspiration, Satan.

If we fixers feel good when we have repaired or washed something, or have been used to help restore a relationship, what may God feel when he repairs something broken? In that sense, he is the Maintenance Director of the universe. The writer of Hebrews said, "Jesus Christ... for the joy set before him... endured the cross, scorning its shame" (Hebrews 12:2). Jesus' self-sacrifice was required to repair all the damage our rebellion against God did to his earth system, to his image in us, and thus to his Name that has been distrusted and despised as a result. He looks forward to a joyful reward.

My wife, Maxine, and I have enjoyed the fulfillment of seeing God restore fractured marriages to joyfully God-centered partnerships. We have celebrated as he restored imprisoned criminals to joyful lives of positive spiritual influence. Who can imagine God's joy in restoring one wandering heart to loving him for his sake?

God's satisfaction will be complete when he has restored his Name by restoring earth and heaven—including all its populations of every kind of being, starting with humankind—to their Edenic rightness, order, and beauty. Parts of Isaiah 53:10–12 read: "Though the LORD makes his life an offering for sin, he will see his offspring and prolong his days.... After he has suffered, ... he will see the light of life and be satisfied.... By his knowledge my righteous servant will justify many, and he will bear their iniquities.... He will divide the spoils with the strong, because he poured out his life unto death, and was numbered with the transgressors. For he bore the sin of many, and made intercession for the transgressors."

Whether we enjoy the results of inserting a missing floor joist, of seeing a broken marriage healed, or of being used by God to help rescue a lost life, such joy is but a single sugar crystal compared with the rich feast with which God will celebrate when he has finished putting restored mankind back in place in his restored earth and heaven, thus restoring his Name as the Good Creator, all in and through the sacrifice and resurrection of Christ Jesus.

Eternity in our glorified, restored state, on a renewed, restored earth, with all systems restored to their created function and purpose, will be the most exciting experience of using all of our amazing capacities that reflect God's to become more and more acquainted with him and his amazing creation. No one will be bored. Ever. For God is infinite in every characteristic and attribute. No limit exists to knowing him. No one will be able fully to fathom God.

SECTION 2

THE STORY OF THE NAME

The architect's supreme accomplishment

A certain architect and his partners were glowing with satisfaction over their newest project. The spacious mansion had every feature that a discriminating customer might need or even wish. And some features no customer ever had asked for, not even the one who had commissioned the firm to build the showplace. From every angle the edifice demonstrated the magnificent design for which the firm was renowned. Every change of light and angle revealed new details, all in perfect balance.

The firm's landscaper had designed and planted each garden with the superb taste for which she, too, was renowned.

The partners had planned the mansion to be the signature showpiece of their designing and building skill, one that would bring the world's wealthiest and most discriminating customers to their door. They had drawn and built it together. So they shared the pleasure of the finished product.

As they walked through on their final inspection, admiring every detail, the partners said to each other, "We've made our name with this place."

That night their main competitor and rival broke in and planted an odor generator deep inside the heating and cooling system. The device produced a penetrating stench like a roadkill skunk's carcass, like rotting carp. The system's blowers carried the reeking odor throughout the palatial mansion. Soon it permeated every rug and carpet, every curtain, every blanket, every pillow, and every towel.

Immediately, the partners ordered repeated washing and cleaning of every article and surface. Nothing removed the odor. So they replaced every moveable item. Only then did they realize that the stench had penetrated every piece of carved woodwork, every plastered surface, the framework that held those surfaces, the insulation, and even the concrete foundations and floors. Their deodorizing efforts were useless. So was the mansion.

The customer canceled his contract and demanded refund of his deposit. Other potential customers lost interest. Wherever the odor spread, the firm's name died with it.

Stage 1

THE GLORIOUS NAME ESTABLISHED IN CREATION

Chapter 1

The Creator's name is Elohim

The first two chapters of the Story's first "book," the Bible's *Genesis* (meaning *beginnings*), set the stage. God is the only character on that stage. God introduced himself by name as history's main character, its hero.

"The beginning" does not mean the beginning of God himself. As we'll see, God describes himself as existing and operating before he invented the time in which the Story takes place, and continuing to exist after he finishes his purpose for time. God's creatures experience events consecutively in time, each event following the one before it. Since we live inside the goldfish bowl of time, our vocabulary contains only words related to time. We have no words that deal with timelessness. This is our reason for saying "in the eternal past" when we really mean before time began. God exists outside time; he is timeless. He knows all our moments of time simultaneously.

But God's own existence is not the subject at this point. The human storyteller through whose pen God told his Story assumed his reality. Why would God need to describe his beginning when he had no beginning?

So, "In the beginning"—words that have to do with time—must mean either the beginning of time itself and all the things that exist within time or, more likely, the beginning of the Story that is taking place in time and space.

The word *God* in the Hebrew language is *El*, also spelled *Eloh*, *Elohim*, and other variants. Sometimes the word is used generically, of other "gods," or even of all deities people worship. Sort of like *a* king, *the* king, and *King David*. In Genesis 1:1, God is a personal name. Not *a* god, or even *the* God, but *God*.

When a writer used *El* or *Elohim* for a human who was responsible for leadership, it was translated as *master, lord,* or even *sir*. Used of God, *Elohim* revealed a few blinding rays of his glory: his majestic gravity, dignity, fullness or magnitude, and authority.

The heart of all history always has been about the Name.

Some readers ask something like, "If the Bible is God's Story, why was it written as though someone were writing *about* him like a biography, instead of by him, as an autobiography?" The answer is that the Story is about God's relationship with his primary creation, mankind. Man's story is part of God's Story. They who doubt this need to read the whole Story with this question in mind as they read: "Is this plot God-centered or man-centered?" When they read the Gospels, they should ask, "Are these biographical records man-centered or God-centered?"

In fact, God wove man into his Story so intimately and inseparably that he even had men record its events. Most often he gave those people freedom to tell their parts of the narrative from their own points of view. Yet, to produce an absolutely accurate record of God's involvement with people (2 Peter 1:21), the Holy Spirit oversaw their writing. They described their own interactions with God as they became acquainted with him through his names revealed in those interactions. God dictated—word for word—other parts of the Story.

Another common question is "How did this being named God come to be?" He certainly had no mother or father. No inventor designed and built him. The Story describes him as timeless, always being—in our time-bound terms, forever past, present, and forever future. Since no other being existed before him, we will have to depend on what he later said about himself, as he described in another of his names that he disclosed in a conversation with Moses. That name is the key element in the God who identified himself to Moses as "I AM" (Exodus 3:13–14), meaning that God exists by himself and in himself. No one gave God life, and God depends on no one to keep him alive. Instead, he is the source of everything else that exists. He *is* life. No one created him. No one birthed him. He depends for his existence on no one and no power outside himself. He simply *is*. Theologians describe this as God's *self-existence*.

God had no starting point, and he never will die. This explains why no one gave God his name, I AM, or any of the other names by which he identified himself—why he had to name himself.

"Creator," by his own use, appears to be one of God's three favorite names. The others are "King" (Provider, Shelter, Shepherd, Protector); and "Savior" (Rescuer, Restorer). His proper name in this part of the Story is Elohim, God. Elohim's first activity is creating all things. Only later is this creative work ascribed to God by the formal name Creator.

In this part of the Story God revealed himself in his activity of creating. Therefore, in this role we could almost cite his name as Elohim (God) creating, Elohim (God) Creator, or the creating Elohim (God). He showed the kind of creativity that every human inventor desires.

God not only took responsibility for creation; he took credit for it. He designed it, imagined it, built it, and energized it.

God was about to introduce into that fabulous environment his main supporting character, man. But to do so properly, he needed to set the scene ... or, more accurately, construct the scene. Until he started creating, nothing but God himself existed. He constructed everything out of nothing but his own imagination and purpose. Stage after stage, day after day, God expressed his brilliant and powerful mind by *speaking* the earth and the universe into existence outside his mind.

In each creative act, God "spoke," and the object appeared (Psalm 33:6, 9, *The Message*).

One of the popular PBS weekly TV episodes of "Antiques Road Show" (February 5, 2018) featured a pearl ring set in clusters of diamonds. The show's jewelry appraiser said that the combined street value of the ring's precious stones and metal amounted to about $10,000. However, when he pointed out three tiny initials carved inside the platinum band, everything changed. The initials were those of the famous New York jeweler who had crafted the ring nearly a century earlier. Said the appraiser, "These initials at least triple the value of this ring … to $30,000 or even $40,000!"

In creation, God established his brand. The universe reveals its Inventor's intelligence, power, variety, and beauty. It shows his organized, systematic, wise, and endlessly generous creativity (Revelation 4:11) and providential care. Creation established God's right to judge his creatures' usefulness to fulfill his purpose for it.

Finally, God finished creating, arranging, and giving life to every detail of the scene and had every particle and subsystem properly functioning in perfect harmony with every other particle and subsystem in the whole vast single system.

That system not only looked *good,* but it *worked.* It functioned. It was healthy. It sustained the life God put into it. In that word *good,* God described his system, and each particle of it, as worthy of himself. God was justly proud of all his creative work, of his intricately beautiful workmanship. The system was worthy for him to place his signature in its corner. God had produced in material form the beautiful picture he held in his mind. All the objects glowed with vibrantly living color in their proper places in the composition. That was the visual dimension. And in its audio dimension, the symphony hummed with perfect harmony and rhythm, ready for the melody. The scene was ready.

Into that moment of readiness, the Story inserts what I describe as "a divine pause." To better understand the meaning of that pause, we need to take a brief side trip.

The divine pause

Two plural pronouns included in one sentence hint two things. They suggest the enormity of what God was considering. In human terms they suggest a pause for consultation: "Let *us* make man in *our* likeness" (Genesis 1:26). And they indicate plurality in the Creator.

Notice the difference between his previous words of creative command and this word of collaboration. The previous creative fiats had been "Light, be ..." and "Animals, be ..." Here God was not giving an order. This *said* was conversational, indicating discussion or collaboration. For when he said, "Let us ... ," God introduced another element into the Story (Genesis 1:26). Yes, God was talking to himself. But in a way different from how we humans talk to ourselves, more like our "with himself."

For "*let us*" hinted at another feature of God's being. It is a feature so different from our existence and experiences that earth's finest minds cannot fully comprehend it.

That feature is this: besides being a real spiritual being who could imagine something and then with a word of command bring it into existence out of nothing but his imagination-fired volition, God is plural. Normally it is contradictory grammar to fasten a singular to a plural, as in "*he* said, let *us*." But that is the way the Hebrew language—in which God had Moses write this part of the Story—formed this sentence.

In fact, in this narrative the very first name, *Elohim*, God had

Moses use for him is plural. It's not that he is one of several gods but that in his oneness he is more than one. Since I'm trying to keep this from becoming so technical that I get lost and you stop reading, I'll move on shortly after just this: careful readers of the whole Story recognize that in "Let us" God was introducing the other two members of the triune godhead: the eternal Son, later identified as the Angel of the Lord, Jesus the Son of Man, and the Christ; and the eternal Spirit, later identified as the Holy Spirit. Later in the Story we also learn that among God's many names is Father. So the developing picture is of Father, Son, and Holy Spirit creating together, and here pausing in that work to discuss their, or his, plans for the next step. As the Story develops to its climax, the reader will become aware that the second Person of this triunity is its central character. The plot reveals Jesus, the Christ, as God—God made known in Jesus Christ. The Story reveals God as and in Jesus (Luke 24:27; John 5:39, 46; 17; 2 Timothy 3:15; etc.). But that is getting ahead of the story.

For a further exploration of this, the interested reader would do well to notice the word *one* as it is used in both Genesis 2:24, about the union of Adam and Eve, and in Deuteronomy 6:4, about God. In both cases, the single *unit* consists of more than one *person* acting in loving relationship.

With that incomplete and inadequate consideration of God's triune being and Name, and to maintain the Story's original tone, we will return to it in its native mix of singular and plural. The slight pause in the Story describes the three Persons apparently in conference, God taking counsel with himself, deliberating about creating man, saying, "Let us make man in our image."

Please try to imagine, as reverently as possible, parts of what the conversation in that planning conference *could have* included:

> "Man is to be not just a machine, a vegetable, or a slave. He will be our friend (1 Samuel 15:22; Job 42:7; Psalm 25:14; Jeremiah 9:24; Matthew 11:19; John 15:5, 14; Romans 5:11;

2 Corinthians 5:12; Philippians 3:10). He will fulfill our purpose for him by revering us above all others, giving himself to us in praise, awed worship, and devoted service of love while we give ourselves to him in loving provision, meaning, and oversight. Such a friend needs a mind that can learn, think, know, contemplate, understand, appreciate, and respond to us. So he needs spiritual, physical, and emotional senses that let him admire us and gratefully appreciate the environment we have prepared for him. He needs a spirit that can be amazed at our wonders and at us—his highest Gift. He needs a volition that can choose to love us and walk with us, and freedom to do so. He will need the ability to recognize, appreciate, and choose noble goodness.

"If we want humans to enjoy the pleasure of our company forever, while we enjoy theirs forever, we need to give them human-sized elements of our character. They will need personalities enough like our own to be able to recognize us and our triune qualities, and be attracted to us. Soul mates forever. We are far too vast for them ever to fathom completely, but they will need enough curiosity to keep trying to do so. We will be their glory as they reflect some of ours. And even though their bodies will be physical enough to live in a material environment, they will need predominantly spiritual natures to be able to connect with us and exist forever in our realm.

"If we want humans to love us, we need to give them hearts that can feel and act. And if we want that love to be pure, we must grant people freedom to choose it and to cooperate gladly in achieving our purposes for them. We will have to take the risk that they may choose to reject us.

"If man is to be rightly focused on his completeness in us, we must give him a conscience capable of doing so. He must be a living soul. He must be energized by and driven by that soul, fully aware of our spiritual values and goals so that he can share them with us and cooperate in them as we do.

"Our goodness must create goodness that can generate more goodness. If we want humans to partner with us in populating earth with people who bear our likeness and name, we must give them the capacities, desires, and organs that make them capable of doing so—the ability to give life to another who will be able to give it to others. We must make them relational in nature, like we are. We must give them generous and even sacrificial hearts like ours. Human reproductive systems will need to be able to replicate in the tiniest detail their genetic record and material so as to produce real people who bear not only their likeness, but ours, too. So, we will give males some of our masculine characteristics, and females some of our feminine qualities. The sexes must be different enough from each other to require not only teamwork in reproduction but fascination with each other's complexities and capacities. And they will need the emotional intelligence and instincts that make it possible for them to form and maintain permanent, healthy and intimate family and clan relationships that perpetuate our values.

"If we are going to give people the joy of being our agents in caring for our earth, to have dominion over it, they will need reflections of our ability to rule. They will need some of our understanding, wisdom, compassion, imagination, vision, ability to make decisions, and other capacities for management.

"If we expect people to share our creativity, we will need to equip them with the capacities to imagine their future and evaluate their past, as well as to be analytically aware of their present environment and its resources.

"Humans are going to need highly complex systems and sub-systems of life. They will need systems of nourishment and digestion, of circulation to carry that nourishment to every part of their bodies. They will need systems that sustain each of the senses through which they stay in contact with their environment. They will need networks of nerves that communicate with each other in every part of their bodies and with their managing brains so that all their systems will work together smoothly. Brains will need capacities for connecting observations and evaluations, for creative thinking, solving problems, and planning, as well as for memory, self-identity, and responsibility. They will need internal systems of healing that protect and maintain their health. They will need hormonal influences that regulate all the systems, including growth and limiting growth. And to avoid boredom and confusion, no two people can be precisely identical.

"But as a precaution, we will keep in our own hands the matters of actually giving and ending human life. We'll share with man semi-autonomous control of his life—his heart beat and his breathing—but we will maintain final responsibility for his first breath and his last heartbeat. He must never be able to forget that his life derives from ours and depends on ours, and that in every way he remains responsible to us. Cut off from us, he cannot fulfill his role in our Story, or even stay alive in all these ways."

The three Persons considered all the angles and consequences of making man in their own likeness. With all the foresight that only deity possesses, he (they) looked down the halls of time and beyond time, seeing the enormity of what their highest creature could and would do with the freedom they planned to grant him. They agreed to go ahead—and to pay the price of doing so (Ephesians 1:9–11; 2 Timothy 1:9 ESV).

This part of the written Story is brief. It closes with the profoundly pregnant words, "So God created mankind in his own image, in the image of God he created him; male and female he created them....

God formed a man from the dust of the ground and breathed into his nostrils the breath of life, and the man became a living being" (Genesis 1:27; 2:7). Then God fashioned woman from the man's side.

The worlds of water creatures, air creatures, and land creatures have life and breath by the decree of God. But when God breathed his own life into *Adam's* nostrils, it was different from animal life. It included God's *spiritual* life, the capacity to know and love God. Man lives, and lives spiritually, as the product of the very breath of God himself. This is the living part of man that reflects the very likeness— the image—of God. God built into man some of his own qualities or characteristics. Enough so that he and man could *know* each other and *love* each other. God and man were united in spirit.

> God created people to be moons to his sun,
> reflecting his image to earth.

But to grasp the meaning of the rest of the Story, we require another brief side trip.

God's purpose for creating man

Why did God create humans? Why did he create earth to be the beautiful and suitable environment for humankind? Why did God create anything? These questions puzzle all people to some degree. That curiosity is one of the primary evidences that humans are more than an accidental coincidence of chemical matter. And more than animal life. They ask questions about themselves and their environment.

An invention is under its creator's final control. He designs his machine, his object, or his service to fulfill a purpose, usually to meet a human need. He envisions a limited objective for his invention. The truly rational person, who knows he is but the creation of Another, seeks to know and fulfill the purpose for which that Creator designed him, for he senses that only God fully knows the *good* purpose for which he created him. It is God's enemy, the purveyor of death, who says to man, "You know better than God does what is good for you. Make up your own mind about your purpose."

Nowhere in this initial part of the Story did God *state in one sentence* his ultimate purpose for creating man. However, countless thoughtful seekers have sought the answer by analyzing the whole Story along with this part's commands, characterizations, conversations, assertions, hints, theology, and examples. The narrative grasp of the Bible recognizes how God created mankind to play roles in the epic drama of his Story, and cast humans as players in it. Believers understand that he has assigned us special roles. "He called us with a holy calling ... according to his own purpose and grace, revealed by the appearing of our Savior, Jesus Christ" (excerpts from 2 Timothy 1:7–10). To fulfill those roles, he equipped us with everything we need: "power, love, and sound minds," the discipline of self control.

For the moment we'll consider those specific purposes that God stated and implied in this part of the Story.

The first jumps out at us. God said, "Let us make man to carry our likeness ..." (Genesis 1:26).

Reflect God. Since God is pure good, pure love, pure righteousness, and pure joy, we can understand that his purpose to magnify and multiply the radiance of these qualities, reflected in billions of his family members populating the globe, is not a self-centered, narcissistic, tyrannically authoritarian demand. It is the only right and possible motive of generous love. Pure love wants to multiply objects of that love, people who can enjoy and return it in grateful praise. Pure glory wants more beings to enjoy it and share it. God's purpose for man grows out of his full and properly placed confidence that the reflections of his own good qualities are his best gifts to share with us. Humankind is the moon to God's sun, the multiplied reflections of his radiance. We are designed to be givers, born to give. That reciprocal, mutual (but not commercial) love exalts God's Name.

Reproduce images of God. God's first word to this newly minted couple, these earth persons who reflected himself, was the blessing of "Be fruitful and increase in number; fill the earth" (Genesis 1:28; 4:1). God's ultimate purpose for creating human sexuality was to perpetuate and exalt his name by populating earth with multiplying reflectors of his own brilliance, his Name.

God's first mandate to human beings, to produce a new generation of good people who would produce the further generations that would populate the earth, was an expression of the fact that beings who truly live by God's life produce more life. They give. They love to give. They give life. Here is the foundation of all healthy sex-education.

That life, along with its giving spirit, came originally from God. One of the unanswerable mysteries that puzzle all honest evolutionists is how supposedly spontaneous chemical combinations and later unintentional selection of features eventually produced human *moral values* such as altruism. Honest evolutionists think they can trace the development of *physical* characteristics and features. But they have no idea how physical features produce *spiritual, moral, and emotional* qualities. The Story's record of purposeful creation by a moral Creator answers that mystery.

God jealously guards the glory of his name of Creator—of being Life! He knows that only those who enjoy themself—who fully *live*—can enjoy human fulfillment. Worshiping substitutes and believing lies can lead only to death.

Here lies the ugliness of the contemporary so-called "right to choose" movement, which arrogates to the individual woman the supposed inalienable right to terminate the new life she is carrying within her. She, with her supporting society, presumes that the baby is hers alone and that its existence and continuing life are hers alone to decide. That presumption ignores not only the rights of the baby's father and the community but even more the right of the baby's Creator, life's Source.

Rule. God's second word repeated to Adam what the Persons of the Trinity had just said to each other: "Let them rule over the fish of the sea and the birds of the air, over the livestock, over all the earth [its systems], and over all the creatures that move along the ground" (Genesis 1:28). God appointed people to take care of ("rule") his other creatures, to be his stewards, trustees, or caretakers who exercise dominion over his created realm (Genesis 2:15). Humans would represent God's interests in managing the beautifully intertwined and interdependent elements of the environment.

Relate. Most religions teach that their deity is far off, either unreachable or very hard to reach—assuming it is the kind of god one would want to reach. The Story's God created man to be his friend. He made himself accessible to man. Man was not just a prized object to stand in God's trophy case as the lifeless symbol of God's inventive genius. He is the living, throbbing, creative image of God who can know him, recognize his worth, and respond to him in trusting love.

Reverence. Reverential respect that is afraid to disappoint would be the basis of the relationship. Respect is the basis for every good relationship. As God made human bodies to be temples or dwelling places of the Holy Spirit (2 Corinthians 5:1), he wanted to be first in people's thoughts, affections, and plans. They could know with God what he told them and think with God about those things. They could feel loyalty and affection for God. They could choose to love and please him and fear to displease him. In trustfully loving God they could know they were giving him the joy of their worshipful love while they enjoyed his loving fellowship.

And they would **rejoice** in their relationship with God. One whole book of the Story, Song of Songs, describes an ideal human romance. Metaphorically, it also describes God's ideal for his relationship with humanity. So, besides being a wonderful dialogue of human marital love, in this Song God speaks to his beloved as a groom to his bride. God constantly repeats this theme throughout the Story, sometimes in the most intimate spiritual terms. The Bible's "marriage" of God with man, in all its ideal dimensions, is an expression of how those who bear God's image also relate joyously to him.

When we describe God as good, we mean that all his attributes are good. God is good in all his ways, just as he is holy in all his ways, wise in his use of all his powers, and just in every expression of every one of his characteristics.

It is supremely important to God that he be known for his goodness. Therefore, man's original goodness reflected his Creator's. And even more to the point, it is God's pure goodness that Satan has chosen to malign as much as any of his qualities. When someone describes another as having lost their faith in God, what they usually mean is that they have lost their faith in God's goodness. They were disappointed in their expectations of God. When a darkened mind does not get from God what they thought was good, they think God is not good.

So, throughout the Story, God's goodness in himself, and as a reflected element in man, is a matter of great aspiration and tension.

The developing Story will describe ways in which God wanted this good relationship with humanity, this eternal walk in the garden, to develop. He wanted people to have the blessing of knowing him more and more fully. The friendship, founded as all healthy relationships are, in respect, was to be one of mutually joyful friendship.

Man's relationship would not be limited to that with God. As the drama began to unfold, people were to relate to their spouse, and to all others, as those who also bear God's image and name.

That is all this part of the Story plainly says about God's *purpose* for creating humankind. We might expand those single words to: "Reflect me", "Reproduce my likeness", "Rule for me", "Relate to me", and "Enjoy me." Or, to emphasize the essential moral quality of all this, "Be good like me," "Multiply my good likeness," "Take care of my good world," and "Be my good friends."

Magnify. What is the effect and result of man reflecting God, reproducing godly people, ruling earth properly, and relating to God as his friend? The result magnifies God's creative genius—in two senses of the word.

First, man's goodness exalts and perpetuates God's name. If "the heavens declare God's glory" in inanimate revelation of God's creative genius, how much more does God's vastly more complex creation, man, magnify God's name in intelligent gratitude and intentional cooperation with his Creator's mandates, starting with reproducing lovers of God? Second, man multiplies the qualities of God's name throughout the world as the lives of all Adam's descendants reflect them.

So the logic is this: in fulfilling God's original mandates of reflecting God, reproducing generations of those who carry God's image, ruling earth for God, rightly relating to God, and reverencing God, man *magnifies* the *glory* of God's great name as he established it in that creative work.

Every one of man's deepest, truest, and most lasting desires and aspirations—for essential goodness, for meaningfully creative and useful work, for meaningful relationships, for posterity, for recognition—is satisfied only by fulfilling their overriding purpose to exalt God's glory (Deuteronomy 11; John 4:4–15) by properly bearing his name and reflecting his likeness. Humans find their true glory and joy in reflecting and magnifying God's glory.

Chapter 2

The glory of the image

God is not the *Father* of a horse, a diamond, a planet, or a color. Even though all those are God's creatures and inventions, they are not his kin. God is the "Father of spirits" (Hebrews 12:9). Every attribute of the pure human spirit, intellect, affections, and will reflects a corresponding divine attribute that indicates derivation, resemblance, and intimacy. God made man to reflect his own abilities and energies (Genesis 2:7) in a physical human environment.

Do people *look like* God? No, and yes. Humans cannot look like God because God is pure spirit—that is, spirit without body—while a human is a spirit clothed with body. Pure spirit has no physical content to be seen, or to look like anything. God is different from us, other than us, holy, as in separate, other. Hence he commands that we not even attempt to make images of him to worship. Spirit is invisible. God is spirit. A human is a spirit clothed with a body.

At the same time, in another way people *can* look like God. If the human body's limbs and organs are the tools by which one expresses and lives out the values, decisions, purposes, and affections of the human spirit, a human's body in some degree expresses *God's* spirit. He created human bodies in which that reflected spirit of goodness, wisdom, and freedom live. A person's actions can make him look like God in action.

THE GLORY OF THE IMAGE

Have you ever found yourself in the presence of a truly godly person? What let you know that they were such? Didn't their eyes sparkle with interest and even caring compassion—that of God? Didn't you get a whiff of godly joyous peace, regardless of their circumstances? Weren't you the beneficiary of their simple goodness? When human faces and body language radiate the wisdom, the goodness, or the love of God, in that sense people look like God. Can a human hand heal a diseased body without being godlike? Doesn't that healing hand look like God's?

Other than in the incarnate Jesus, we cannot attribute to God a physical human body. It would be blasphemous for people to try to limit God to such a body. But still, just as the human body is the material image of the spiritual soul, it may be that, in a limited way, the image of God in humankind *expresses itself* in the various physical characteristics and capacities of the human body. When God revealed himself to humans in their physical environment, sometimes he looked like a person (Ezekiel 1:26-28). And when he joined humanity in the Person of Jesus Christ for the purpose of rescuing, redeeming, and restoring us, he took on a real, working, eating, drinking, sleeping human body (Philippians 2:5-8; 1 John 1:1-3; 4:2-3; etc.). In the mysterious splendor of taking on a human nature, the second Person, Jesus, showed us the fabulous perfection of what God looks like in a human body. "The Word became flesh and made his dwelling among us. We beheld his glory, the glory of the only Son, ... full of grace and truth" (John 1:14).

When he finished creating man, "God saw all that he had made, and it was *very good*" (Genesis 1:31, emphasis added). God felt proud of his highest and best invention. He had fashioned people to be capable of all the relationships, activities, and plans for which he had designed them. He had placed them in a richly pristine environment that provided everything they could possibly need or desire. As God celebrated that first Sabbath, it was as though he leaned back against a tree, folded his arms, and said, "This is good work. I'm glad to put my good name on man and his environment."

What makes humanity God's showpiece? How did humans differ from all other merely "good" creatures? How did people especially reveal and reflect the glory of their Creator, an exclusively spirit being? Why was God proud to put his name and likeness on this creature?

"So God created mankind in his own image, in the image of God he created him; male and female he created them." Adam carried the special reflections of the masculine aspects of God's moral nature. Eve wore the special features of the feminine aspects of God's moral nature. Their bodies truly were temples of the living God. Together they were the place of God's dwelling on earth. Their unique sexual and gender characteristics were capable of expressing the highest degree of spiritual, intellectual, emotional, and intentional ecstasy in the bodily union that creates and sustains the new life that perpetuates God's name on earth.

Centuries later, Israel's King David reflected, "You have made man a little lower than the heavenly beings, and crowned him with glory and honor. You have given him dominion over the works of your hands; you have put all things under his feet. ... O Lord, our Lord, how majestic is your name in all the earth!" (Psalm 8:5–9).

In all this likeness, man was "the image and glory of God" (1 Corinthians 11:7). The Creator put some of his radiance on and into humankind. The creature's glory reflected that of its Creator. God was establishing and multiplying the divine Name on earth in and among people.

Newly created man was blessed with amazing faculties, a few of which he shared with the animals. They included man's five senses or capacities for awareness of their environment. They also included the sensory systems that gave them awareness of themselves. These systems include the senses of pressure, itch, temperature, pain, thirst, hunger, direction, time, muscle tension, and gravity; the capacity to sense without looking where body parts are relative to other body parts; the ability to maintain balance and sense body movement in terms of acceleration and directional changes; awareness of stretching in organs such as the lungs, bladder, stomach, blood vessels, and the gastrointestinal tract; and the ability to be aware of blood-borne hormones and drugs. Add the mysterious abilities sometimes to sense the presence of others or to "feel" that someone is focusing attention on us. But these features have to do with man's body, many in common with animals.

The image of God had to include man's spiritual capacities. As created, they had to be without imperfection, corruption, or any principle of sin of body or soul. God-likeness must have included man's self-consciousness, their awareness of their essence and self, of personal identity, of the "me" that could relate to other persons. A person can stand outside themself to analyze themself, stopping to observe and critique the person who inhabits, animates, and controls their body to accomplish the goals they set for themself. They can think about their own feelings, beliefs, and behaviors. They can imagine the future, and their plans for that future. They can know their environment, how it affects them, and how they affect it. They can know other people and communicate with them, influencing their feelings and behaviors. A human conscience—one's sense of morality—can evaluate the relative rightness of their behaviors with and toward those others, either approving or condemning them. God gave humans the capacity to make decisions, to act intentionally about their moral judgments, and to conduct themselves in conformity with them. An image bearer can plan how to get things done. They are a builder. Most important, the image included one's capacity to know God.

Later in the Story, Jesus' messenger John summed up all of God's awesome features in the simple but profoundly rich word *love*. "God is love." If any word could sum up newly created human likeness to God, it must have been this one. And since the Bible's love is not a feeling but an intentional action of benefitting the one loved, God created Adam and Eve fully equipped to love in some semblance of the way God loved.

The most basic element of a person's likeness to God is the fact that they are *alive*. God—the *living* God, the eternal One, always the immediately past, present, and future I AM—shared with man some of his essential quality, *life*. Man possesses life, the human life that relies on and multiplies God's living nature. Such is human life in all its magnificent expressions of energy, awareness, and purpose, especially the capacity to *give* intentionally and rationally, to pass on some of God's life to another.

Newly minted man shared God's nature of being a living *spirit*. God, a spirit without a body, produced man, a spirit living in a body. Perhaps that nature explains why every normal person hungers for eternity, expecting to live forever. Their most basic nature resists dying. Their every instinct is to perpetuate themselves and their name, personally and through their progeny. The expectation of continuous existence is another reflection of their Creator's eternal nature.

But in all their goodness and magnificence, man was not God. The difference between God and his creature man was twofold: first God, the *infinite, limitless* Spirit, produced man, a *finite, limited* spirit. God knows *all* things; man can know *some* things. In his immensity, God at all times rules everything everywhere and beyond everywhere. A human can be only *some*where. God's power is limited only by his own pure character. A human's power always is limited by their Creator's sovereignty.

Second, God is spirit that is not confined to a body; he gave man a body in which to house his spirit. It was a body suited to the beautiful environment God already had arranged. But that body also limited one's presence to the place that body inhabited.

The first two people shared God's spiritual and moral capacities to know truth, righteousness, and holiness (Ephesians 4:24; Colossians 3:10). God gave them self-consciousness, including awareness of themselves, of their Creator, of their similarities to their Creator, and of their environment. He gave them self-possession. They could relate intentionally with others, give themselves to others.

They could know; understand, remember; think; analyze (including analyzing their past, present, and future forecasts); synthesize and correlate information and ideas (recognizing both the parts and their meaningful places in the systems to which they contribute); organize; plan; feel; and make the free, self-determining decisions that produce and maintain right relationships—the relationships that constitute righteousness.

No animal, vegetable, or mineral could claim the moral and spiritual correspondence to their Creator that man could. The image of God in man consists in that which links him with God's personality, a rational, self-conscious, self-determining personality, capable of joyful fellowship with their Creator.

Animals act but are bound by created instinct to behave only as God programmed their behavior. God gave man freedom to evaluate and *choose* behavior. The first two people *were* good.

A human's likeness to God distinguishes them from the brute animals also in that while man's body links him to the earth from which God molded it, God's image also links one spiritually and morally to their Creator. Neither the most regal lion, the most resourceful ant, nor the strongest elephant can claim such honor. Neither the strongest force of gravity nor the breathtaking vastness of the countless solar systems in the still-expanding intergalactic cosmos can claim the honor of bearing I AM's *image and likeness*. Watermarks of the Creator's genius, yes. But not his likeness. God gave that likeness to humankind alone.

We have noted that the Creator's nature also is triune. He is one Being in three Persons. His essential nature is that of ideally related, unified plurality. God is a relational being. The developing Story reveals the Father, the Son, and the Spirit eternally maintaining constant, uninterrupted, unblemished harmony of mutual trust, affection, and purpose. Such a relational Being creating living man in his own likeness gave him a fundamentally relational nature, the need and capacity for relationships. Man was capable of intentionally forming, nourishing, and maintaining good relationships with their environment, within the God-reflecting parts of their own personality, and with other humans. Man was *righteous*. Yes, God created two people, a relational unit. The first man and woman together made up original humankind.

Still, Adam must have realized that God had not created him to be his equal. God had not cloned himself into man. The "image" meant only that mankind *resembled their* Creator, that they *reflected* enough of his qualities to be able to fulfill their intended destiny of enjoying, knowing, and loving God. Adam must have recognized that a creator always remains superior to what he invents.

Each quality of likeness to God was only a partial reflection of the limitless glory of the Creator. Human intelligence was limited, leaving some mysteries for God alone to know completely. Human freedom and ability to make choices were subject to God's final judgment and benevolently authoritative control. Human creativity enhanced first the name of the superior craftsman from whom it came. Adam did not radiate personal glory. He was not a sun, but a moon reflecting his Creator's radiance. And it would take the combined billions of reflections of God's nature spread through earth's total eventual population to reflect God's glory most fully. *Most* fully, not completely, for God's splendor is infinite.

For example, God did not tell Adam and Eve everything he knows. Two factors control this. First, the timeless God created time, then created humans to live within the confines of that time. Not enough time exists in which God could communicate to time-limited man everything he knows.

Second, all the greatest minds of all time combined into one super genius mind is not large enough or quick enough to learn and contain all that is in God's infinitely vast mind. Our reflections of God's glory are merely that—reflections. We exist to adorn, exalt, extend, magnify, and enjoy the glory of *God's* unlimited mind. It is a good idea for us to content ourselves with grasping what God has chosen to tell us. We don't need to know *all* his reasons for creating us, or for anything else that he does—just those he has told us.

Yes, the first pair must have recognized their Creator's superiority over the greatest of his creatures. "… the King of kings and Lord of lords, who alone is immortal and who lives in unapproachable light, whom no one has seen or can see. To him be honor and might forever" (1 Timothy 6:15–16).

The Story's evaluation of just-created mankind in their pristine environment is, "God saw all that he had made, and it was very good" (Genesis 1:31). Everything else was "good" in itself. Adding people made the system "very good."

God was so pleased with his work that he spent the last day of creation week celebrating (Genesis 2:2, 3).

Imbedded in all this is the main point of creation's record. In creation, God established the glory of his Name as the super-genius architect, designer, and builder of all that is. Every influence, relationship, and connection of every interrelated and interdependent energy, particle, part, and subsystem of the vast and intricate system reveals the transcendent heart and unfathomable mind of its Creator. Particularly his showpiece, man. Creation established God's name. His splendor, reflected in mankind, enhanced and multiplied his radiance. No wonder that God was properly proud of his creative work, and of the result, his creation.

The Creator is God. Elohim God is the only one capable of creating this amazing cosmos. Elohim is the good God, the Most High, who produced the good creation.

In the next part of the Story, when God began to interact with his just-created Adam and Eve, he began to use another of his names.

Chapter 3

I Am, Yahweh Elohim

The second chapter of Genesis reviews parts of the creation story outlined in the first chapter, adding new detail. And it adds a new element of God's name. Yahweh is added to Elohim. Yahweh Elohim, the Lord God: "When the LORD God made the earth and the heavens, …" (Genesis 2:4). The Story later develops the fuller meaning of Yahweh. Here, because God had Moses use it in describing creation's details, the name's meaning seems to be *the only God who can create something out of nothing.* Elohim Yahweh, essential being, is the Source of everything outside himself. As life itself, he is all other life's Source and ground of being. The sovereign God is sublimely superior to his creation in every way.

A note in the Scofield Bible suggests that the Story introduces the name Yahweh Elohim at this point in the creation narrative especially in relation to mankind. It was natural that the newly minted Adam and Eve would wonder about their source, their beginning. If we had just come into existence, wouldn't it have occurred to us to wonder how we got here? It didn't take generations of people for that universal question to arise. It's not only small children that ask, "Mommy, where did I come from?"

The Story does not mention such a conversation. Perhaps God

just added his identity Yahweh—Essential Being—to Elohim, to hint to the two all they then needed to know. "I am the Essential Being who inhabits eternity. I formed you. You derived from me, sovereign God. You began in me, my mind, my heart, my will. I am your Source, your Everlasting Father." That is how God wanted the first humans to know him.

Since God created everything that exists outside himself, and since that everything derives its being from him, that makes him the being who matters most. Countless times during the Story's development, God reminded other characters that it was *he* who created. His creation established his Name.

Since all other life not only came into existence by God's creation but depends on him for its continuing existence, disconnection from God is death. His reason for warning Adam and Eve to avoid eating fruit from Eden's tree of the knowledge of good and evil was that doing so would result in their deaths (Genesis 2:16–17).

Why have we spent so many pages on the first scene of the Story? Because God displayed his creative brilliance and genius in man. Adam and Eve were God's crowning achievement, his masterpiece workmanship, the centerpiece of all creation. But even more, because in designing mankind in his own image *God forever connected his name with his creatures*. God wants all rational beings in the heavens and on earth to know that he is mankind's Creator. The goodness of God's name forever rides on mankind and their care of God's good earth.

Further, understanding the rest of the Story depends on recognizing God's creative work, particularly as it involves creating and restoring mankind in his image. Restoring the image on which God's name rides so prominently is major in the Story. We can grasp God's *restoring* work only in light of his original creative work.

God's image in humans is central and vital to his Story, because God expects all people to recognize his likeness not only in themselves but in all other people, too. As Jesus later formulated in what has become known as the "Golden Rule," he expects us image-bearers to recognize and treat every human being as a fellow image-bearer.

It's no wonder God repeatedly and proudly referred to himself as Creator. Later in the Story, he refers to himself with more than twelve synonyms and variations of Creator, including Architect, Builder, Creator of the ends of the earth, Father of Lights, Former of All things, Maker of heaven and earth, and Potter. Imbedded in *Potter* is the right of molding, remolding, rebuilding, and restoring. No wonder God loves to be known as Creator. His workmanship was worthy of his imprint. The cosmos and its showpiece, mankind, adorned his name with the glory it deserved. In mankind as well as the galaxies, God revealed the radiance of the glory of his creative life. In all creation, and especially in man, God established his Name. God. Creator. Good Creator of the good creature. Essential Being, the living one, the source of all life.

If God endowed the first human brains with genius-like capacities, then we can see not only how Adam and Eve reflected God's image but how much they must have enjoyed exploring the infinity of God's attributes. The brilliant Adam not only understood the fauna of the garden but was able to name each species of it in all its variety. And they could *know* God! They had the ability and capacities to know him whom to know aright *is* eternal life (John 17:3). They felt the wondrous, awesome honor, above all other earthly creatures, of knowing, exploring, adoring, enjoying, and serving the God who gave him life in his own likeness. The living, infinite, good, right Designer of all things. Here was the glory of life in Eden!

The Story gives no hint of how long this idyllic friendship continued. Any guess is only that.

Why do I say this in the past tense? More than to indicate historical fact. Because of what happened next.

Stage 2

THE NAME SOILED IN THE FALL

Chapter 4

The Name distrusted

Every story's plot includes a conflict. At least one. A conflict requires a hero and a villain. Any story's protagonist and antagonist compete for something prized by both. What is at stake in the Bible's plot line are God's power and his reputation as right and good, his trustworthiness. In oriental terms, his "face." In Bible terms, God's Name.

The Bible Story's second stage introduces its villain, Satan, and its main conflict, his efforts to depose God and ascend his throne to rule over mankind, to usurp God's Name and role on earth. The third chapter of Genesis describes the initial engagement of that war.

> Sin started with deadly competition for the Name.

The beautiful serpent that sashayed into the garden coveted and competed for the Name and the throne that went with it. Secretly, Satan wanted humans' worship, not *along with* God, but *instead of* God. He lusted to be God. But since he was a created being, he knew he was not strong enough or clever enough to win a faceoff with God. He would have to content himself with gaining rule over some of God's prized creation. To secure that rule he needed an agent through which to act. Satan needed to trick humans into worshiping himself instead of God, while at the same time trashing God's beautiful creation. To gain the trust of God's creatures for his own name, he had to lower their trust in God and his Name. He had to persuade Adam and Eve that God was *not* good, *not* worthy of worship, and manipulate them into putting himself above God.

Hoping to lower God's name so as to make his own seem higher, Satan used all his evil attributes, setting out to prove to innocent humans that their Creator was not trustworthy, not believable, not truly good, and therefore not to be obeyed. Since manipulation involves self-serving ends, and loss to the one being manipulated, it always requires careful deception. Satan, the master liar, the father of all deceit, was confident that he was up to the task (Revelation 12:9).

Satan knew that God risked his name by connecting it with that of humans, creating them to reflect his own character, and giving them freedom to stay close to himself. So Satan pretended to be even more concerned for Eve than God was. And even though God had warned his most highly prized creatures, they ignored his cautions. Subtly at first, then increasingly openly as he gained traction in Eve's mind, the serpent approached her with questions, innuendo, and accusations about God's character and Name (Genesis 3).

Apparently blinded, at least temporarily, to God's glory, perhaps by Satan's outstanding beauty, Eve became susceptible to visions of her self-elevation to godhood—just what Satan intended. Whether an effect of his first question only made her susceptible or whether it was the seed, Satan sowed in her heart the beginning of what ruled him, pride. Her name became more important to her than God's Name. This was the poison that would drive all descendants of that original pair for the rest of time: the deep hunger to compete for personal mastery over all other beings, the sense of being the center of the world.

Satan's influence always has depended on cunning deception. He was contradicting God's truth, literally turning knowledge upside down. God had said, "My creation is good; man is *very* good." Satan implied to Eve, "Your situation is *not* very good. If you follow me, you and I will make it better." He was making lies seem like truth and God's truth seem like lies. And in the process he was doing all he could to wreck not only God's good Name but everything about his good creation.

Soon Eve would learn that she *needed* a superior God. That God had designed her to operate best under his good rule, depending on him for life and all its gifts. But she would learn it the hard way, through trying to live without him.

Satan's clever conversation with Eve first led her to doubt her understanding of what God had said, then to doubting his goodness and his word. Doubt planted in her the spirit of deprivation. Satan then infected his victim with pride, the sense that she was her own god, that she knew better than God, especially of what was right and what was wrong.

With this foothold, Satan bared his teeth against God's warning of death: "You will *not* die. Look how *good* that fruit looks! It will make you *good*, like God!" (Genesis 3:4–5)

Eve must have thought, *That fruit looks deliciously good. Since God does not care about us, we will need to take care of ourselves. Satan is right. I'm as good as God. I know good and evil when I see it, too. I can run my own life, thank you. My name is worth as much worship as God's. I am fully capable of assuming the role of final judge of what is good and what is evil. I can even judge whether God is right or wrong. I can decide if he is good or evil.*

In the mother of all living, the devil had succeeded in trashing God's name. Those seeds grew into unbelief and arrogance that resulted in outright, rebellious disobedience to the plainly stated will of God.

Where was Adam during this conversation? The text does not say. Adam apparently stood silently by, not protesting her descent into Satan's world of deceit. We get a hint from Paul's first letter to Timothy in "Adam was not the one deceived" (1 Timothy 2:14). Maybe he was somewhere else tending the garden. If he overheard what Satan was telling Eve, he failed her—terribly. He neither protected her from Satan's lie nor said anything to stop her. Weakly, he went along, eating what he knew God had forbidden as well as she did. He utterly failed to be the leader and protector God intended. God had equipped him to *rule* the environment. But he failed to guard even his own home. God assigned him responsibility. Almost every Story reference to mankind's sinfulness traces its cause to *Adam's* fall.

Consequences

> The finest apple branch shrivels
> when cut off from its tree.

Apparently immediately, the enormity of what Adam and Eve had done by believing Satan instead of God began to dawn on the fallen pair. Their first realization was shame. Eve gasped, "Oh Adam, I'm naked!" He replied, "So am I!" (Genesis 3:7). Shame? Over the *good* bodies God had fashioned for them? This may have been false shame or real shame. Or some of both. Their self-respect—proper self-confidence—had died. They were ashamed that they had not lived up to their name or God's. Ashamed that they had violated the divine image in them.

They were ashamed of trying to be their own gods, and in doing so losing the goodness with which God had created them. They had known goodness, but now knew only lack of it. They were ashamed for being responsible for losing it.

These causes of their shame converged in shame of their sexuality. But not because they had misused, abused, or perverted their sexual capacities. The sexual shame was only in their minds, deceptively planted there by Satan to separate them from each other and from God. Their sexuality, the highest gifts of mutual marital love, giving, joy, creativity, bonding, and procreation, along with the organs with which to express them, became a false focus of their spiritual shame.

Ideal sexual intimacy, with its mutual self-exposure and vulnerability, combined and blended with mutual giving and receiving, all conscious of the presence and joy of God, became tainted with shame, not because the intimacy itself is evil but because Satan had warped their minds to *think* it is evil.

Satan's gift to man was shame. Shame and its sister, a sense of inferiority, grow from guilt. Shame breeds comparison, competition, arrogance, and pride, exactly what Satan wanted for them. True confidence, with which God had fully furnished Adam and Eve before their fall, grows out of humility—seeing ourselves as God sees us. The image of God deserves confidence. Evidences of death reminded the pair of their sin. Their very genetic makeup was corrupted.

In a clumsy attempt at modesty, they gathered some large leaves and twisted the stems together to hang over their shoulders as crude aprons. The world's fashion industry had its inception.

Humanity's descent had begun, into the inky, stinking depths of moral, spiritual, psychological, social, economic, and every other kind of corruption and death. Not into *goodness*, but into death.

Satan must have smirked as his plot began to unfold. The decay of death began to set in. The couple's belief in his lies had given him moral control over their spirits. The pair no longer recognized or honored the beautiful glory of their own being that came from God and belonged to God. Death had damaged and obliterated much of the image of God in them. From then on they would tend to forget and ignore the dimmed reflections of their likeness to God that, unknowingly but certainly, they had lost.

Because their goodness was now missing, hunger for righteousness spread throughout their bodies and souls. That awareness of loss of righteousness was one of the few vestiges of original human goodness that remained to them.

Mankind had died to God. Still at work in Adam's mind, Satan manipulated him to blame God for having made a huge mistake in creating him.

Adam had done more than cut himself off from God's fellowship. He became God's enemy (Romans 8:7). Apparently, along with other deadly effects of Adam's fall, Satan planted in his heart that resistance against the Heavenly Father. It's no wonder that Jesus, while he was here, made a major effort to restore trust in "the Father," "my Father," "your Father," and "our Father."

During the conversation that ensued, God called Adam to account for what had happened: "Who told you that you were naked? Have you eaten from the tree that I commanded you not to eat from?"

Adam replied, "The woman *you* gave me tempted me to eat." Death corrupted the most intimate relationship. Marital abuse had begun. Adam became willing to shift blame and even worse, in this case, to *accuse* God!

What had been Adam's joyful God-centeredness and admiring love for Eve became narcissism. Their newly warped sense of self-centered worship had to justify itself.

Eve, infected with the same virus of fear, also pitch-forked the blame: "The serpent deceived me, and I ate." Indeed, he had deceived her.

The reptile that had become Satan's agent of deception received God's first curse: "Forever you will crawl in the dust" (Genesis 3:14).

Along with his first pronouncement of sin's effects and consequences, Yahweh gave his first hint about how he eventually would solve the problem of evil Satan had just introduced into his good creation. Evidently the couple's sin did not surprise him. He informed Satan of the plan that he'd had in mind from the beginning: "I will put enmity between you and the woman, and between your offspring and hers; he will crush your head, and you will strike his heel" (Genesis 3:15). As Satan someday was going to strike the heel of Eve's descendant, that Heel would crush his head. Thousands of years would pass before Jesus kept this promise.

From this point on, every page of the Story, in the dimmest tint or most vivid brilliance, would add its brushstroke to the predictions of the restored Eden and the restored image in mankind. From struck heel, suggesting divine self-sacrifice in conflict, and crushed head, intimating the serpent's defeat, to plainly detailed descriptions of the Restorer who was to come someday, the Story progressed. The coming Savior would restore the image of God in humans, the likeness that we ruined and lost. In the process, the predicted Jesus would restore God's Name. Every color and detail of the Story would add another level of understanding of the Creator who would become the Re-Creator, the Restorer of mankind and Eden.

It must have been with deep sadness that God explained to the couple the life they had forfeited, the sentence they had brought on themselves and their environment. No vindictiveness edged his voice as he reminded them of the consequences of buying into Satan's lies about him. Perhaps tears slid down his cheeks and his voice broke as he told them they had not lived up to their potential, or to the divine name they bore.

By ruining mankind, Satan also ruined the system—the environment—that depends on human custodial care, their mandate to "rule." Thistles and thorns began to crowd out the luxuriant crops that had been flourishing. Previously vegetarian animals became carnivorous. Death spread from people, infecting the animal and vegetable worlds that God had trusted to them.

Death's darkness deepened. The pair's choice to trust Satan's scheme to acquire a name for themselves broke the circuit of their spiritual connection to their Creator. When they sought equality with God, their union with him disconnected. Every part and every relationship within God's good system suffered disruption. Satan's lies that replaced God's truth switched off the light of joyful living in their souls. They became blind to God and to his presence in their lives. They cut their spiritual ties. As the apostle Paul much later described fallen man, "Although they knew God, they neither glorified him as God nor gave thanks to him, but their thinking became futile and their foolish hearts were darkened. Although they claimed to be wise, they became fools ..." (Romans 1:21-22). Although God still was everywhere around them, they lost the spiritual faculty of being able to recognize him accurately. The inevitable result of separation from the living God, life's only source, was death.

Worst of all, Satan had tricked them into damaging, despoiling, and maligning God's Name by bringing death to his living image in humans. When Adam fell into the trap, he became Satan's agent to continue and multiply all his other malicious attacks on God's glorious Name. Satan's jealousy of the Righteous One is the real source of human sin, the fountain of all human suffering and degradation.

It would take the man and the woman the rest of their now limited lives to experience all that death meant. The normal attitudes of the creature toward the Creator were gone, along with those toward the other creatures. They had muffled their ears to truth, blindfolded their minds to true beauty. They lost their former sense of being responsible entities.

Perhaps one reason God did not allow the fall to annihilate *every* aspect and quality of his image in man was to leave us reminders of what we once were, and of what we still can be, motivating us to hunger for restoration.

God himself must fix our nature.

The pagan Menya people of Papua New Guinea grasp this better than most "civilized" people. Missionaries with Ethnos 360 Mission carefully taught them about how God created all things, then man. And how Satan had tricked man into listening to him instead of God. And how that distrust of God brought death into the world, corrupting not only man's conduct but their very nature. Hearing these facts, a Menya woman, Rita, said, "Adam's nature remains in us. God is not pleased. We can't escape this—our nature. We still have it. Their sinfulness remains in us. We cannot fix it. God himself must fix our nature. Only he can do it."[5]

THE NAME DISTRUSTED

Satan's vicious hatred for God and his prize creation set out to increase the effects of mankind's death to God. Sin's dying convulsions proved to include:

Loss of their center in the Creator and Sustainer, their
    joyful life purpose and meaning;
 loss of their supreme love;
  loss of the Source of self-respect;
   using others as objects of selfish desire and lust
      instead of loving them;
    passing blame, including blaming God for the gift of
      moral freedom,
     in the process ruining his Name among men;
     judgmentalism, attempts to assume God's judgment bench;
    peevish, angry tempers;
   hard-heartedness;
    murder and hatred;
   taking advantage of others;
    unbelief and suspicion;
     presumption and attempted use of God
       instead of trusting and obeying him;
    pride;
   unfaithfulness to word and vow;
   disloyalty;
    indecisiveness;
     deception; untruthfulness, and deceit of every
       degree;
     injustice;
    poverty;
     impurity of thought, word, and action;
     covetousness;
      all idolatry;
       fearful hoarding;

squandering improvidence;
sins private and public;
irreverent and selfish prayer;
misused time;
unnecessary dependency;
competition, conflict, and war;
selfish jealousy;
small and mean objectives;
all the diseases of mind, body,
emotions, and spirit,
starting with shame and the guilty
conscience;
all pain, starting with birthing labor
pains and unfruitful labor;
and eventually,
the grave.

Under Satan's manipulation, man had infected God's whole created system with death. Death was much more than the personal penalty for capital crime. It was the inevitable consequence of separation from God. With what must have been gut-wrenching horror, Adam and Eve began to realize what death meant. Every interrelated part and subsystem of creation began to fall apart. The system on which God had proudly inscribed his Name began to disintegrate. Creeping death took over everything.

Spoiler Alert!
In terms of the stage,
the Bible's Story is not a tragedy,
but a comedy.

Yet along with describing the kinds of death they had brought on themselves, on their descendants, and on their environment, God gave the first couple some hope. He promised that in a limited, handicapped way they could still accomplish at least some of his purposes for creating them, starting with populating earth with people, even though now only through pain.

Stage 3

THE NAME ENLARGED IN HISTORY

Chapter 5

The conflict for name continues

It was not long before another level of horror struck the young couple: their first realization of genetic sin and consequent continuing death.

Out of the intimate mutual knowing of their love, Eve gave birth to a son. The wonder of Cain's birth, the first in human history, struck her in just the way it should have. She exclaimed, "I have borne a *seed*, a man, a person in the image of God! Sharing with God's creativity, I have gotten a man!" (see Genesis 4:1). Eve made history by giving her son a name, Cain, that meant precisely what she wanted it to mean.

Within a few years, she bore another son, Abel. The text does not mention the daughters who also must have been born.

The Story likewise includes few details of the family's growth. It is not difficult to imagine what Adam and Eve must have felt as the family grew and grew up. They must have delighted in cuddling each new expression of the lingering image of God. But they must have writhed in regret as they saw in their children the same mixture of delightfully innocent smiles and instinctively self-centered manipulations we see in all our infants.

Satan was not done with his plots to denigrate God's name and to ruin God's plan for restoring it. Although his name does not appear in every subplot of the Story, his work is plain, as person after person, family after family, nation after nation displayed the deadly effects of disrespecting, disbelieving, and distrusting God's name, disobeying his good laws that, had they been obeyed, would have brought life.

So Adam and Eve watched their firstborn, Cain, grow up at least a willful rebel, determined to do things his own way, regardless of what Adam and Eve tried to teach him about God and his good ways. They knew they were responsible for passing on to him the spiritual DNA of that rebellion—the death gene—, the kind of free thinking that opposed all that the image of God was supposed to produce.

Was Cain jealous over what every generation and culture of later history has noted: loss of the full attention of his parents when baby Abel was born? Or was he infected with the angry spirit of deprivation and victimization that is the result of ingratitude and resentment that reveals an essentially bad attitude toward God—what God labels as an "evil" heart? Perhaps some of both.

Since Cain was born dead to God, he was blind to the vestiges of God's likeness in Abel. Maybe he misinterpreted Abel's devotion to God as religious arrogance and judgmentalism toward his own rebellious behaviors.

At any rate, what should have been Cain's admiration for his brother's trusting and obedient spirit toward God became jealousy and accusation (1 John 3:12). The parents must have been pleased to see Abel's positive response to their teaching. But they must also have been worried about Cain's unruly, independent spirit, his desire for self-exaltation, that showed in his frequent disobedience to God's clear commands.

As they grew into manhood, both sons followed Adam into agriculture. Abel specialized in animal husbandry, becoming a shepherd. Cain cultivated crops.

The crisis came at harvest time. In obedient faith and token of stewardship, Abel gave God the best and fattest of his flock, showing his gratitude and willingness to sacrifice future wealth, as well as present income. Cain knew as well as Abel did that God expected him to bring offerings from the flocks to sacrifice in faith (Genesis 4:4 with Hebrews 11:4). In his typical proud independence and petulant reluctance, he brought to his own altar some of his grain and produce.

Cain's resentful heart revealed itself even more plainly when God told him he was pleased with Abel's offering, but not with his. He dropped his head trying to hide the dark look and flared nostrils of angry discontent that were disfiguring his face. But he could not hide his guilty heart from God.

Cain's offering was unacceptable to God, not on some arbitrary grounds and not only because he gave an offering from the crops he had raised instead of the animal sacrifice God desired. God knew Cain offered his "creative" offering out of an ungratefully resistant heart, for the faithless purpose of attempting to gain favor with God instead of showing gratitude for God's forgiveness pictured in the sacrificial lamb.

After challenging Cain to examine his motive, God warned him that he had put himself in serious danger. "If you do not do what is right, sin is crouching at your door; it desires to have you, but you must rule over it" (vv. 6–7).

But instead of producing the intended repentance, God's rebuke only further hardened Cain's jealous wrath. His self-centered view, his self-exaltation, blinded him to God's goodness. His misplaced rage over Abel's blessing from God took such control of him that, rejecting God's warning and yielding to Satan's murderous malignancy, he began to plot his brother's death. He never stopped to think, or didn't care, that his brother bore God's image. Abel's righteous life was too great an aggravation. Cain's view of life had to rule. Abel was in the way. As a mere obstacle, he had to go.

So, while they were away from the farmstead together, far out in a field, Cain struck, killing Abel.

In that fatal blow the first family fractured with history's first

evidence of a man letting Satan rule their heart;
   its first joyless, envious, legalistic religious sacrifice;
      its first marvelous birth shadowed by its first human death;
         its first murder, struck against the image and name of God, which
            is the excellence of human nature;
      its first premeditated murder;
     its first fratricide;
       its first war, and first religious war;
         its first martyr;
           its first funeral of a child before their parents;
             with all its grief,
               shame,
                 sorrow,
                   and regret;
                     and the first banishment from human society,
                       foreshadowing eternal death alone in outer darkness.

Cain's selfish jealousy trumped the brotherly love that ought to have wanted Abel's name and progeny to continue. He thought only about having eliminated his brother's competition.

Cain further revealed his wickedly loveless heart—his true character—when God asked him where Abel was (v. 9). Instead of showing remorse, to imply his innocence Cain replied with his now infamous insolent diversionary tactic, "How should I know? Am I my brother's guardian?"

The attempted evasion didn't work. Cain learned again that God knows everything. With as much sadness as he had felt as he informed Cain's parents of the deadly consequences of their unbelieving act in Eden, God replied to Cain's pretended innocence, "Look at what *you've* done! Listen to what I'm hearing. Your brother's very lifeblood is crying out to me from the ground into which it is soaking, begging me for justice for being denied the right to live. Now you have put yourself under a curse. The earth that drank your brother's blood will

THE CONFLICT FOR NAME CONTINUES

refuse any longer to give you its fruit. You will become a perpetually fear-filled fugitive and vagabond, ever running from your guilty conscience as you try to find a way to earn your living."

Cain began to realize the appeal of home, and the special presence of God there, both of which his actions now had forfeited for life (Genesis 4:13-14). But shame over loss of his security and of damage to his own name only added resentment to his still rebellious heart. In self-pity and self-justification, he lashed out with insolent accusation, "God, your punishment is too harsh! I don't deserve it!"

Imagine what Adam and Eve must have felt. Cain, their firstborn, who ought to have perpetuated the honor of the first family's name, and with it the Name of his parents' Creator, was exiled—by God himself. Many of the generations he later founded demonstrated that they had inherited his evil-hearted instincts, further maligning his Name by multiplying the corruption that ended only in the flood of Noah's day.

Further, the family's only other son was dead. As far as they could see, their mandate from God, to multiply people who bore God's image and name, was as dead as Abel. The deep heaviness of the consequences of their original distrust of God, now demonstrated in Cain's blot on God's name and his own, nearly suffocated them as they realized how it had infected their family. Instead of perpetuating the image of God in their sons, they had birthed children infected with the same doubt and distrust of God they had accepted from Satan in the garden. They must have felt as guilty as Cain did.

From then on, the battle has raged. God has continued to work, against opposition, to reveal more of himself. And to restore and justify the glory of his good Name so that men can know him as he really is, trust him, and experience true living in exalting him in loving obedience. Satan has been darkening the Name, tearing it down so that people will not believe God and will live without knowing him, therefore demeaning his glory.

Satan has been more than successful. Inserting God's name or values into almost any conversation in today's America results in discomfort at best. God—at least the God of the Story—is not an attractive object. One's view of God is supposed to have nothing to do with their politics, their business, or the national conversation. The average person permits God only a narrow slice of their weekly time, if any. Many treat God as an angry, judgmental spoilsport. They view his ideas as old-fashioned, irrelevant, certainly unscientific. God's Name gets little, if any, respect. Even for many "Christians," God is only a benign old Santa Clause in the sky, whom as often as not they blame for inattention and heartlessness. Satan seems to be winning.

One example: In the American national debate over personal rights, how often is an unborn child recognized as bearing the image of God? How often does a woman who is demanding her "right" to decide the fate of her unborn child say, "I don't care whether my fetus carries God's image! It is my possession about which to decide." And to what degree did the U. S. Supreme Court consider God's image in each fetus when it legalized the decision about opting for an abortion as the final right of the mother?

In order to teach us how helpless we are, God has allowed Satan to be so successful that it is difficult to see God's image remaining in mankind, let alone having them gratefully proud to bear his Name. See the first three chapters of Romans.

Job, the pawn of Satan's hatred of God

Although scholars included the narrative of Job's intense sufferings in the poetical writings that are grouped near the middle of the Old Testament, that famous man probably lived very early in the Story, perhaps even before Abraham. His story reveals mysteries we could not otherwise have known. It gives us unearthly glimpses into what sometimes goes on in heaven between God and his enemy, Satan. It demonstrates how God protects his sheep from Satan's most malicious plots, even when he gives Satan rope to test and torment a godly believer.

Job's story describes just one set of Satan's hateful attacks on God's Name, the name that Job properly bore. As far as the record goes, Job apparently never learned that the real cause of all his suffering was nothing in his own life, but actually was Satan's attempt to hurt God by hurting one of the finest examples of those who bore his name and his image to a high degree.

As the story climaxed, God revealed to Job wonders of which he never had dreamed. Wonders that only God could perform. Wonders that gave perspective to Job's very real suffering. Job learned that he was not the center of the world, or of time. He learned things that *only God can do*. His last recorded words were, "My ears had heard of you, but now my eyes have seen you. Therefore I despise myself and repent in dust and ashes" (Job 42:5b–6). As good as he was, Job had learned that it's all about the Name!

The narrative does not tell us whether in his encounter with God Job ever learned the Satanic source of his suffering. The story does let its reader know that God is giving Satan room to do his worst, but that in the end the God who created and *controls* the mightiest animals of earth will bring Satan's evil intentions to an end.

But Job certainly learned vital facts about God and about his relationship with God. And he learned that in every person's story what matters most is his respect for the God who does wonders no human can do.

In the development of the Story's plot, Satan only *seemed* to be winning that cosmic battle, for God repeatedly acted to reestablish his Name among earth's people.

The worldwide flood

The second demonstration of genetic sinfulness has its record in the first historic culmination of accumulated human evil. God documented the evidence that all mankind was incorrigibly corrupt. With history's only worldwide flood, he drowned all but the one remaining faithful family (Genesis 6–8). That mass execution intended to scrub from earth mankind's Satan-inspired corruption, disinfecting it and leaving it ready to start over with Noah and his family (Genesis 6–9).

Those events made it undeniably clear that the same unbelief corrupted the DNA of all Adam's children, and their children's children to the last generation. And neither they nor the children could do anything about it. Those were some of the darkest days in the family, when they all realized they were helpless in the clutch of death. They could not repair themselves. They could not fix each other. The essential seed of sin, disregard and denigration of the Name, not only produced all the personal and social evils of all time but infected the very genetic makeup of every new generation.

In order to fulfill his purposes for humankind—to exalt his Name by and among his people—God found it necessary to wipe out or sideline rebellious generations, each time starting over with a new line of humanity. If he destroyed *all* mankind he would annihilate his own image in them, an unthinkable possibility. So in each case he retained enough to begin a new line, in this case Noah and his immediate family.

But even with that warning so fresh in the family memory, Noah's great-great-grandsons (Genesis 10:21–31) agreed to build a permanent brick ziggurat as high as heaven "so that we may make a name for ourselves" (Genesis 11:4). Instead of enjoying worshiping God, they hungered to be worshiped—for a name as high as that of God himself.

The Story's main conflict that began in Eden,
—Satan's competition for the Name—
continues today,
as he continues to manipulate people into the pride
that is willing to judge God, disbelieve God, disobey God,
defy God, and even deny God,
and then pretend he does not exist.

Abram/Abraham

When Noah's descendants demonstrated in their hearts and in their behavior the same corruptions of God's name and image their drowned ancestors had, God began another new family. In a sovereign and gracious decision, God chose a pagan, Abram, to head that new family of faith.

God demonstrated his grace by revealing himself to Abram, appearing to that idol worshipper in the pagan environment with which he was saturated. The first part of that story is included in Genesis 12, that of God's orders for Abram and his family to leave Ur for a destination known only to God.

God had a plan that included Abram. He did not share it in detail with him in Ur. Only later he informed him of parts of it, ways in which God would use Abram to restore his Name.

Whatever conversation the account omits, combined with the promises it quotes, must have convinced Abram that God was both real and worthy of his trust. Repenting of whatever idol worship he may have practiced, with the faith God gave him, he obeyed. God recognized Abram's obedience to result from his new faith. In and from this man, God developed a human confidante (Genesis 18:16–33) and from his grandson, Jacob, whom he renamed Israel, he built the nation of Israel.

Since the *el* portion of Israel's name derives from God's own Name, *Elohim*, from that time both the man Isra*el* and the nation Isra*el* literally bore God's name. The new nation was to be a model of those whom God restored to friendship with himself, a sample intended to attract the trust of the rest of the world. Before Israel could choose to be the people of God, he chose to be their God, to put his Name on them. God *made* them his special people, without regard to what they may have deserved. God wanted to display to all the world how he could make those who trust and obey him as their God into a nation of righteousness, justice, peace, health, and prosperity. Thousands of years later, the nation still is known by his name, Israel.

> God wanted to display to all the world
> how he could make those who trust and obey him
> as their God
> into a nation of righteousness, justice,
> peace, health, and prosperity.

God graced Israel to know him intimately and commissioned the family/nation to bless the rest of the world by carrying his Name to it and being his instrument to bring his Messiah into it (Genesis 12:2–3; 13:14–17). That explains why Israel has been the object of Satan's special hatred, temptations, and attacks throughout the rest of human history. God's friend is Satan's enemy.

But God did not equip them to make that special calling and command fully effective. He did not change their natures. He did not restore his image in them. Their fulfillment of their part of the covenant depended on their own obedience. That obedience remained their responsibility. Had they fully obeyed, they would have enjoyed God's full blessing, making the most of living in his good land (1 Chronicles 28:8). Judaism remained primarily a performance-based response to God. God could be counted on to keep his part of every covenant he made with man. But mankind had yet fully to learn the impossibility of living up to any covenant with God, the total helplessness of man to complete the will of God, and the full meaning of the "death" about which God had warned Adam in the garden.

Chapter 6

God introduces more of his names

To show the power of his name, in a remarkable series of events, Yahweh gave Abram powerful promises—"covenants." He was calling Abram and his descendants to play a major role in his Story, both in a special land and in the whole world. Through them God would make both Abram's name and his own name great as Abram cooperated with him to bless *all* people. God hinted that he would send humanity's Savior, the Messiah, through a later generation of his descendants, this new people (Genesis 12:1-3; 17:1-8). With the last covenant, God changed his friend's name to Abraham.

God kept his covenants with Abram, giving him prosperity and respect.

His nephew, Lot, shared both. But in a shortsighted and self-serving move, Lot settled in Sodom. Soon after, and almost accidentally, Sodom fell into the hands of an area king named Kedolaomer, who on the way home from a successful military campaign looted the town and carried off captives, including Lot and his family.

Learning of the disaster, Abram gathered his small security force for a rescue operation. Successful, he brought home all the loot, along with the captives, including Lot and his family.

As they were returning, Melchizedek, a man about whom we know very little except that he was King of Jerusalem and priest of God Most High, came to greet and bless Abram. This was his blessing: "Blessed be Abram by God Most High, Creator of heaven and earth. And praise to God Most High, who delivered your enemies into your hand" (Genesis 14:19-20).

God introduced this name, El Elyon, the Most High, exalted, elevated God of Israel, in order to distinguish himself from all other gods, especially from all the pagan gods other peoples had invented. And by his own choice he had chosen Israel to be his especially blessed, protected, and treasured people. Israel was to be special because their God was the only living deity.

Abram, recognizing Melchizedek to be a legitimate priest of his Most High God, gave him a tenth of the spoils.

When the king of Sodom saw Abram's act of worship, he said, "Give me the people and keep the goods for yourself."

Abram replied, "With raised hand I have sworn an oath to the LORD, God Most High, Creator of heaven and earth, that I will accept nothing belonging to you, not even a thread or the strap of a sandal, so that you will never be able to say, 'I made Abram rich.' I will accept nothing but what my men have eaten and the share that belongs to the men who went with me'" (Genesis 14:17-24). He was determined to trust only God, and to give only him credit for the victory.

Not long after Abram recognized his Creator, Elohim Yahweh, in this new light as "God Most High," God renamed him Abraham and revealed more of his plans for him and his descendants.

Along with that expanded covenant, God revealed another of his names to the man whom billions of people have recognized as their spiritual forefather. God said, "I am God Almighty; walk before me faithfully and be blameless. Then I will make my covenant between me and you and will greatly increase your numbers" (Genesis 17:1-2).

As Abraham—a former pagan idol-worshiper— believed the light God gave him and lived accordingly, God gave him more and more understanding of his names. *Elohim Yahweh* gave Abraham awareness that he not only is the *One Who Inhabits Eternity as Essential Being*, the *Creator* of all other life, but also the *Almighty God; the supreme God; the terrible, awesome, all powerful one*; and *Shaddai, the Provider*, nourishing and sustaining all life as the *all-sufficient, full-breasted one*. Abraham knew God was as trustworthy as the finest, most respected father, and as caring and providing as the most beloved mother.

As we already noticed, God later renamed Abraham's grandson Jacob "Israel," which means, "he struggles with God" (Genesis 35:10). Since the *el* portion of his name means "God," Isra*el* literally bore God's name. The nation he founded still is known by his name. God graced Israel to know him intimately, and commissioned his nation to bless the rest of the world by carrying his name to it.

Much of the Old Testament details national Israel's story, and its place in the Story, as the grand example to the rest of the world of how God cares for those he chooses to bless with the honor of knowing him as their God. And that history does not hesitate to record how God deals with his beloved nation when they forget who he is, the God who has chosen them for the special blessing of bearing his Name.

God established his Name with Abraham, Isaac, Jacob/Israel, and Joseph, and later with Moses, in each of their circumstances that seemed at first so contradictory to his goodness. But those circumstances tested each one, preserving them until they saw the glory of God's goodness, the glory of the Name.

Chapter 7

An even higher view of I AM, Yahweh

Jacob/Israel's story includes how his sons, jealous of the way he gave their brother, Joseph, special treatment, sold him to traders, who in turn sold him to an Egyptian high official. The story includes Joseph's eventual providential rise from slave and convict to vice-ruler of that world power. When a famine hit Canaan, Israel took the remainder of his family to find food in Egypt, where they were reunited with Joseph, now become their rescuer. Israel's descendants remained there for four centuries, multiplying into a horde of two million that a new pharaoh saw as a potential threat. To maintain control of them and at the same time to profit from their presence, he enslaved them, mercilessly forcing them to build his cities.

When God had had enough of Egypt's incorrigible mistreatment of his chosen people (Exodus 3:9), he chose Moses, a Jewish political refugee from Egyptian oppression (Exodus 2) to be his agent to emancipate them. But Pharaoh evidently did not know that Moses was a Jew. Or that his daughter had compassionately preserved him from the king's edict ordering genocide of other Jewish baby boys. Or why she raised the boy with all the privileges of a son in the palace.

But Moses became aware. He had been in his godly parents' care long enough to learn what it meant to be one of God's chosen. Long

AN EVEN HIGHER VIEW OF I AM, YAHWEH

enough to learn how God had spared his life for a special purpose. Long enough to reverence the Name and swear allegiance to it.

Long enough to withstand the temptations of royal education, luxury, privilege, and potential power. As a responsible young man, when he saw the enslavement of his fellow Jews from which God had preserved him, he recognized his predicament. Carefully, and obviously with the Holy Spirit's illumination, he considered his alternatives. Many hundreds of years passed before the Spirit explained Moses' decision: "By faith Moses, when he had grown up, refused [any longer] to be known as the son of Pharaoh's daughter. He chose to accept mistreatment along with the people of God rather than to enjoy the fleeting pleasures of sin. He regarded disgrace for the sake of Christ as of greater value than the treasures of Egypt, because he was looking ahead to his reward. By faith he left Egypt, not fearing the king's anger; he persevered because he saw *him who is* invisible" (Hebrews 11:24–27, emphasis added). To Moses, it was all about the Name.

Forty years later, Moses found himself learning more lessons of leadership by caring for his father-in-law's balky sheep and in the process losing the last shreds of the bravado of palace privilege. God's call to that fear-filled shepherd required special persuasion. To get Moses' attention, God appeared to him in the now famous burning bush. When Moses pled personal insignificance and inability for the assigned task of emancipating his people from Pharaoh's enslavement, God promised to stick with him through to success.

That was when Moses asked, "Suppose I go to the Israelites and say to them, 'The God of your fathers has sent me to you,' and they ask me, 'What is his name?' Then what shall I tell them?"

God said to Moses, "I AM WHO I AM. This is what you are to say to the Israelites: 'I AM has sent me to you.... The Lord, the God of your fathers—the God of Abraham, the God of Isaac, and the God of Jacob—has sent me to you.' This is my name forever, the name by which I am to be known from generation to generation.

"Go, assemble the elders of Israel and say to them, 'The LORD, the God of your fathers, the God of Abraham, Isaac, and Jacob, appeared to me and said: I have watched over you and have seen what has been done to you in Egypt. And I have promised to bring you up out of your misery in Egypt into the land of the Canaanites, Hittites, Amorites, Perizzites, Hivites, and Jebusites—a land flowing with milk and honey'" (Exodus 3:11–17).

We've already seen that Yahweh means "the Existing One" or "the Self-Existing One." He derives his life from no other source. He depends on no one for his existence. Another attempt to express this name that is so mysteriously far above human experience is "He that is who he is." The name derives from the Hebrew word *havah*, meaning "to be" or "to exist." It also suggests "to become" or, specifically, "to become known"—indicating the God who reveals himself unceasingly.

The subsequent events in Egypt demonstrated that the same Essential Being who had created the earth and its people out of nothing; who had brought their ancestor, the idol-worshiping Abraham, out of his unbelief to recognize Elohim as Most High God, and also into Canaan, promising it to his descendants; and who now had kept his promise to multiply Abraham's descendants into a vast nation, even under anti-Semitic slave conditions, was smart enough and persuasive enough to release them from Pharaoh's grip and restore them to the land he had promised them centuries earlier.

At first, the cocky young pharaoh flexed his biceps at Moses' message from I AM. He snorted, "Who is this the LORD [Yahweh God], that I should obey him and let Israel go? I do not know the LORD and I will not let Israel go" (Exodus 5:2).

God replied through Moses, "When I stretch out my hand against Egypt and bring the Israelites out of it, the Egyptians shall know that I am the self-existing one" (Exodus 7:5). Pharaoh soon learned who Yahweh was.

Through ten sobering interventions in nature, both human and subhuman, and *in order to re-establish his Name in the world*, God did

AN EVEN HIGHER VIEW OF I AM, YAHWEH

rescue his nation from Egyptian slavery. Even the power hungry and tyrannical pharaoh finally recognized God as *caddik*, the Righteous One—straight, right, and faithful to the standard of his nature and covenants (Exodus 9:27). Enslaved Israel learned that the God who had chosen them to be his special people *was* their Glory and Strength, the Holy One of Israel, the Righteous Judge of all the Earth, The Lord their Righteousness. Everyone surrounding Egypt and Palestine at the time heard the dramatic stories of the miracles God performed to free his people from Egyptian slavery (Exodus 5–12).

In these interventions, God established his Name, not only in Israel but among the surrounding nations, as I AM, the self-existent, ultimate being. Four hundred years after Yahweh emancipated Israel from Egypt, pagan Philistines still felt fear about how he had treated the Egyptians for their disrespect of his name (1 Samuel 4:5–9; 6:5–6). He showed himself fully capable of all that his name hinted: "I will be what I will be. I will be all that is necessary as occasion shall arise, including legislator, provider, judge, rewarder, redeemer, and emancipator."

God went on to preserve his people from their enemies, invasions, and famines.

One example is God's memorable rescue of his special nation from the murderous revenge of the Egyptians. Only about a week into their pilgrimage from Egypt toward their promised land, God *led* them into what appeared to be a trap. They did not know that their Mighty One was about to do something that would encourage them for generations, while it made their enemies then inhabiting that land quiver in fear. God led them through a mountain pass to the very shore of the Red Sea, knowing that the Egyptian pharaoh and his chariot-mounted army were almost at their heels to bring them back to Egypt. Only when the refugees found themselves trapped between the advancing army, the mountains on both sides, and the Red Sea in front of them did God open the water for their escape and then close it over the heads of the pursuing Egyptian army. Exodus 14:31, coupled with

Isaiah 63:12 and 14, make that point: "When the Israelites saw the mighty hand of the LORD displayed against the Egyptians, the people feared the Lord and put their trust in him and in Moses his servant.... [God] sent his glorious arm of power to be at Moses' right hand [and] divided the waters before them, *to gain for himself everlasting renown* ..." (emphasis added). God intended the whole drama of his rescue of Israel from Egyptian slavery to exalt *his Name* among them and among the surrounding nations. He intended their invincibility to showcase his. God's Name was at stake.

At least Moses got God's message. Although he failed God on more than one later occasion, he never again lost faith in Elohim Yahweh, I AM THAT I AM, I WILL BE WHO I WILL BE, the Mighty One of Israel.

Forty years later, even though the nation had failed to live up to their name, which also was the name of God that they bore, God dropped an invisible dam across the spring-flooded waters of the Jordan River so his people could gain access to that long-promised country. Safely across the dry channel, their new leader, Joshua, ordered their tribal leaders to bring rocks from the still empty riverbed. After using the rocks to build a stone memorial pillar, he said, "In the future when your descendants ask their parents, 'What do these stones mean?' tell them, 'Israel crossed the Jordan on dry ground.' For the LORD your God dried up the Jordan before you until you crossed over. The LORD your God did to the Jordan what he had done to the Red Sea when he dried it up before us until we had crossed over. He did this so that all the peoples of the earth might know that the hand of the LORD is powerful and so that you might always fear the LORD your God" (Joshua 4:21–24).

God intended both miracles to do more than rescue his people from slavery and give them a beautiful land. Those events were part of his strategy to use Israel to let *everyone* know about his pure goodness and power that takes care of those who trust him. It's all about the Name.

After God emancipated his favored nation from Egyptian slavery, he met them in the Arabian Peninsula at Mount Sinai, where he renewed both his covenant with them and their identification with him (Exodus 19:30).

The beautiful Aaronic benediction found in Numbers sums up how God's name and that of his people intertwine. He put his Name on them. "The Lord said to Moses, 'Tell Aaron and his sons, "This is how you are to bless the Israelites. Say to them: 'The LORD bless you and keep you; the LORD make his face shine on you and be gracious to you; the LORD turn his face toward you and give you peace.' So they will put my name on the Israelites, and I will bless them."'" (Numbers 6: 22–27).

This benediction closed a major section of God's instructions for His beloved chosen nation. Using Moses as His selected leader, God had rescued them from Egyptian slavery. Through Moses, he had revealed to his people his great power and tender love. Also through Moses, he had instructed them in the special ways they were to live so as to represent his Name properly among the pagan nations. This was God's special blessing for those who properly lived up to his name that he had placed on them.

God wanted the new nation to know that he held them close to his heart. He had such special love for them that he put his name on them. Their success and prosperity would show how God cared for those who trust him enough to obey him. God wanted them to have the honor of helping pagan nations around them know, trust, and love him. He was holding up Israel as a model for all nations to see how he protected and cared for those he chose to hold close to his heart. He was inviting all others to enjoy the same care he showered on Israel, the people of his name. The nation literally bore *God's* name.

In that new land God gave his people a system of animal sacrifice to remind them of his forgiving nature and to foretell in it his coming self-sacrifice. It was not due to bloodlust that God required bloody sacrifices. He was reminding his people of what he had warned Adam and Eve: that death is the result of sin, and that God himself would provide the atonement for all sin in his own future death on the cross of Calvary. Thus, the multiplied animal sacrifices of the Old Testament system of worship featured constant reminders to them to be thankful that God would provide himself a sacrifice, just as he had done on Mount Moriah in providing a substitute ram in place of the death of Abraham's Isaac. Every festive journey to Jerusalem, the place God chose for those bloody sacrifices, became another expression of gratitude for God's forgiveness in self-sacrifice.

The bulk of the Old Testament part of the Story records Israel's checkered history of failure to live up to that description of those chosen to bear God's name and of the revivals God sent. Repeatedly the nation fell to Satan's alternative schemes that denied or besmirched God's name among them and their neighbors. Repeatedly, God sent revivalists to restore the Name by reminding Israel to live up to it.

We'll not be able to devote a chapter to each of the stories in which God gradually revealed all of his hundreds of other names. Each showed to his beloved nation, and through them to the world, the radiance of another of his character qualities. Instead, we'll briefly mention only a few, with references to the sub-plots in which God revealed them:

The God who sees me (*El Roi*, Genesis 16:13).

The LORD my Shepherd (*Jehovah Jireh*, Psalm 23) is closely related in sense to El-Roi, expanding on God's shepherding and providing care.

The Jealous One, (*Kanna*, Exodus 20:5) rightly zealous for his name and glory, warning against following helpless gods, knowing that he was his best possible gift to Israel.

King, the immediate, personal and corporate Prince (*Jehovah Ha-Melech*, Exodus 23:17, Numbers 23:21), caring, protecting, ordering, ruling, governing, guiding, providing, and judging for his people's best interests, demonstrating true royalty in his shepherding care of all that he created.

Gracious and compassionate God. (*Jehovah El rahum wa hanun erek appayim werab hesed weemet*, Exodus 34:6), This long name describes God as longsuffering and abundant in goodness and truth.

Rock, the steadfast, safe retreat (*Cur*, Deuteronomy 32:4, 15, 18). At least 28 names and titles express the safety to be found in God by those who trust him. These include Dwelling Place, Fortress, Hiding Place, High Tower, Keeper, Rock of Refuge, Shelter, Shield, and Stronghold.

The living God (*Elohim Chayim*, Joshua 3:10). The name emphasizes that Israel's God is the only living, alive deity, vs. all other lifeless gods that are made by people.

Holy God (*Elohim Kedoshim*, Joshua 24:19), infinitely different from, other than, and above all other beings in every characteristic, including being morally superior to all.

The LORD of hosts, Commander of the Army of the LORD, Head of Israel's army, Mighty Warrior, omnipotent God of hosts (*Elohim Sabaoth*, 1 Samuel 1:3; 4:4; 17:45), over the multiple ranks of agencies and beings: men, warriors, stars, angels, or powers in every form of moral & physical power and majesty. Hence, *The Message* consistently translates, "Lord of the angel-armies".

God who Saves (later spelled *Joshua*, and then *Jesus*), Savior, Redeemer, Restorer (*Jehovah Yashaw*, Isaiah 60:16). Throughout the Story, God emphasized and reemphasized that people are so helpless in their sinful lostness that only he himself is capable to rescue, redeem, and restore their likeness to their Creator. Many of the Messianic predictions indicated that it would be in his own self-sacrifice that he would accomplish that restoration.

The Lord is our Righteousness (*Jehovah-Tsidkenu*, Jeremiah 23:6), emphasizes God's moral rightness and justice in all his relationships with all his creatures. Synonyms include Father of the Fatherless, Protector of Widows and Orphans, Holy Father, Holy One of Israel, Righteous Judge of All the Earth, Just and Mighty One, Lawgiver, and Upright One.

These few sample names hint at God's infinite vastness and character.

No wonder Jesus' apostle, Paul, repeatedly taught the eternal danger of failure to recognize the supremacy of the Name. See Romans 1:18–32 and 11:7, 8.

All accumulated human languages do not possess enough names to describe and express all of God's qualities and attributes. We are left relatively speechless in any attempt to do so. Yet the Bible gives us enough examples to make us realize just how infinite He is.

> You are worthy, our Lord and God,
> to receive glory and honor, and power,
> for you created all things,
> and by your will they were created
> and have their being.
> —Revelation 4:9–11

Chapter 8

God rejected as wise guide

After leading his beloved people to the rich land he had promised, God gave them his judges to protect and guide them as they gradually and painfully learned to trust *only* him as their provider. God repeatedly said that he did those miracles to establish his Name as supreme.

The new nation operated as a theocracy under God's immediate kingship. As king, he ruled. Rulership meant that God took responsibility for caring for all aspects of his peoples' lives— their domestic, religious, educational, social, and governmental welfare. Everything revolved around and depended on God's blessings. God was more than a distant Creator. He was their good Guide, Shepherd-King, Provider, Protector, Commander-in-Chief, and Judge. He cared.

As Creator, God was and is the responsible owner and overseer of all his creation. God was Israel's *sovereign* King. He was in charge.

But as they became established in that rich land under that personal rule of God, the same thing happened to Israel that happens to others who forget the true source of their riches. The Old Testament book of Judges tells part of that repeated cycle of sad stories. The people began to worship the corrupt man-made idols God had warned them against. They adopted the corrupt morals of those gods.

As discipline, God gave the remnants of the defeated natives strength to resist, harass, and even rule portions of the land. When the people of God finally realized the reason for their trouble, they begged God to give them relief. When they did, God would give men or women—"judges"—strength to defeat or drive out the oppressing enemy. Or to rally the people to do so. Through those judges, God would reestablish his personal rule over them, sending back peace and prosperity. A few years later, the nation again would forget who gave them that peace, and begin again to follow the corrupt pagan gods. And again God would send the promised discipline of enemy oppression (Judges 2:10–23), followed by a new rescuing judge when they again repented.

One of those judges was the famous body-builder Samson. Apparently Samson became that hero during one of the worst of Israel's periods of national decay. For while earlier judges had brought spiritual revival with their liberations, Samson was anything but a spiritual or moral hero. Even though God sent him through a miracle birth, clearly intending him to rescue Israel from Philistine oppression, he became a product of his godless culture. He was a willful, cocky womanizer from his youth, and for the most part his parents gave him what he wanted. They only mildly reproved his narcissistic ways. Yet, possibly because he was the best God could find among the idolatrously corrupt nation, he gave him physical strength to kill scores of the oppressive Philistines. God associated that power with Samson's uncut hair. But the strength itself was supernatural, God's.

At the height of his fame as a Philistine killer, still another woman attracted Samson. Delilah was the equally legendary Philistine beauty. The Philistine rulers bribed her to trick Samson into revealing to her the clue to his strength.

Why did God include Samson's story in his Story? The Philistines celebrated their capture and blinding of the Israelite hero with these boastful words: "Our god [Dagon] has delivered our enemy into our hands" (Judges 16:24). God had established Israel to be examples of those who worshiped the true God. When the Philistines captured God's man, they thought their god was stronger than Israel's. It's all about the Name.

But Dagon, a mindless and voiceless idol, did not warn them that Samson was growing a new head of hair.

The fully re-muscled Samson died burying three thousand Philistines along with himself under the demolished roof of Dagon's temple.

From that seeming moral low point, everything got even worse for God's nation. Idolatry spawned every form of personal, sexual, economic, religious, and social immorality that led even to civil war among the tribes of cousins. Some of the evils they perpetrated make the reader's blood run cold.

Several more cycles of religious, moral, and governmental decay left the nation an anarchy in which "everyone did as they saw fit" (Judges 21:25). The Story plainly describes the consequences experienced by a nation that despises, abandons, or ignores God and so denigrates his Name.

Chapter 9

Israel Rejects God as her King

We have seen a bit of God's appreciation for the title King. He created people to benefit from depending on his wise, caring supervision and protection, his rule as Shepherd-King. Through his prophet, he said, "*I am the* LORD, *your Holy One, Israel's Creator, your King*" (Isaiah 43:15). The term expresses both the sovereign ability and the care God exercises for the good of his beloved people. He loves the trust well-treated subjects offer their caring, protecting, providing Monarch, Yahweh Ha-Melech.

Man has misunderstood and misused the role of king for so long that the title typically leaves a bad taste in our mouths. The true role of a king is not that of a tyrant demanding service from all his subjects to meet his own needs and desires. Corrupt kings have earned that reputation. Corrupted by the power and wealth of high office, they have abused their role for their own ends. God's personal rule is that of one strong enough, rich and powerful enough, caring enough, and responsible enough to bear the burden of taking good care of everything and everyone in the whole realm that is under his watchful rule. This is God's true role with his creatures and all his creation. He exercises immediate, personal, caring, ruling oversight that protects and provides for his beloved people. As we have said, such rule is *theocracy*.

Only God himself is capable of such a responsible task. Only God is incorruptible. All mere humans are corruptible and less than capable. God's adversary, Satan, is less than capable of the rule he seeks to usurp. Already corrupted, he craves only the power of the potentate. Not the power to bless, but to boss. And to gather benefits. He cares nothing about the true welfare of people. A killer at heart, he wants only their submission to feed his selfish ends. He is happy to manipulate them to that purpose.

God had bound himself in a covenant of kingship over his beloved Israel. Moses, who knew God's heart, told them, "If you pay attention to these laws and are careful to follow them, then the Lord your God will keep his covenant of love with you, as he swore to your ancestors. He will love you and bless you and increase your numbers. He will bless the fruit of your womb, the crops of your land—your grain, new wine and olive oil—the calves of your herds, and the lambs of your flocks in the land he swore to your ancestors to give you. You will be blessed more than any other people; none of your men or women will be childless, nor will any of your livestock be without young. The Lord will keep you free from every disease. He will not inflict on you the horrible diseases you knew in Egypt, but he will inflict them on all who hate you. You must destroy all the people the Lord your God gives over to you. Do not look on them with pity and do not serve their gods, for that will be a snare to you.

"You may say to yourselves, 'These nations are stronger than we are. How can we drive them out?' But do not be afraid of them; remember well what the Lord your God did to Pharaoh and to all Egypt. You saw with your own eyes the great trials, the signs and wonders, the mighty hand and outstretched arm, with which the Lord your God brought you out. The Lord your God will do the same to all the peoples you now fear. Moreover, the Lord your God will send the hornet among them until even the survivors who hide from you have perished. Do not be terrified by them, for the Lord your God, who is among you, is a great and awesome God. The Lord your God will drive out those nations before you, little by little. You will not be allowed to eliminate them all at once, or the wild animals will multiply around you. But the Lord your God will deliver them over to you, throwing them into great confusion until they are destroyed. He will give their kings into your hand, and you will wipe out their names from under heaven. No one will be able to stand up against you; you will destroy them. The images of their gods you are to burn in the fire. Do not covet the silver and gold on them, and do not take it for yourselves, or you will be ensnared by it, for it is detestable to the Lord your God. Do not bring a detestable thing into your house, or you, like it, will be set apart for destruction. Regard it as vile and utterly detest it, for it is set apart for destruction" (Deuteronomy 7:12–26). That is true ruling. God is the true King.

God did not forget that covenant. He used his judge-prophet Samuel to rescue Israel from another uprising of Philistine rebellion (1 Samuel 7:2–17). Even though their national misery had been the consequence of their abandoning God, failing to keep their part of God's covenant, and even though God was faithfully keeping his part of his covenant with them, the people again concluded that God was not protecting them the way they thought he should be.

So the tribal leaders got together to appeal to Samuel. They said, "Appoint a king to lead us, such as all the other nations have" (1 Samuel 8:5). They had become used to God's gift of the abundant milk and honey of Canaan. They took it for granted, thinking it was their right, just as some today feel that prosperity and good health are their *right*. They forgot their honor of representing to their neighbors the Name of the God who had chosen them for that special favor. They were greedy for what looked like the greener grass of their neighbors, the larger wealth of the Joneses. Stupidly, they were asking Samuel to help them reverse their role with those neighbors, elevating them and their kings as their heroes instead of representing God's righteousness to them. But they were insulting God, implying, "You are not good enough for us! We want a brand we can trust to do us good."

Just as Eve earlier learned that God had created her to depend on him and so *needed* him, the new nation was about to start learning its first political lesson, that no form of human government can substitute for God's caring rulership. Israel *needed* God's direct rule.

Displeased as he was with the leaders' misguided demand for a king, Samuel still relayed it to God.

The Lord answered Samuel, "Listen to all that the people are saying to you; it is not you they have rejected, but me. But warn them solemnly … about what the king who will reign over them will do."

Samuel did so. With a vengeance. His warning included startling alerts about how a king would draft their sons and daughters into his army and his farm and palace staffs. He would tax them heavily, even confiscating their property and goods. He concluded his warning with, "When that day comes, you will cry to God for relief from the king you have chosen, and the LORD will not answer you in that day."

It was not that God would abandon his rebellious people. Forsaking them would ruin the credibility of his Name among their enemies. For the sake of his own Name, God would only discipline them by withdrawing his protection and the closeness of his fellowship for a while. Samuel tried to encourage them with, "For the sake of his great name the LORD will not reject his people, because the LORD was pleased to make you his own" (1 Samuel 12:22)

The leaders responded by only repeating their request.

So began one of the fascinating major subplots of the Story, one that still continues. Through failed government after failed government, God still is teaching Israel, and all societies, that only he is our true King. Only he really cares about all people and nations. Only his personal rule is free of corruption. Only he is powerful enough to protect anyone from all enemies. Only God is mankind's true and trustworthy King of Glory and King over all kings (Psalm 24:7–10; 42:10; 1 Timothy 6:15).

God chose to grant Israel's request for a king, partly as another disciplinary measure. They soon learned that no human could withstand the corrupting influences of trying to assume God's place among and over them.

Israel's first king, the tall, dark, and handsome Saul, so full of human potential, ended his term falling on his own sword in shame over military failure that resulted from arrogant disobedience of God's clear commands (1 Samuel 31:4).

All the kings of Israel were the nation's substitutes for God's immediate rule, protection, and care. Yet with all their corruptions, God condescended to use those kings as his agents of that rule.

The second of those kings, and the best, was the illustrious David. We met him already, properly representing God's name to Goliath and the Philistine army. Having been a shepherd, he most effectively reflected God's kingly qualities and behaviors. His own love for God gave him understanding of God's caring Lordship over his people.

When God had made David's realm secure, the man who understood God's heart prayed a very special prayer. It included: "Who am I, O Lord GOD, and what is my house, that you have brought me thus far? ... Therefore, you are great, O Yahweh. For there is none like you, and there is no God besides you ... making himself a name, ... And your name will be magnified forever" (excerpts from 2 Samuel 7:18-29 ESV).

But when even such a good king succumbed to power's inevitable corroding influence, he did so hugely, combining adultery with murder. How God brought David to repentance is a beautiful story in itself. See 2 Samuel 11:1-12:25 and Psalms 51 and 32.

The rest of Israel's kings, to one degree or another, became Satan's agents of evil idolatry. Instead of leading the people to God, most led them away from him, and consequently from the morality he represented. And all, either in their closeness to or distance from God's character, also became in themselves predictions of the eventual restored kingship of God himself.

The third of those kings was Solomon, David's silver-spooned and gifted son. Solomon started out well, humbly obeying God. With the

ISRAEL REJECTS GOD AS HER KING

wisdom God gave him in answer to his first request, Solomon peacefully expanded the realm to its largest and most prosperous scope. At the apex of Solomon's rule, Israel's holdings stretched from the boundary with Egypt on the south and the Mediterranean coast on the west all the way to the Euphrates River on the northeast, encompassing much of modern Syria, Jordan, and part of the Sinai Peninsula. God expanded Solomon's fame to Sheba in southern Arabia or eastern Africa, straddling the present day Gulf of Aden. Note the description of 1 Kings 10:1: "When the queen of Sheba heard about Solomon and his relationship to the LORD, she came to test Solomon with hard questions." But Solomon allowed his lust for collecting women, and his consequent hundreds of pagan wives and concubines, to turn his heart from God to their idols. "The LORD became angry with Solomon because his heart had turned away from the LORD, the God of Israel, who had appeared to him twice" (1 Kings 11:9). God demonstrated his sovereignty by letting the kingdom disintegrate as rapidly as he had built it (1 Kings 11–13).

Solomon finally learned his lesson, for he closed his lifelong search for wisdom with these words: "Now all has been heard; here is the conclusion of the matter: Fear God and keep his commandments, for this is the whole duty of all mankind" (Ecclesiastes 12:13). He recognized God as Israel's—and his—true King. It's all about the Name.

During the period of the kings, as discipline for the nation's constant distrustful disobedience, God allowed invasions of idolatrous neighbors to wield his correcting sword. As any good father puts his loved but unruly child on a time-out stool, during those eras God set Israel aside from intimate friendship with himself and from the privilege of living in his land. In the face of constant accusations of being unfaithful to his promises to them, God justified his faithfulness by repeatedly reminding Israel of how completely he had kept his promises to them (see, e.g., Psalm 105:5; 33:9). Those promises included the discipline they would receive if they abandoned him for idols.

Every good king should have reminded the nation of the goodness of the God they forgot, and in some way pointed to the day when they would acknowledge God as their only true King to watch over them again. The miseries of living under every evil king should have moved them to turn back to him, the only truly Good One.

Two Old Testament historians recorded, "… Jerusalem, the city that Yahweh has chosen out of all the tribes of Israel, to put his name there." (1 Kings 14:21; 2 Chronicles 12:13 ESV). Had Israel's capital lived up to that name, it would have become known to all history as the city of righteousness and justice, of crimeless safety and security, of resulting prosperity that blessed the whole economic world, and of refuge from all the selfishly heartless cruelties and inequities of the other cities and nations. It would have burst with creative ideas and programs, not only for the arts but also for human development and social relationships of every sort. But, with sadness, God had his prophet Jeremiah tell his people how disappointed he was in them: "'As a belt is bound around the waist, so I bound all the people of Israel and all the people of Judah to me,' declares the LORD, 'to be my people for my renown [name] and praise and honor. But they have not listened'" (Jeremiah 13:11).

Those who revered God's name honored him and those created in his likeness. Those like King Manasseh of Judah, one of the last kings mentioned in the Old Testament, who desecrated and blasphemed God's name with his idolatry, showed their disdain for him. Showing how monumentally important this is, God said of Manasseh's descendants and his people, "I will banish Judah from my presence … and I will reject my chosen city of Jerusalem and this Temple where my name was [supposed] to be honored" (2 Kings 23:27 NLT).

Nationally and individually, God wants to be known in every heart as the good King, for he knows that only he is pure good. He knows that no person can truly prosper under any other rule. He himself—his Name—is his best gift to people. For any fallen human (and we all are) to believe such about himself would be arrogant conceit, the worst sort of narcissism. For the pure God, any less awareness would be not only the worst false modesty but impossible.

As Israel gradually abandoned their trust in God, putting their faith in the idols of the surrounding nations, their moral life degenerated at the same speed, and with it their self-respect. After God fulfilled his warning to deport them, the historian described the miserable populace as being just like the idols they worshiped: they "became worthless [nothings]" (2 Kings 17:13–15).

At each failure, Satan must have laughed.

Chapter 10

The Poetry exalts the Name

We mentioned Job's role in the Story earlier, as part of human history, instead of here, where its poetic literary structure has placed it. Other poetic sections include the "wisdom literature," Proverbs, Ecclesiastes, and Song of Songs. The poets express humankind's spiritual yearnings for restoration, for reunion with God. Each plays an important role in the Story, and of this history and understanding of the Name, but this is a condensation of that narrative.

The Psalms

The Old Testament's history in poetical form expressed human awareness of the centrality of God's name and his restoring work in and among people. From the deepest gullies of human complaint and the highest peaks of achievement, God's people have lifted their voices to heaven. In the best-known psalm, David twice acknowledged, "[The LORD, my Shepherd] refreshes [restores] my soul" and "leads me in righteous paths for his name's sake" (Psalm 23:3). Notice *who* restores a soul—God. Notice also his *stated purpose* for doing so—the sake of his name.

Sixty-five of the psalms weep over some loss or pain. But in each

THE POETRY EXALTS THE NAME

of them is a turning point where cries of joy dry those tears. Their common turning point is where God makes himself known to the sufferer, comforting him with his presence. It's all about the Name.

Of all men, King David, the "man after God's own heart," recognized more fully than most the supremacy of the Name. It affected every situation of his life, even his failures, and echoes through every one of his songs. In one, he rejoiced, "I've thrown in my lot with you, God" (Psalm 26:1–2, *The Message*). In effect, David was saying, "My God, I realize that only you are worthy, so that only union with you can restore me."

The psalmist exalted God with 31 of his names, each with a special meaning. Three of these are Yahweh our Maker (95:6); "LORD of all the earth" (97:5); AND *Yahweh Rapha, the* "Yahweh Who Heals" or restores health (103:3), the Great Physician who heals the spiritual, physical, and emotional needs of his people. Psalms 93–99 and others extol God as King of all the earth. The 100th invites all nations to join in thanking and praising God for his goodness. Psalm 80:7 calls on God to "restore us, God Almighty (or God of hosts, *Elohim Sabaoth*).

The psalmist repeatedly exclaimed, "Give God the praise, glory, and blessing due to his name!" (96:1–9). His life's true purpose and joyful fulfillment, along with other devotees in the very presence of God, was the exaltation of God's name weekly, daily, hour by hour, and eternally. This is what all people owe God.

Psalm 83 repeatedly links the name of God's people with God's name. God frequently reminded his beloved nation, Israel, that he had chosen them to be his people. He had become their God in order to magnify his Name among the nations by showing those nations in Jewish lives what it was like for a people to be blessed by having Yahweh as their God. Isaiah 43:1, 10ff, with John 5:41–44, says the same. When Israel failed to live up to their name as the people of the living God, God told them, "[I will] blot out your transgressions, for my own sake" (Isaiah 43:25). They deserved annihilation for their idolatry. It was for the sake of his own reputation with the surrounding nations that God did not give up on Israel. If he had, Israel's enemies would have had excuse to accuse him of being no more powerful than their own manufactured idols (Exodus 32:11–13).

The psalmist also recognized that in spite of their short memories of God's power, it was for the proper protection and preservation of his own Name that God rescued his people, Israel, from their enemies: "Yet he saved them for his name's sake, to make his mighty power known" (Psalm 106:8).

"Like your name, O God, your praise reaches to the ends of the earth" (Psalm 48:10).

"But you, Sovereign LORD, help me for your name's sake; out of the goodness of your love, deliver me" (Psalm 109:21). The psalmist submitted to God's will, trusting him to intervene in his trouble, for the sake of God's reputation of being the only loving, distress-relieving God.

Isaiah

Since that great prophet couched many of his messages from God in choral, poetic form, let's listen to his message in this section of poetry rather than in its normal place among the Major Prophets. Isaiah 45:1–13 and 48:9–11 are two examples of how God superintended history in ways that should have caused the people to recognize his great Name. He addressed the first in a prophecy to Cyrus, the Gentile potentate of Persia, who was not yet born, introducing himself by name to that pagan as Creator and inviting and urging his attention. He addressed the second to Israel, warning them again that they who bore his name had turned deliberately deaf ears to his personal appeals.

The message of Isaiah 63:7—64:12 describes another Israelite disciplinary situation that God designed to "make for himself a glorious everlasting name." The event marks one of the few Old Testament references to God's names of both Father and Potter. Later, Jeremiah amplified the latter as he described the Potter restoring the flawed lump of clay into a pot of usefulness and beauty (Jeremiah 18:6–17). Someday that usefulness and beauty would enhance and adorn God's name as the supreme Potter.

Through Isaiah, God contributed to our grasp of his identity as the Coming One who would restore his Name among men. In a hint also toward the new birth, the Holy Spirit would do what no human could do, miraculously create Messiah's incarnate life in a virgin (7:14). Isaiah well summed up these predictions with "For to us a child is born, to us a son is given, and the government will be on his shoulders." That baby's descriptive names would include "Wonderful Counselor, Mighty God, Everlasting Father, Prince of Peace. Of the increase of his government and of peace there will be no end. He will reign on David's throne and over his kingdom, establishing and upholding it with justice and righteousness from that time on and forever. The zeal of the LORD Almighty will accomplish this" (Isaiah 9:6–7). In self-sacrifice that Promised one voluntarily would bear the guilt and consequences of humanity's sin (Isaiah 52–53). He yet is to be revealed as "a rebuilder of walls and a restorer of homes" (Isaiah 58:12).

Chapter 11

The Prophets plead for the Name

Throughout the duration of the kingdom, God sent messengers—"prophets"—to call the people of Israel and their leaders back to himself and his Name. As the spiritually deaf nation drifted further from God, he multiplied those messengers. The Old Testament collects their multiplied messages as the Major and Minor Prophets. Those prophets united their voices to plead for Israel's return to God that would restore his Name among men and result in their revived experience of his fellowship and blessing. Constantly, they gave the nation and its leaders predictions of eventual discipline if they did not return to exclusive worship of God, along with promises of redemption and restoration that would accompany their repentance.

Implied or specified in each such call was the promise that eventually God would take on human identity in order to himself atone for humans' constant sinning. He would come as the nation's true caring, rescuing, self-sacrificing, restoring King. The King would be a direct descendant of King David (2 Samuel 7:12–16), born to a virgin who would name him Immanuel, meaning God with us (Isaiah 7:14), in a specific village, Bethlehem (Micah 5:2). And that King would act and speak in such a way that it would be clear that it was God himself who was restoring the nation and humankind (e.g., Isaiah 9:6–7). Each such call to repentance added details about the character, work, and identity of that Messiah, so the people would not fail to recognize him when he arrived. One collection of these predictions includes 365 separate direct Old Testament references and hints regarding Messiah. Brush stroke by brush stroke, the prophecies filled out the portrait of what Messiah would be like in his coming incarnation. An example is the beautiful and well-loved extended prophecy in Isaiah 52–53.

God did not want his people to miss Messiah when he came.

The prophets passed on to the people these messages with such competence that centuries later, when Jesus had finished that predicted work on earth, with these words he took two of his disciples on a tour of the whole Story up to that moment: "Beginning with Moses and all the Prophets, [Jesus] explained to them what was said concerning himself in all the Scriptures" (Luke 24:27).

Again and again God encouraged the nation with promises like, "I will teach them my power and might. Then they will know that my name is the LORD" (Jeremiah 16:21). And "This is the covenant I will make with the house of Israel after that time," declares the Lord. "I will put my law in their minds and write it on their hearts. I will be their God, and they will be my people" (Jeremiah 31:33).

Predicting Israel's eventual repentance from their habitual idolatry, Jeremiah quoted God: "If in a truthful, just and righteous way you swear, 'As surely as the Lord lives,' then the nations will invoke blessings by him and in him they will boast" (Jeremiah 4:2).

The appeals and warnings rejected

As later the same prophet was observing the demolished remains of Jerusalem, bemoaning the end of the kingdom for that era and mourning their lost opportunity to give witness to other nations as to God's goodness, God gave him a very special message of hope. Basing its fulfillment on the fact that he was the Creator, who also had established the nation, he promised to restore the nation completely: "I will cleanse them from all the sin they have committed against me, and will forgive all their sins of rebellion against me. Then this city will bring me renown, joy, praise, and honor before all nations on earth that hear of all the good things I do for it; and they will be in awe, and will tremble at the abundant prosperity and peace I provide for it.... I will make a righteous Branch sprout from David's line; he will do what is just and right in the land. In those days Judah will be saved, and Jerusalem will live in safety. This is the Name by which it will be called, 'The LORD our Righteousness'" (from Jeremiah 33).

Man's reflections of his Creator's reputation are so important to God that he had Ezekiel repeat his words over and over to his idolatrous people who had "put shame on his name" by worshiping idols instead of him. The scene was this: God had established a reputation—a name—as the God more powerful than the demonic magic of the Egyptian ruler's advisors, more powerful than Pharaoh himself, who at that time ruled the known world. Yahweh, the God of the Israelites, and their leader, Moses, had claimed those slaves as his special people out of all the other nations. He had proceeded to bring Pharaoh to his knees as he opened the waves of the Red Sea to be Israel's escape route, and then closed those same waters over Pharaoh's army as their grave. Earlier, the psalmist specifically had credited this rescue to God for his purpose of maintaining his Name: "Yet he saved them for his name's sake, to make his mighty power known" (Psalm 106:8). Then for forty years God fed, watered, clothed, shod, and protected the refugee slaves in the desert as they migrated toward their promised destination, and then gave their rag-tag, weaponless "army" victory over all the massed military might of Canaan.

As far as the surrounding pagans could see, Israel's God was not great enough to maintain their loyalty or moral obedience, for at almost every opportunity God's people joined the idol worship and sexual degradation of those neighboring nations.

This, undoubtedly to Satan's delight, seemed to put God in a bind.

To maintain his Name for goodness and morality, God considered wiping them out. But he knew that doing so would give those surrounding nations excuse to laugh at his inability to maintain the respect of even his own favorites. Ezekiel 20:8–9, 14, 22, 27, 39 repeats: "But they rebelled against me and would not listen to me; they did not get rid of the vile images they had set their eyes on, nor did they forsake the idols of Egypt. So I said I would pour out my wrath on them and spend my anger against them in Egypt. But for the sake of my name I did what would keep it from being profaned in the eyes of the nations in whose sight I had brought them out…. In this also your ancestors blasphemed me by being unfaithful to me…. 'Go and serve your idols, every one of you! But afterward you will surely listen to me and no longer profane my holy name with your gifts and idols.'" Yahweh concluded this prophecy by repeating, "'You will know that I am the LORD when I deal with you for my name's sake and not according to your evil ways and your corrupt practices" (v. 44). Six more times God repeated the same theme through just one of Ezekiel's prophecies.

Speaking of the beginning of the same exile, Ezekiel repeatedly quoted God as saying, "Then they will know that I am the LORD, when I disperse them among the nations and scatter them through the countries." Thirteen times in five consecutive messages through Ezekiel (chapters 12–17) God repeated that essential point: "*Then* they will know that I am the LORD" (emphasis added).

But he also promised, "I will give them an undivided heart, and I will put a new spirit in them; I will remove from them their heart of stone and give them a heart of flesh" (Ezekiel 11:19).

God's good Name is everything, to him, and to everyone. More such declarations will be found in Ezekiel 22, 24, 25, 26, 28, 30, 34, 35, 36; 38:23; and 39:6–7, 25. Ezekiel's primary ministry, it seems, was to remind Israel of how, when their prosperity was supposed to enhance God's reputation among their neighbors, their idolatrous corruptions instead were diminishing that Name.

Other prophets also reminded the nation of God's commitment of his Name to restore them. One was Nahum, who, before God finally deported the southern two tribes, "Judah," to Babylon for national discipline, said, "Yahweh is restoring the majesty of Judah and Israel" through the final defeat of mighty Nineveh (Nahum 2:2).

Heroic Daniel's prayer (Daniel 9:7–8, 15–19) demonstrated the same identification of God and his Name with his people and their bad reputation. Note how Daniel prayed that God would act "in keeping with all your righteous acts.... We do not make requests of you because we are righteous, but because of your great mercy.... For your sake, my God, do not delay, *because your city and your people bear your Name*" (vv. 16–19, emphasis added). Daniel cared more for God's name than for his own. And he lived in the way he knew would most enhance God's name in the pagan Babylonian, Median, and Persian cultures.

God used Daniel to give witness to the power of his name among the powerful non-Jews of his day. Among them was the king who had conquered Israel, the brilliant but proudly pagan and ruthless Babylonian Nebuchadnezzar. He took Israel's most promising people to his capital. Among them was Daniel. By diplomatically standing up for Yahweh, Daniel earned Nebuchadnezzar's respect for himself and for his God. Nebuchadnezzar took several faltering steps toward Daniel's God (Daniel 2 and 3), but did not submit to God's sovereignty. Then God changed Nebuchadnezzar's brain chemistry and nerve connections, causing a form of insanity that made him live in the woods like an animal for seven years (Daniel 4:1–33). When God restored Nebuchadnezzar's mind (1:34), the world's mightiest king of the day recognized God's name as supreme (1:35–37).

God used Daniel through the remainder of Babylon's rule. He reminded one of Nebuchadnezzar's successors, Belshazzar, of his sovereignty when that tin ruler in a drunken stupor denigrated God's name by considering him no different from the Babylonian idols (Daniel 5:3–4). God literally wrote Belshazzar's formal accusation

THE PROPHETS PLEAD FOR THE NAME

on the wall (vv. 5–28). Giving Daniel ability both to know and then to interpret the mysteriously appearing words, God reminded Belshazzar of how he'd had to use insanity to bring his predecessor, Nebuchadnezzar, to submissive faith in his name. Belshazzar died the same night, leaving no evidence of any change of heart.

God continued to use Daniel as a top-level administrator and advisor through the Median empire and into at least the beginning of the Persian—the forerunner of modern-day Iran. During those years, through Daniel God gave the world the written political-military outline of how he would work out his Story in the rest of human history. Those predictions have been fulfilled so accurately that critics of the Bible still claim that Daniel must have lived after the events, for no one could have predicted the future in such detail. In that misleading conjecture, they ignore the fact that the outline still is being fulfilled now, just as God gave Daniel the ability to predict.

King Solomon had said, "The LORD told my father David, … 'Your son whom I will put on the throne in your place will build the temple for my Name'" (1 Kings 5:5).

Speaking likewise through another of his prophets, Amos, God faulted Israel for "profaning my holy name" by a long list of their moral corruptions (Amos 2:7). Then he closed a lofty description of his true glory with "the Lord is his name" (9:6). Since God had identified himself as Israel's God and had chosen that people to be his special people, their conduct reflected on his person, and therefore on the name that described that person, that identity. Their idolatrously immoral conduct did not corrupt God himself, of course, but it did damage his name among the nations that worshiped other gods. Israel's monstrous immoralities gave their neighboring idolaters every reason to think, *If the Jews live like that, their god must be okay with their behavior. If Yahweh's people are like that, he must be like that himself.*

To the contrary, Isaiah (42:6) declared that God originally called the nation to demonstrate his righteousness, to conduct themselves as a light for the Gentiles. Righteousness is not only one of God's absolute qualities, and it not only describes and regulates all his other qualities, but it also is one of his many names: "This is the name by which he will be called: The Lord Our Righteous Savior" (Jeremiah 23:6).

Throughout the centuries of patient working with Israel, God sent his prophets, constantly predicting that he would one day live and rule as a human servant-king among them. In the coming One, the Messiah, God would restore his name (Deuteronomy 18:15; Isaiah 11:12; 28:16; 52:13—53:12; Ezekiel 37:24, 26–27; etc.).

Amos summarized Yahweh's message to unbelieving Israel: "If you refuse to know me as Shepherd, Protector, and Provider, you will learn to know me as Judge of all unbelief and violence. My name is the Lord God of heaven's armies" (see Amos 4:1–13). Isaiah repeated that warning: "I am the Lord; that is my name! I will not yield my glory to another or my praise to idols" (Isaiah 42:8).

God committed his name to fulfilling all these promises and predictions.

Many of his prophets died at the rebellious and conscience-stricken hands of those who rejected their messages.

Chapter 12

Israel forfeits God's land

God repeatedly took action against Satan's pretend gods, his substitutes for himself the real, *living* God. He did so in order to keep the hearts of his people Israel trusting himself as their only real source of life and prosperity. But their continued spiritual adultery, as God so vividly described it, more and more severely tried his patience. He sent prophet after prophet to try to revive their obedient faith by both direct warning and by parable, sometimes acted out. Those prophets faithfully and repeatedly alerted them that God would have to send his agents—foreign enemies—to bring his disciplinary invasions on them. If they didn't listen, finally he would have to banish the nation to exile in pagan Babylon. His land would not welcome them back for seventy years. The repeated warnings fell on deaf ears.

First, God removed his presence from the temple (Ezekiel 10:18–19). The people still did not repent. Eventually, God's discipline required temporarily putting an end to Israel as a kingdom. Ever faithful to his covenant and his name, God dispersed the nation from its homeland into pagan, cruel Babylon. Then Nebuchadnezzar came with his brutal armies, burned Jerusalem to the ground, flattened its walls, including its temple, and carried off to Babylon all but a few of the poorest farmers (2 Kings 25).

God kept his word, seventy years later moving Cyrus to send home the few aged survivors and their children and grandchildren. Not once since has the nation turned to idols.

But their hearts never really returned to God.

The periods of the Story encompassing Israel's occupation of the promised land under God's direct rule, under the judges he gave them, and later under the kings they begged for to replace God, demonstrated over and over that while God kept his part of his covenant with them, they were incapable of keeping their part. Their defacement of God's image in themselves and his name on them was too far advanced. The intended model of obedience to God and his law that produces safety and prosperity failed. Satan's strategy seemed to be succeeding. God's name was not worth much in that world.

Those failures contributed to the Jewish vocabulary a long list of Hebrew and Greek words that describe the meanings of words underlying *sin*. The list included missing the mark, error, fault, concrete intentional wrongdoing, iniquity, transgression, lawlessness, ungodliness, and a number of other specific wrongs. The Story later shows that these are the natural expressions of the sinful governing principle or power that grips every human being. The essence of all sin is what began in Adam's fall, disrespect and disregard for God's Name, as though he were insignificant, unworthy of worshipful obedience, and other than what he represents his Name to be. Sin shows in raising self over God. All sins grow out of this one. The disrespect led to outright, rebellious disobedience. And all the corruptions of individual and social life. It is dangerous to deny and forget the glory of God's name.

Every person in every generation of every nation lies helpless in the grip of that sin. All sins point to the conclusion that humans are helpless to restore themselves. Only the Creator can re-create anyone in his image. This explains why God demonstrates his grace in

ISRAEL FORFEITS GOD'S LAND

granting to his elect the gift of repenting faith. For in its essence, faith is reverence for God, as revealed in his Name.

What always is most at stake? It's all about the Name.

God marked the end of the Old Testament narrative of his special people, Israel, with a final and summarizing word through his spokesperson, Malachi: "'My name will be great among the nations, from where the sun rises to where it sets. In every place incense and pure offerings will be brought to me, because my name will be great among the nations,' says the LORD Almighty [*Elohim Sabaoth*].... Surely the day is coming; it will burn like a furnace. All the arrogant and every evildoer will be stubble ... ' says the LORD Almighty [*Elohim Chayim*].... 'But for you who revere my name ... the sun of righteousness will rise with healing in his rays.... See, I will send the prophet Elijah to you before that great and dreadful day of the Lord comes. He will turn the hearts of the parents to their children, and the hearts of the children to their parents; or else I will come and strike the land with a curse'" (excerpts from Malachi 1:11 and 4:1-6). That Sun of Righteousness, of course, would prove to be the Messiah, Jesus Christ. That Elijah would turn out to be John the Baptist, Messiah's honored herald. Those were God's last words to humans for four hundred years.

As we will see later, Israel did reject their sun of righteousness. And just as certainly, God struck the nation with a curse, the immediate climax of which was Rome's sacking of Jerusalem in a.d. 70. That curse was lifted partly in 1948 with Israel's reestablishment as a nation, and partly remains in force as its many enemies still want to bulldoze Israel into the Mediterranean Sea.

God *will* fulfill his promise to restore his Name through restoring his treasured Israel, as well as the pagan Gentile world that he has been using to discipline them. For almost two thousand years the nation's surviving remnants have been living outside the special land God gave them, and under the harsh rule of the nations that worship man-made gods. In one of the greatest but least noticed miracles and mysteries of mankind's history, for all those centuries Abraham's descendants have maintained a clear ethnic identity even while scattered among the world's other nations. "Nothing is too hard for God!" While since 1948 Israel has been in only a beginning stage of national restoration in their own land, God has promised them a glorious future when he opens their hearts fully to know and exalt him in the way he has planned for them all along (Romans 11:5, 26). "[The Lord] will pour out on the house of David and the inhabitants of Jerusalem a spirit of grace and supplication. They will look on [him], the one they have pierced" (Zechariah 12:10). It will take more supernatural work—another of God's true miracles—to give spiritual sight to still spiritually blind Israel. His name rides on his ability to keep his word. It's all about the Name.

> One of the greatest but least noticed miracles
> of mankind's history
> is God's preservation
> of the ethnic identity of Abraham's descendants
> even while they have been scattered
> among the world's other nations
> where they often have survived genocide,
> with no country of their own until 1948.

The Story has included frequent narratives of the competing gods—actually inert objects of misguided loyalty set up by Satan's influence, all reflections of helpless self—and religions that all the peoples of earth have depended on. Even specially blessed Israel had finally succumbed. Each such people group found all their substitutes for God—"I AM," the only ultimate Reality—to fall short. Baal worship proved helplessly hollow (1 Kings 18). The followers of Ashtoreth perverted sex to a god-like stature that led them to sacrifice their infants in the fires of her Molech consort idol. Toward the end of Israel's history in the land, about the time of her disciplinary dispersal into the surrounding nations, Buddhism had its origin in

THE PROPHETS PLEAD FOR THE NAME

India, trying to fill the emptiness left in lives and cultures that long since had abandoned the Name. The same period produced Persian Zoroastrianism, although some historians see seeds of that religion at a much earlier time. It was in such a culture that God used Daniel, one of Babylon's Jewish captive refugees, to give his witness to the mighty King Nebuchadnezzar. The story of that monarch's spiritual pilgrimage is included earlier. And it was in his Persian successor's palace that God used exiled Esther to preserve his people from otherwise certain worldwide annihilation at the hands of anti-Semite Haman.

Chapter 13

Then heaven went silent

Malachi's messages from God to Israel were to be it's last. He summarized Israel's disrespect for Yahweh. God had had it with Israel. If they refused to listen, he would stop appealing to them.

The silence lasted four hundred years. God sent no prophet to his people, by then dispersed into many lands. No priest received an answer to a national prayer. It was as though the void lamented, "Israel, you haven't really listened to God once. When you seemed to turn an ear, it was only to get something out of him—relief, relaxation, or riches. You never really cared about his Name or his plans or his feelings. You never got the point. You never appreciated your only real treasure. Now learn from his silence just how valuable he is."

It was not that God took a four-hundred-year nap. He kept preparing the world's stage for the Messiah he repeatedly had promised. Even though he had scattered his people throughout the world, miraculously they maintained their necessary Jewish pre-Messianic bloodline. To hold themselves together in those distant communities, the Jews developed a system of synagogues that constantly reminded the people of their identity. Even quasi-Jewish groups promoted the expectation of Messiah. Liberal ideas of Judaism opposed by conservative ones—the new Sadducees vs. the new

Pharisees—and both void of true faith—nevertheless perpetuated Judaism as a system by preserving the text of the Old Testament.

God readied the non-Jewish world for good news by moving Greece to develop its language and philosophical ideas to serve the entire Roman world. He moved Rome to build an infrastructure of highways and seaways that knit together nations all around the Mediterranean Sea. He was paving those roads to carry his heralds worldwide. He influenced thinkers and writers to stimulate hunger for the human liberty only God could provide.

He allowed Rome to subjugate Israel so that it was crying out for that liberty almost as loudly as it had during its captivity to Egypt centuries earlier. Yet in clever accommodation to Jewish economic value to the realm, Rome's local King Herod rebuilt Jerusalem's ruined temple to its highest magnificence.

By the end of the four hundred years, Greece had unified the civilizations of Asia, Europe, and Northern Africa and had established its universal language with its logic and learning. Rome had hammered the whole world into one submissive empire and made all parts of it accessible with its fine roads. The pagan religions revealed themselves as morally bankrupt. The Dispersion of the Jews from their homeland around the world, carrying with them their synagogues, the Scriptures, and their monotheistic religion, had made known everywhere their expectation of a Messiah.

As in the days of Esther and Xerxes God preserved his people without once being named as responsible for having done so, the four centuries of silence were not due to God's inactivity. Silently, he was completing preparations for the Son's birth into humankind.

Most of all, God's silence created in the hearts of his people a longing for words from heaven that could be satisfied in no other way. From earlier Babylonian and Persian captivity, and from dispersion among the world's nations, Israel had learned the danger of idolatry. From heaven's long silence were they learning to listen, and to listen carefully, when God would speak again?

For some, the longing for Messiah's arrival was growing deeper and more intense. All human efforts to restore the lost relationship with God, to restore their likeness to God and his goodness, and their mistaken ways of ruling themselves without God, had ended in failure. Israel groaned under Roman rule. More and more people were realizing that they had no solution to the death they had brought on themselves by trusting Satan's lies about God. If humanity were to be rescued, restored to their original likeness to God, God himself would have to do it. Only God's personal action would or could restore everything, including his name.

The hints as to how he would do so were everywhere in the story. God's multiplied promises of a Messiah-Savior-Restorer were becoming more and more appealing.

The Old and New Testaments

The New Testament's stories about God's life on earth in the person of Jesus, the Christ, continue the narrative of his work to restore his image and name in man. From that perspective, the Old Testament set the scene that would be inhabited by the Jesus of the New Testament.

When man had fully proved himself so spiritually and morally dead as to be incapable of climbing back up to God, *God came to be with mankind*, in Jesus the Christ, who was both Son of God and Son of Man, and so properly carried both names (1 Timothy 2:5; Hebrews 12:24). Only such a one could fully represent God to people while he also represents all people to God (Hebrews 4:41; 10:21).

What most imaginatively creative human novelist could have invented the idea that before people knew they needed rescue, and even before they existed, God would plan to become human in order to reconcile them to himself, rescuing and restoring them to his original image and purpose? (see Matthew 13:35; 25:34; Ephesians 1:4; 1 Peter 1:20; Revelation 13:8; 17:8).

Yet the New Testament details how God became Jesus, Emmanuel—God with us—the Messiah, and how he lived, died, and came back to life in order to vindicate and restore his Name among men. It also tells the stories of some of the effects of Jesus' life on much of the known world of that day, expands on Jesus' teachings, and forecasts the rest of the Story.

The first of Jesus' biographers, Matthew, included in his narrative of Jesus' life and teaching quotations from many of the Old Testament's predictions that God would send the Messiah to reign as King.

Stage 4

THE NAME RESTORED IN CHRIST AND HIS PEOPLE

In the first sentence of the first chapter of his Story, God had introduced himself by name as history's Founder and main character: "In the beginning, *Elohim* created the heavens and the earth" (Genesis 1:1). Now, thousands of years later, the most vivid way in which God made himself known to lost mankind was by coming into their environment in the form of a human being with a name. From the moment Adam and Eve allowed Satan to blind them to the glory of knowing God intimately, God had begun pointing them to that day when he would most clearly make himself known to them, in the sacrificial Lamb of God, come to take away the sin of the world (Genesis 3:15, 21). During the centuries that followed, as we have seen, he regularly made more predictions that included details of the coming Restorer's life and work. When God took on that human flesh, on earth in Jesus fulfilling those predictions, his humanity was so complete that most people did not recognize the God-man for who he really was (John 1:9–11; 4:25–26; 5:19–45; 6:41–59; 8:12–59; 10:22–39; 14:7–20; 17; 20:26–28).

By becoming human, Jesus took the initiative to restore God's name among people. He capped that display with the most convincing act of the *good* deity it was possible to offer: he sacrificed himself in place of those who fully deserved to die such a death (Isaiah 53:4-11; John 3:16; 1 Peter 1:18-21; 3:18; 2 Peter 1:16-17; 1 John 2:2, etc.). Most of the world did not realize it, but in that act Jesus restored God's true Name and his image in man. Life's Creator came to restore the life that man in his rebellion against God had forfeited (John 1:1-14; 3:16, 36; 5:24-29; 10:10; 11:25-26). Life's Originator reversed sin's death sentence, restoring true life (1 John 5:11-12). He gave the lie to all Satan's false accusations about God. God is not the heartless tyrant Satan and bitter people have made him out to be. No, God is good, so good as to absorb in himself all the pain that all sins of all people have earned (Isaiah 53:4-11; Acts 11:18; Romans 2:4; 3:25-26; 8:3). This was the ultimate expression of the Name, the self-sacrificing One (Ephesians 5:2; Hebrews 7:26-27; 9:26-27; 10:12). Yes, the ultimate expression of love, one of the chief qualities of God's true character, is self-sacrifice, and therefore a primary evidence of deity. Matthew, Mark, Luke, and John told that story.

Chapter 14

The promised Restorer arrives as the King

God broke his 400 years of silence with his most important revelation of all. He took on human form—with a human name.

God did not make his entrance among mankind in a spectacular way, such as princes of earthly kingdoms would have. No parade marched before him. He wore no rich robe or jewel-laden crown. Oh, God had touched the heart of the local king Herod to call for a census that drew a young engaged couple, supernaturally pregnant with the King, to Bethlehem, the ancient birthplace of his ancestor, King David. In fact, even though an angel pre-announced his arrival in a similarly miraculous birth to a previously barren older Elizabeth, he made the Prince's pregnancy announcement only to the baby's mother, Mary; his foster-father, Joseph; and a few shepherds. And although God placed a new star in the sky to mark the occasion and the place of his birth—the predicted Bethlehem—apparently only several discerning astrologers in a country far to the east noticed it.

Yes, God had chosen to enter earth's scene through a miraculous human birth. The second Person of the godhead, God the Son, became a human baby. That humble birth mysteriously united the nature of God with that of mankind (Philippians 2:6–11; Hebrews

1:2–3; 2:14), so that he was known as Son of Man while remaining Son of God. All his human faculties, organs, and senses worked normally and perfectly. This totally human baby carried the full image of God, somewhat as Adam had carried it before his fall, but complete, because he was God. He was morally perfect, without blot or even taint (Hebrews 4:15). With only voluntarily and temporarily restricted use of some of his divine powers (Philippians 2:7), he yet was fully God (John 1:1–2, 14, 18; 8:58; 10:30, 37–38; etc.).

To be sure, it was a miracle birth in another way. Mary, the young woman who bore him, had never known a man sexually. But her neighbors did not know that. So her betrothed, the young carpenter the angel had informed of his intended bride's supernatural pregnancy, had to overcome his own and society's taboos and temporarily give the baby his name and nurture.

So plenty of divine evidences marked the special birth. A *very* special birth. But not one of celebrity or royal pomp. No uninformed observer would have predicted that this baby, born in a barn, his first crib a cow's feeding trough, would grow up to have a name rightly praised by billions of followers. For thousands of years. And forever beyond time's end. The promised King was on earth. But few recognized or treated him as a royal prince, because he was not like the kings of earth. He was the original King, the true Shepherd of his people. So he came quietly, humbly, as the unostentatious servant he was. The servant's towel came first. It would prove him to be the promised true and original King come to restore true righteousness and justice.

Neither Mary nor Joseph had to think about or discuss a name for this child. His heavenly Father had taken care of that. He sent his angel to inform the couple, "You are to give him the name Jesus [*Yahweh-Yashua*], because he will save his people from their sins" (Matthew 1:21).

Jesus is I AM

The Greek spelling for *Jesus* transliterates the Hebrew *Joshuah*, a shortening of Yahweh-Yashua. This beautiful name means "Yahweh is salvation"—a pregnant clause, to say the least. It means much more than "God saves;" it asserts that God *is* salvation. Just as other compounds with "Yahweh" identify God as Shepherd, King, and the Lord our Righteousness, Yahweh-Yashua sums up his purpose for becoming human. We already know that the name Yahweh represents the One Who Inhabits Eternity as Essential Being, the Creator of all other life. Compounding it with Yashua means that Jesus not only is the I AM who rescued Israel from Egyptian slavery, restoring her to the dignity of being reflectors of God's image, but the Redeemer and Restorer of humanity from the ravages, eternal consequences, and power of all sin.

"Jesus" was the Son's personal, given name. "Son of God" was his heavenly family name. "Son of Joseph" was his local identifier, for that Nazareth builder had accepted the role of guardian for Jesus.

The other key name by which Jesus became known later was Christ, or the Christ. Christ is the Greek equivalent of the Hebrew word *Messiah*. Its fundamental meaning is "the Annointed One" or "the Annointed King." Jesus fulfilled the prophet's predictions, beginning with that of Genesis 3:15—"he shall crush your head"—that stoked the hopes of all Jewish people. Those hopes were that Messiah would rescue them from their oppressors—especially from Satan's long domination—and reestablish or restore God's rule on earth. So the common Jewish view was that Messiah was their returning King. As real and royal a ruler as King David.

The word of the King's birth did get around. Angels announced it to shepherds. The Holy Spirit notified an aged and godly Jerusalem native, Simeon, that the expected Messiah had arrived. Earlier the Spirit had told him he would not die until he saw "the Lord's Christ." So eight days after his birth, when Joseph and Mary brought Jesus to the temple to have him circumcised, Simeon recognized the special infant (see Luke 2:28–32). The same day the Holy Spirit also moved an aged prophetess, Anna, to declare the significance of the baby to those "looking forward to the redemption of Jerusalem" (Luke 2:38).

And Herod, the king who had called for the census that brought Joseph and Mary to Bethlehem, heard about the birth from the eastern astrologers who had followed the miraculously moving star as far as Jerusalem, inquiring after the birthplace of "the king of the Jews." Herod's fear of losing his throne led him to plot a way to eliminate this baby he thought must be a challenger to his throne. An angel outwitted him by warning Joseph in a dream that Herod's killers were coming. The young family escaped to temporary safety in Egypt. The tyrant's jealousy for his crown, aggravated by his fury at having been outmaneuvered, pushed him to massacre at least scores, and maybe hundreds, of babies in Bethlehem. He could allow no competition for the power he wielded.

Only when the angel later told Joseph and Mary that Herod had died did they venture back, settling safely 65 miles north of Jerusalem in Nazareth.

There they raised their son, the Son of God. The couple either homeschooled Jesus or relied on the local synagogue school to help them fill his mind and heart with the truths of his heavenly Father's words and ancient works. Joseph, a faithful Jew, never forgetting the miracles surrounding Jesus' birth, would have made sure that Jesus' life was saturated with the history and teachings of his people. Mary, no less godly, so well versed in the Scriptures, would have cooperated eagerly in Jesus' education. Jesus' bright mind easily memorized the facts of the Story he had come to advance, including all the predictions of his arrival and life. His heart beat with the deep meanings of those words.

Joseph also apprenticed Jesus as a builder. He wisely balanced spiritual nurture with the skills of a respectable trade by which Jesus could earn a living. Jesus grew to be a real man in all senses of the word.

So the spiritual always was primary. And as Jesus grew toward adolescence, his awareness of his real nature and its reason rapidly increased.

One year the family made its annual festive pilgrimage to Jerusalem to celebrate God's deliverance of his ancient people from Egyptian slavery. After the festivities ended, Mary and Joseph prepared to leave for home. Thinking that the precociously responsible Jesus was with friends or relatives in the entourage, they went on without him. He was not with those friends but deeply involved in conversation with teachers in Jerusalem's temple court. A day elapsed before the couple realized Jesus was not with them, and days more before they found him back in the city. They could not help but notice that "everyone who heard him was amazed at his understanding and his answers" (Luke 2:47 ESV).

Mary scolded Jesus for upsetting them. Innocently, he replied, "Why were you searching for me? Didn't you know I had to be in my Father's house?" (Luke 2:49 ESV).

Earlier we noted how God's name rides partly on man's. Among observers on earth and in the heavens, mankind's fulfillment of God's plan for them, or their failure to do so, affects God's Name as the good Creator. All of the first Adam's descendants share in his failure to live up to that Name. The ultimate man is Jesus, the God-man. He is the last Adam (Romans 5:12–21), the representative man on whom the full responsibility lies to fulfill man's potential. Jesus' words "I must be in my Father's house [about my Father's business]" indicate that even at the age of twelve he was fully aware of that role.

So this was neither childish lapse nor adolescent rebellion, but Jesus' expression of his deep awareness of his unique nature and mission. Jesus knew he was here on a mission, to reveal God to the world in his own life and work. It was an awareness that Joseph and Mary should have recognized. Devoted obedience for both his Father in heaven and his foster father in Nazareth filling his heart, he went home with Joseph and Mary and his brothers and sisters. There he continued to grow "in wisdom and in stature, and in favor with God and man" (Luke 2:52). Not only his family, but also his neighbors and carpentry customers, must have recognized something very special about Jesus. He was beginning to make a name for himself. A *good* name. A prince's name. The name Adam forfeited.

But Jesus, already entering his adolescence, showed no other usual signs of kingship. Servant leadership, yes. Common kingship or ordinary officiousness, no.

In Nazareth, Jesus was known as Joseph's son, but he also knew that Son of God was his earlier name. He, the first person in human history to perfectly bear his Father's image and name to do so, lived up to that Name.

Another 18 years passed without record as Jesus continued to mature, preparing to accept the crown of Israel—and humankind.

Chapter 15

The Introducer prepared

God had been developing another subplot, one essential to the oriental culture.

A Nameless executive

As part of my work with Bibles International, the Bible society of Baptist Mid-Missions, I once traveled to South Korea to find and interview officers of the company that was printing large numbers of high quality Bibles for the American market. Could they satisfy our demanding printing specifications economically, using our digitized texts, and, being closer to some of the Asian groups that would use the finished books, reduce our shipping costs?

In Seoul, I inquired where such companies were likely to be located. Then I took taxis and buses to their locations. I knocked on the doors of their managers. When I introduced myself, they looked suspiciously at me and gave me only limited attention and information. When I finally convinced them that I was the officially appointed director of a U.S. Bible society that was doing business on four continents, they began to take interest in me.

Only later I learned that many Asian cultures like the Korean assume that a person who must introduce himself is a nobody. Persons of significance always have someone else introduce them. Had I known this, I would have arranged for proper introduction by someone the printers already knew and respected. I had a name, but they didn't know it until someone they trusted properly introduced me to them.

In the ancient Middle Eastern nation of Israel, no one's identity or reputation, no one's *name*, could stand merely on his own word. The glory of God among men needed an especially fitting introduction.

So God sent John the Baptizer to give the long-promised Messiah, Jesus, an official, culturally acceptable introduction to the world. Centuries earlier, he had promised to do so (Isaiah 40:3).

Actually, the Holy Spirit had arranged John's miracle birth six months before Mary birthed Jesus. John's mother, Elizabeth, was the elderly, formerly barren wife of Zechariah, a priest, and related to Mary, Jesus' mother. The Story does not tell us when Zechariah had stopped praying for a son and heir, only that an angel came to announce Elizabeth's pregnancy in answer to his prayer. The key part of the angel's message was, "[Your son, John,] will go on before the Lord, … to make ready a people prepared for the Lord" (Luke 1:17b).

We know that Zechariah had stopped praying for a son, because now he hesitated over the couple's vanished abilities to produce a child.

The angel, scolding Zechariah over his hesitancy to believe God's statement, while also giving him an authenticating sign, replied in part, "Now you will be mute until the baby is born."

When the speechless Zechariah had to write out for Elizabeth the promise that she would conceive, she was as ecstatic about this as she was over her resulting pregnancy. Three months later, when Joseph's betrothed, Mary, pregnant with Jesus, arrived for a visit, Elizabeth's baby "leaped for joy in her womb." The two amazed women joyfully compared notes on how the God they both loved and trusted was intermeshing their stories with his. Together they recognized the hand of God at work, beginning to fulfill his promises to earlier generations, starting with Eve and then Abraham.

Zechariah was equally ecstatic when his beautiful John was born. He, too, composed a song for the occasion. Its lyrics recognized how God had been fulfilling his promises and predictions of centuries earlier (see Luke 1:70-79).

Early on, John earned the admiration of the neighbors for his integrity and spirit. He did not lose that name when he relocated into the nearby desert, lived off the land, including eating locusts and wild honey, and wore the rough hand-woven clothing of a hermit.

It was partly the respect the traveling revivalist had earned earlier that brought crowds out to hear his startling proclamations. The addresses were all about the One who would "come after me, more powerful than I, the thongs of whose sandals I am not worthy to stoop down and untie" (see Mark 1:7-8).

John so thoroughly did his job of preparing the way for Messiah—in the process sacrificing everything, including his life—that Jesus later declared of him, "No greater prophet ever lived." For the details, see John 1:1-34 and parallel passages, including Matthew 3:1-12; 11:2-19; 14:1-12; Mark 1:1-8; 6:14-26; Luke 1:5-25, 39-45, 57-80; 3:1-20; 7:18-35.

The stage was set. The Glory of God was about to enter it, to inaugurate his reign on earth. Yahweh Ha-Melech, *Monarch of Israel,* the now incarnate Son of God and Son of Man, was poised to receive back his beloved nation as his subjects. Were they ready to submit again to his Lordship they had renounced when they begged Samuel for "a king like the other nations had?"

Chapter 16

Jesus assumes royal kingship as the Lamb of God

The double introduction

Messiah's arrival was so important that two introductions were appropriate.

Jesus' first formal public authenticating introduction took place on the banks of the Jordan River near where John had been preaching, not far from its mouth into the Dead Sea. The Judean crowds John attracted included the religious leaders from the capital. They came to check out the new prophet, since they knew they had not issued him credentials to prophesy. They were lining the riverbank with John's converts and others when Jesus, traveling from Nazareth in Galilee, came on the scene.

Recognizing him, John exclaimed, "Behold, the Lamb of God, who takes away the sin of the world! This is he of whom I said, 'After me comes a man who ranks before me, because he was before me.' … For this purpose I came baptizing with water, that he might be revealed to Israel" (John 1:29–31 ESV).

John must have realized something of what an epoch-changing introduction this was. This superlative man to whom he pointed, who had been maturing in Nazareth for thirty years, was God in human form, coming to inaugurate the work that would end in a bloody self-sacrifice that literally, and eventually forever, would put an end to all of sin's deadly effects. That work would restore God's Name among men as it restored his people to his pure image, and consequently restored the rest of creation to its pristine, vigorous life. His name was Lamb of God.

Jesus shocked John with his reply: "I came to be baptized."

Knowing who Jesus was, John struggled to deter him. "I need to be baptized by you, and yet you come to me?"

Jesus replied, "Let it be so now; it is proper for us to do this to fulfill all righteousness."

Jesus was not rebelling against, not ignoring or overlooking any detail of God's law, but was fulfilling every right thing to do. While not demonstrating the personal repentance John's baptism also symbolized, for he had nothing of which to repent, Jesus' baptism assumed responsibility for the multiplied failures of all people to honor God's name. Only that authoritative explanation persuaded John to baptize him.

The second authenticating introduction was even more dramatic.

Just as John was raising Jesus—still praying—from the water, Jesus looked up and saw heaven opened and the Spirit of God descending in the form of a dove, lighting on him.

Along with this startling visual came a voice, clearly from heaven: "You are my beloved Son; I am well pleased with you" (Mark 1:11). It was as though the Father were shouting to the Son, "Look who you *are*! You can do it! Go for it!"

> By joining mankind in earthly life,
> Jesus shined the glory of God
> into the world's moral midnight.

Humans are incapable of forming adequate abstract ideas of the divine Being. But we can understand something of him through metaphor, especially *relational* metaphors that also are familiar. God himself chose the highest, best, and most universal human relationship he had created, the parental, to represent himself and Jesus' relationship with him. "You are my beloved Son." Perhaps that explains why Satan spends so much effort to turn men into cold, distant, corrupt father tyrants, in the process distorting the very concept of fatherhood.

Our Father in Heaven

One of the reasons Jesus took on humanity was to restore to mankind the original relationship of Adam to his Creator, to turn the hearts of fathers to their sons. That motive and that intimate relationship led Jesus, the last Adam, almost exclusively to use *Father* as his endearing name for God and for his addresses to God in prayer. And to teach his followers to do the same.

Could God's motives for using these ideal Father and Son metaphors have included making him more accessible and more attractive to us? The last Adam, the Son of Man (used by Jesus 83 times to identify himself with the common, despised race of sinners), the "exact imprint of [God's] nature" (Hebrews 1:3) in human form, is the clearest and best revelation of God. This was truly *good news*. God, the real God, the good God, was here. The King had come! "Your Father who is in heaven" became Jesus' favorite reference to God (Matthew 5:45; 6:1, 9; 7:11; etc.). It became a major emphasis in Jesus' teaching. When Old Testament Jews thought of God as Father, it was in a national sense, as George Washington was the "Father" of the American nation. Jesus was correcting, amplifying, and warming that concept. He was introducing God not only as Creator, but also as the warm, personal, caring, intimate Father of individuals.

Jesus' heavenly Father—vocally—and the Holy Spirit—visually—had united to give their authentication of Jesus, the Son, to the assembly of sinners—repentant and resistant alike—and their religious leaders. The Glory of God had arrived among men. But not with a king's normal trappings.

Months later, John and others in the riverside crowd who became Jesus' disciples had reason to give their witness of this divine authentication of the arrival of the Messiah so long promised and anticipated (John 3: 25–36). In Jesus, the Son of Man and Son of God, God had united himself and his Name inseparably with his creation, man.

Still later, when detractors expressed their disbelief of Jesus' claim of Messiahship, denying that he was the life-giving and life-judging God-King, Jesus referred to this event at the river. "You have sent to John and he has testified to the truth [of who I am]" (John 5:33). He was reminding them that His Father, through his prophet, had properly introduced his Messiahship to the world. Jesus went on to inform them of the highest witness to his identity, that of his heavenly Father himself. Name is everything. God personally had properly verified and introduced the greatest name in human history, Jesus, the Messiah Christ—come to restore God's Name by restoring all things.

The nation as a whole had yet to be convinced. Why didn't Jesus act like other kings? Jews and non-Jews alike demanded more proof that Jesus had the right to that Name.

The restoring King meets the original usurping destroyer

It is difficult to overstate the significance of what Jesus did immediately after the Father's voice from heaven introduced him at John's baptism. Knowing that he had come "to destroy the works of the devil" (1 John 3:8) with which that enemy had been maligning God's name for so many centuries, Jesus, the incarnate God, deliberately made himself available to Satan for his first hand to hand battle in the war. With the Holy Spirit's guidance and aid, he put himself in the place, and in the condition, for Satan to find him at his physical weakest. That place was Satan's temporary turf, the wild desert he had made of God's originally beautiful world (Romans 8:19–23). Jesus was inviting and challenging the devil to an encounter that would put an even greater emphasis on the reason for his incarnation. Since it was Satan who lay behind the fall, it was he that Jesus needed to defeat at every step of his restoring work. The first clash was at hand. Satan, certainly having heard about Jesus' monumentally submissive baptismal introduction and heavenly affirmation, chose to try to end Jesus' ministry before it began.

The miracle of incarnation gave God a body on earth that Satan could attack physically and personally. When Satan tempted Jesus— the second and last Adam—he tried to seduce him with the same tricks that had worked so well on the first Adam. But in more sophisticated form. He tried to trick incarnate God—Jesus—who came to rescue man from their corruption as a greedy taker, into acting in the same greedy way he had tricked Adam into heading the race of takers. This explains why Satan used the same essential tactics on Jesus, the last Adam, that he had used successfully on the first Adam and Eve. He offered Jesus shortcuts to glory: food without productive work, dominion without demand, and satisfaction without sacrifice. He wanted Jesus to deny his own nature, the very nature of God as the Giver of all givers (Matthew 4:1–17).

Satan was more subtle with Jesus than he had been with Adam. He first tried to persuade Jesus, literally starved from forty days of fasting, to use his miracle power to satisfy his ravenous hunger with loaves of bread he could make from the desert stones. He easily could do this *if*, Satan hissed, Jesus was who he claimed to be, the Son of God. But with the Sword of Truth, Jesus parried, "It is written that 'Man shall not live by bread alone, but by every word that comes from the mouth of God.'" He would not use God's power for selfish purposes. He would depend on his Father to supply his needs in his own time.

Then Satan tried to manipulate Jesus to manipulate the Father into a spot where he had to do what Jesus asked. Repeating his insinuating goad about Jesus' identity, he suggested that he jump off a temple pinnacle, trusting that "God will command his angels to catch you ... so that you don't strike your foot against a stone."

Jesus replied, "Again it is written, 'You shall not put the Lord your God to the test.'" If God puts himself on a spot, he will come through, but no one else has that right. Such a jump would have been an audaciously presumptuous—and therefore suicidal—leap for empty glory.

Finally, the devil, showing him all the kingdoms of the world, boasted, "All these I will give you if you will fall down and worship me." This was the adoration Satan had coveted ever since he had let his self-respect devolve into narcissism. Deceived and deceptive, as all narcissists, he was offering a supposedly quick, painless, cross-less way for Jesus to reclaim earth's rule.

Recognizing the cruel lie, Jesus replied, "Be gone, Satan! It is written, 'You shall worship the Lord your God, and him only shall you serve'" (in so many words, "I didn't come to bow to you, but to bring you to my feet").

Unlike the first Adam, Jesus didn't cave. His encounter with personified evil had shown Jesus' power over the strongest enemy of God and mankind.

Jesus had reclaimed the first beachhead in the great war of reversal. The King had returned.

"Satan left him, ... for a while." He had begun to feel on his head the heel of Eve's progeny.

More credentials of Kingship

Two of those who became best acquainted with Jesus wrote extensive reviews of his life. One of them, Matthew, wrote especially to Jewish believers and unbelievers. Repeatedly he showed how Jesus came as the long-predicted Messiah King of the Jews, God living among men.

Matthew's tracing of Jesus' genealogy proved his human descent from King David. He showed how what Jesus did and taught fulfilled all the Old Testament predictions about Israel's King who was to come. He emphasized the major theme of Jesus' teaching and preaching, the nature of the kingdom of God—his personal kingship—that he had come to reestablish and restore. Matthew portrayed how Jesus' works proved his right to the royal title as both Son of God and Son of Man. In the most complete of the three records of Jesus' famous sermon on the mountain, Matthew showed how he established his kingdom's constitution and bylaws, the New Covenant's codification of God's eternal law. He piled up evidences to prove that for the world from that day until he comes again, he built the foundation of the microcosm of that kingdom in the Church, his beloved Bride that includes both rebirthed Jews and rebirthed Gentiles.

In doing so, Jesus restored the true meaning of God's name as King, Yahweh Ha-Melech. As Messiah-King he was the sovereign Creator who alone has the right to rule, and to do so out of his goodness, rightness, and wisdom. He proved himself to be divine Shepherd King, the Care-giver, Protector, Defender, Provider, and just Judge.

The ancient Israel that rejected God's personal rule thought of him as a failed shepherd, incapable of protecting them or providing for them as they thought they deserved. Under the curse of Satan's misinformation, Israel of Jesus' day had lost their national and personal awareness of God's real character. The nation largely had come to see him only as a legislating taskmaster and an angry "hanging judge," the one to blame for every bad situation. We can understand their view to the degree that we know many Americans who view God either as an ethereal Santa or an unscientific and irrelevant spoilsport and critic.

In his own character and conduct, Jesus came to restore Israel's awareness of who God really is—the true knowledge of God as Shepherd King (Matthew 4:17; Mark 1:14-15; John 1:1-18, 45-51; 14:6-11). He was not only God *in* a human but *the God-man*. Every move he made, every gesture, every word he uttered, radiated and sparkled with divine goodness, glory, and authority. The glory of

God moved among men. The heart and drive of Jesus' mission was to restore God's name through restoring mankind in God's image.

In Jesus, God made himself visible to human eyes, audible to human ears, solid and warm to human touch. Jesus was God on earth, real, available, and knowable to humans in human terms. He was the exact representation of God, "the exact imprint of his nature" (Hebrews 1:2–3). Denying himself the royal perks he had enjoyed in heaven, he lived out the attitudes of the true Servant-King, humbling himself to the point of the voluntary sacrifice of his very lifeblood (Philippians 2:6–11).

The Shepherd King also was divine Friend. He would provide what his people needed in order to be all that he had created them to be and do—reflect his magnificence to the whole universe. Jesus' passionate love for the Father's righteous Name and for his people would lead him to die for them as their sacrificial lamb (John 1:29, 36). Yet he would die as the rejected King of the Jews—and rise from death to validate and vindicate his name and his claims to the whole world. It's all about the Name!

Chapter 17

The King's royal conduct

The Creator, Elohim, always has been King of his creation and to his creation. He has been King in the original sense of being the responsible Caretaker-Shepherd: Yahweh Ha-Melech, Yahweh-Jireh. When God permitted his special nation, Israel, to have their own way by having kings *like the other nations*, he did not relinquish his responsibility as their true King. He did not go off to sulk. He did not renounce those names. He knew that even the best of those human kings would be corrupted by the power and perks of their thrones. Even though he would appoint them as his agents, their reigns always would be distorted reflections of God's ultimate rule. God knew that one day he would need to restore his Name of Shepherd-King by reestablishing his personal rule over not only Israel but all nations. That plan was embedded in his oft-repeated promise of sending Messiah—"Anointed King"—to Israel.

In the midst of his narrative about Jesus's birth, Matthew explained that the infant Jesus would become known as *Immanuel*, the name meaning the triune God *with* his people as their long-expected Messiah-King (Isaiah 7:14; 9:6–7; Matthew 1:22–23; 3:17).

Confirming both John's and the Father's credentialing introductions, after telling them this, Jesus conducted himself as their king.

His behavior was that of a true servant king, not that of a selfishly corrupt king such as they were used to having. Jesus refused all the trappings of earthly kings. No pomp or parade for him. He mounted no white charger. Nobody addressed him as "King Jesus." He neither collected taxes nor conscripted an army. He fomented no rebellions against tyrannical Rome or the corrupt Jewish government. He took responsibility to shepherd all, even though only a few recognized his care as true kingship.

The King's royal conversation

Jesus spoke to his followers and the crowds, as well as to his enemies, with the authority of their Creator and King. "When Jesus finished saying these things [the Sermon on the Mount], the crowds were astonished at his teaching" (Matthew 7:28; Luke 22:66-23:4; John 1:1-18). He knew that his words carried the weight and power of his supreme authority, that of God. Those who listened with trusting faith in him as their divine Shepherd found his words to express divine, sublime, freeing truth.

Jesus and the Name, "Our Father in Heaven"–again.

Jesus taught his disciples that they were to address their first and therefore most important prayer to "Our Father in heaven" (Matthew 6:9).

In that model prayer, Jesus introduced his friends to God as his, and their, heavenly Father. The name sums up and conveys all the realities and emotional nuances of what the ultimate Father is to his beloved children: Designer, Creator, Caretaker, Affectionate Watcher, Provider, Guardian, Model, Disciplinarian, Proud Nurturer, Sacrificing Protector, Wise Guide, and even Judge. He was reminding them of what his type, David, had written centuries earlier, "As a father shows compassion to his children, so Yahweh shows compassion to those who revere him" (Psalm 103:13).

> One child's written prayer:
> Dear Father, I hope your name becomes famouse around the world. I love you, and I hope you will get to our needs, in Jesus name, amen.

Jesus did what no natural, sinful human king, even with the highest efforts of his soul and mind, could do: he revealed the pure, good God to mankind. His all-pervading goodness attracted and held followers (John 1:37–39). In his person, Jesus showed the world how the good King God acts, thinks, and feels. He revealed God's fatherly values, his goals, and his objectives (Matthew 5:17–48). In his words and deeds, Jesus showed us what our Father-King does. Literally, he washed his disciple's dirty feet, representing the way God goes about achieving his sovereign goals (John 13:1–17; Ephesians 5:25–27). The good news was that God, the real God, the *good* God, was there; the King had come, doing *good*! Demonstrating the power of God's goodness, Jesus overcame evil with *good*! Jesus' closest friend on earth, the disciple John, wrote of him, "That which was from the beginning, which we have heard, which we have seen with our eyes, which we have looked upon and touched with our hands, concerning the word of life—the life was made manifest, and we have seen it, and testify to it and proclaim to you the eternal life, which was with the Father and was made manifest to us—that which we have seen and heard we proclaim also to you, so that you too may have fellowship with us; and indeed our fellowship is with the Father and with his Son Jesus Christ" (1 John 1:1–3).

In this way God's most spectacularly expressive name is Jesus. Jesus, the "exact imprint of [God's] nature (Hebrews 1:3), is the clearest and best revelation of God. Jesus was and is God, Emmanuel, "God with us." Everything he did and said was totally godly. As a man, Jesus lived up to his name. He showed God to the world.

> God's most spectacular name is Jesus.

Jesus knew the name he carried. He was fully aware that he bore the divine dynasty. He was King God, revealing and representing God to humans.

In one encounter with doubters, Jesus asserted, "If you knew me, you would know my Father also," indicating that he knew he was God in human flesh (John 8:19). God's name and character fully and ultimately rises or falls in Jesus the Christ.

While for good reasons Jesus hid the full brilliance of his deity from some unappreciative eyes during the first part of his ministry, he clearly unveiled it when it became appropriate to do so. Just prior to being betrayed by Judas, Jesus plainly told his disciples, "If you really knew me, you would know my Father as well. From now on, you do know him and have seen him."

Philip said, "Lord, show us the Father and that will be enough for us."

Jesus answered, "Don't you know me, yet, Philip, even after I have been among you such a long time? Anyone who has seen me has seen the Father. How can you say, 'Show us the Father?' Don't you believe that I am in the Father, and that the Father is in me? The words that I say to you are not just my own. Rather, it is the Father, living in me, who is doing his work. Believe me when I say that I am in the Father and the Father is in me; or at least believe on the evidence of the miracles themselves" (John 14:7–11).

> Philip: "Show us God."
> Jesus: "Here I AM!"

Jesus fully understood that God's Name rode on his life, conduct, and reputation. Because he was God in the flesh. It was the glory of *God's* kingship that Jesus revealed.

Earlier, Jesus had warned the Pharisees about the danger of committing unforgivable blasphemy against the Holy Spirit (Matthew 12:32). They had just given Satan credit for a miracle that Jesus knew he had performed in the Holy Spirit's power. So, his warning about blasphemy was his defense of his own essential deity, his Name, and that of the Second Person.

Jesus had a humanly impossible task to perform. Paul later wrote, "The name of God is blasphemed among the Gentiles because of you [Jews]" (Romans 2:24). Alone, Jesus had to correct that impression.

Jesus constantly demonstrated, emphasized, and defended his oneness with the Father that gave him the responsibilities and rights of divine royalty (Mark 14:61b–64; John 7–10, 12, 14, 17). After he restored a lame man's ability to walk, the religious leaders blamed Jesus for "working" on a Sabbath day, a day on which they strictly prohibited any activity that remotely could be thought of as work. Even a stroll of more than a specific few yards. In reply to their accusation of breaking that Sabbath law by instructing his patient to walk, John reported Jesus as saying, "'My Father is always at his work to this very day, and I, too, am working.' For this reason the Jews tried all the harder to kill him; not only was he breaking [their idea of] the Sabbath, but he was even calling God his own Father, making himself equal with God" (John 5:16–18).

At one of Jesus' pre-crucifixion hearings, the high priest interrogated him with, "I adjure you by the living God, tell us if you are the Christ, the Son of God."

Jesus replied, "You have said so. But I tell you, from now on you will see the Son of Man seated at the right hand of Power and coming on the clouds of heaven" (Matthew 26:63b–64).

When the Roman governor asked Jesus, "Are you the King of the Jews?" he replied, "My kingdom is not of this world. If my kingdom were of this world, my servants would have been fighting, that I might not be delivered over to the Jews."

"So you are a king?" asked Pilate.

Jesus answered, "You said it, I am a king. For this purpose I was born and for this purpose I have come into the world—to bear witness to the truth. Everyone who is of the truth listens to my voice" (John 18:33-37).

Believing hearers discovered in Jesus' profound words the spiritually rich life he promised: "I came that they may have life and have it abundantly" (John 10:10). Those who chose not to believe him not only remained guilty and trapped in their sins but became more hardened in them (Matthew 27:22-23; John 1:10-11). Those with minds opened by the Holy Spirit recognized and proclaimed Jesus' kingly character (Matthew 27:11-14, 27-31, 41-44; Luke 23:47; John 1:35-51; 12:12-19). Those with closed minds mocked and resisted it (Matthew 26:59-60; John 19:19-21).

Jesus demonstrated sovereign rulership over all people, Gentile and Jew alike (Matthew 8:5-17), as well as over all things, including nature (walking on raging waves and then calming them with a word; Matthew 8:23-27; John 6:19-21); diseases and disabilities, both congenital and acquired (Matthew 4:23-24; 8:14-17, 27; Mark 5:25-29; 35-42; John 9:1-7); the spirit world (Matthew 10:1; Luke 8:36); that world's evil leader (Matthew 4:1-11); and life itself (Matthew 9:18-33; John 11:1-44; 10:17-18; chapter 20). He healed every kind of disease he met, gave a lifelong cripple the ability to walk, exorcised demons, with a word sent Satan packing, literally called people back from death (John 11), and most stupendous of all, walked out of his own tomb.

Jesus was master of his kingdom's environment and willing occupants. He would take care of the rebels later (Matthew 13:24-30; 24:50-51).

Perhaps rationalistic humanism's worst error is its false exaltation of natural human intellect to the arrogant presumption of being able to judge God. Asserting *righteous* judgeship (John 8:16), Jesus took back his bench of justice, then filled the kingly role of Judge of all the earth (John 5:21-30). He asserted, "Even if I do judge, my judgment is true, for it is not I alone who judge, but I and the Father who sent me" (John 8:16).

Without exception, Jesus used his royal authority to perform kingly works, and only for good: arranging miracle catches of fish, multiplying a small lunch to feed thousands, and protecting his treasured friends from Satanic attack (Matthew 26:59-60; 27:3-4; John 17:12; 18:28-19:16; Acts 10:30). He extended that authority with his disciples (Mark 16:17-18; Luke 9:1).

Although Jesus was "God with us" (Matthew 1:23), in princely loyalty he constantly sought to exalt his Father in heaven (John 1:18; 17:1-26; 20:30-31). His most severe actions against irreverence for the Name were born out of that loyalty (Luke 2:49-52; John 2:12;).

Jesus demolished the artificial racial and political boundaries of his kingdom that men had erected, even though doing so enraged the misguided guardians of Judaism's "justice" (Matthew 28:19-20; Mark 7:24-30; John 5:16-18).

Jesus protected his kingdom during attacks (Mark 3:23-27).

Jesus appointed and sent his chosen disciples as ambassadors of his realm (Matthew 10:1-42; 28:19-20).

Jesus restored God's Name as Creator of a good humankind by being in himself the restored image of God in man.

Jesus was not only the eternal Son in humanity as the Son of God and Son of Man. He also was the second and last Adam, the ideal, perfect human, the unblemished, unimpeded image of God (Philippians 2:5-11), come also to head a new race of the reborn children of God, those restored in God's image, those truly the children of God (Romans 5:12-21; 8:28-30; 1 John). By fully joining humankind in earthly life, Jesus shined the glory of God into the world's moral darkness.

By fully joining humankind in earthly life, Jesus shined the glory of God into the world's moral darkness.

Chapter 18

The King's royal teaching

As in his conduct, so in his teaching, to friend and enemy, Jesus demonstrated the magnanimity and authority of true Kingship.

Jesus began his public preaching with, "Repent, for the kingdom of heaven is at hand" (Matthew 4:17). The words meant what the crowds heard: "See me as I am. I, the King of heaven, am here among you, personally speaking with you. I am your King, the God who lived *among you* in Eden, with the patriarchs, in the Emancipation, in the wilderness, and in the Tent of Meeting in the Promised Land, the one your ancestors rejected as your Sovereign. Still, I stayed with you in Jerusalem and in the Temple's Holy of Holies until you so hardened your ears and hearts against me that I left your presence, abandoning you to your enemies. Now I've returned to bless you again with the presence of God in my Person! I, your eternal King, the Glory of Israel, am here!"

He announced and explained his immediate and long-range plans for his realm, usually using parables to do so (Matthew 13; 17; 19:28–30; 20; 24). He loved metaphor, crafting it to its ultimate power. And he fulfilled all his commitments.

As the model teacher, Jesus constantly maintained a positive spirit, teaching all this as the Good News of the kingdom (Luke 4:43; 8:1).

Even with his necessary condemnations, Jesus had a positive motive, the restoration and preservation of his realm's goodness, righteousness, and justice, of his people's nobility, and ultimately of the Name.

Never supercilious, yet ever maintaining his mostly hidden regal dignity, Jesus always maintained control of his own attitudes and words, his plans, and his influence on all his relationships (Matthew 27:12-14, 34; 26:62-68; Mark 15:2-5, 16-20; Luke 9:50; 23:26-43; John 8:12-59). Thus, he never needed to "pull rank" or to excuse his behavior as "*under* the circumstances" or as "the weakness of the flesh." Not once did he blame his feelings, words, or conduct on some situation or someone else. He never allowed himself to be anyone's victim. Even in the murderously torturing hands of the religious hierarchy and the Roman governor, Jesus asserted, "You would have no authority over me at all unless it had been given to you from above" (John 19:11).

As earlier mentioned, Jesus inaugurated his kingdom's constitution and bylaws—those of his Church—their code of conduct, delivered in what has become known as the Sermon on the Mount (Matthew 5:1-7:27; 22:34-40). In it he taught his disciples the attitudes, values, and conduct of the King's subjects in all relationships, both within the realm and outside it (Matthew 22:15-22).

In that talk, and constantly elsewhere, Jesus demonstrated and taught just what you'd expect from the true King, authenticity and transparency in character and in all conduct and relationships (Matthew 5:8, 11-12, 27-30, 33-37, 43-48; 6:1-8, 16-18, 22-34). Repeatedly he condemned the play-acting hypocrisy of merely behaving religiously. He expected of his kingdom's citizens only what he expected of himself, the true service, the true good works that flowered out of pure hearts that put others' needs ahead of their own (John 13:1-17). His own summary was, "The Son of Man came not to be served but to serve, and to give his life as a ransom for many" (Matthew 20:28).

That kingly service, uncorrupted by any swampy smell, was the highest imaginable, giving to humanity life in all its richest earthly and eternal dimensions (John 3:3–8; plus chapters 4, 10, 11; and 5:1–30).

Jesus did all he could, and said all he could, to make it plain who he was and what his name meant.

Jesus restored truth. Those who listened carelessly to Jesus heard words of revolution. But his ideas were as ancient as the world's formation. Jesus was correcting thousands of years of Satan's intervening lies. In Eden, Satan had conned Eve and Adam by making his lies so appealing that they believed him as he contradicted God's truth. Instead of the promised life and freedom, those lies had brought death and bondage into the world. Now, to *restore* the life that could result only from living the truth, the God-man was restoring original truth. "I have come that they may have life, and have it to the full" (John 10:10). So everything he said restored the truth that is life's source.

Much of Jesus' teaching corrected the errors, misunderstandings, and misinterpretations of God's laws that had accumulated over the centuries. Leaders and people had repeated those errors so often they had become as entrenched as though they were truth. No wonder Jesus' words sounded revolutionary.

Jesus' Sermon on the Mount set the themes of his kingdom's administration. In it he repeatedly took his disciples back to the beginning, to the original intent of his ancient Ten Commandments: "It has been said…, but I say to you …" His words restored the King's original truth. Everything he said corrected some twisting or contradiction of that truth.

He explained that the Commandments had described God's principles of abundant *life* for Israel. Moses declared God's promise: "You shall therefore keep my statutes and my rules; if a person does them, he shall live by them: I am the LORD" (Leviticus 18:5). Paraphrase: "If you really want to *live*, you'll do these things, starting with loving me supremely, taking my Name seriously, … and avoid these that destroy life." Through Israel's model, God also wanted to display to the whole world the multifaceted prosperity he wanted all his image-bearers to enjoy (Deuteronomy 4:5–6). So now Jesus described his kingdom in terms of its conformity with that original law of God. He was restoring the original meaning and purpose of that law, and of all its commands, illustrated by certain of them (Matthew 5:17–48). He explained how *really to live*, how *really* to be in touch with the Father (6:6–15; 7:7–12); the *real* values of his realm (6:19–34; 7:13–14); and the *real and* essential attitudes, conduct, and prosperity of its God-reflecting subjects (7:1–6).

Further, in "Until heaven and earth pass away, not one iota, not one dot will pass from the law, until all is accomplished" (Matthew 5:18 ESV), Jesus reminded the disciples, or for the first time opened their eyes to recognize, that the law is not a list of independent rules but the expression of a whole system of life. He meant that as God himself is the totally integrated perfect sum of his qualities and attributes; and as he created a perfectly conceived and completed *system* of the cosmos; and as he created man "very good," a perfect image of God that reflected the qualities of God in a complete and integrated *system*; so his law was the complete and perfect expression of how man was to relate to him and all other creatures in the wholeness of every part of his life. Failing to do so, "breaking" the law in even the minutest detail, violated the wholeness and perfection of the system, and consequently introduced the opposite of life—death.

In his own life as the second and last Adam—representative man—Jesus would accomplish what no one before him had done: live the complete, perfectly integrated, whole life described by that whole law, vindicating its righteousness while at the same time preparing to make his impending sacrificial death that of the flawless Lamb. He would keep the Law.

So, Jesus was (1) reestablishing the proper view of the law, (2) declaring his credentials for the sacrifice he was going to make, and, (3) as being himself the perfect image of God, giving people a view of the integrity he expected them to live out as "new" men in whom

God would be rebuilding his image. The kingdom's constitution was a whole system, not a list from which one could select some parts for attention while ignoring others. Integrity and wholeness would mark the new life in Christ. In order to fulfill the whole law, every part of man, and every one of his relationships, would need to be made new.

The most profound truth Jesus introduced was the answer to the question of the ages: Could God restore his Name among men and angels? Could he defeat Satan by restoring the divine image in mankind?

The elements of the divine image that had died in Adam's fall required restoration. What Satan had damaged had to be healed and repaired. Mankind's history had proved that he could not heal himself. The Creator was the only candidate powerful enough to restore life in his image. This is the crisis that brought God the Son to earth as the perfect man. In the sight of all the angels, good and evil, and of all the world's nations, how would God restore his good image in ruined humanity? How would he reclaim his name as the Creator of a *very good* humanity?

Jesus answer was, "You all must be born again."

Chapter 19

The new birth restores the Name-exalting image

Jesus used the nighttime visit of a prominent Pharisee, Nicodemus, to put this momentously crucial subject into its vital place in the Story. The Creator of human life in the image of God was about to tell a Jewish Pharisee—and all humanity—that he was restoring that lost image, and why.

John recorded the main points of the well-known interview. Its record is in the first part of chapter 3 of John's account of the Good News about God.

Nicodemus, a member of the Jewish ruling body, the Sanhedrin, was of the Pharisee party. The party already had demonstrated hostility toward Jesus in defense of their erroneous understanding of the kingdom of God, as well as their deafness to what Jesus really was teaching. One night, perhaps bravely overcoming fear of his party's outrage, likely because of his piqued interest in Jesus' view of the kingdom of God, and thoughtfully selecting a time when Jesus would be free to give him personal and private attention, Nicodemus sought out the new young teacher who was attracting so much attention. He spoke on behalf of his fellow Pharisees. But he did not try to trap Jesus in order to belittle him before an audience. And he did not try to impress a crowd with clever questions.

Reports of Jesus' healings attracted Nicodemus. But he had thought further and deeper about them than others had, and Jesus knew it. Perhaps Nicodemus sensed, at least dimly, that each of Jesus' healing miracles restored some aspect of life, or life itself—the image of God Adam had forfeited in his fall. The other Pharisees certainly were blind to that image: they treated sheep as more valuable than persons (Matthew 12:9–12). Perhaps the Holy Spirit led Nicodemus to seek this interview with Jesus, and led John to include the narrative of it, partly because he already had laid in Nicodemus's heart a foundation of faith in God's Word and a sincerity about obeying it, notwithstanding Nicodemus's deeply erroneous understanding of its central story and meaning.

Nicodemus greeted Jesus, "Rabbi, we know that you are a teacher who has come from God. For no one could perform the signs you are doing if God were not with him" (John 3:2). His words expressed respect for the kind of life Christ was living. He recognized that Jesus's main activity had been that of a teacher and healer, one so fully alive that he could give life to others. He did not comment on what Jesus had been saying as a teacher but on his behavior. This observation indicates the substance of his understanding that *God* had sent Jesus. "Rabbi," coming from such a prominent scholar, was no thoughtless honorific. The respect must have been sincere. Only if he really believed it would a member of the Sanhedrin have made such an identification. Nicodemus must have gathered enough information, and thought carefully and long enough about Jesus' identity in light of Old Testament predictions, to have come to this at least tentative conclusion. He wanted to confirm it. Still, he did not recognize Jesus' Messiahship, much less his identity as the Son of God. Jesus knew all this about Nicodemus.

Maybe the Holy Spirit wanted to make rescuing inroads into Israel's leadership and to demonstrate that he has power to enlighten, open, and enliven even such a blindly twisted mind, such a legalistic, self-saving heart as that of a Pharisee. It is possible, even, that the Spirit had brought Nicodemus to a level of disillusionment with Pharisaic misunderstanding of Scripture, pride, and spiritual and social futility that he was ready to see in Jesus what most others, especially his colleagues, did not see: God's true messenger, Messiah, the world's true King.

Nicodemus wanted further light about what he had heard Jesus teach. Here was his reason for addressing Jesus the way he did. He was convinced by the several public miracles—that only the power of God could have produced—that Jesus represented God in his teaching. He recognized that the credentials for authority as a teacher are the demonstrations of actual service. The man who accomplishes useful miracles, who does truly good things, is the one whose teaching about life anyone should trust.

Jesus loved to give such open hearts more truth.

The questions that were bothering Nicodemus, that he sensed only a messenger sent from God could answer, had to do with God's kingdom, his reign on earth. Legalistic religious ceremonialism had not satisfied him, nor had leadership as a theological scholastic. Maybe God was about to reveal to him, and to his countrymen, what it was that his heart told him they were missing. Nicodemus knew, as later the Samaritan woman at the well did, that the Messenger from God, Messiah, was to come to earth to establish God's kingdom. He must have wanted to know whether Jesus was that Messenger, the Messiah, and if he was about to set up that kingdom in all its expected political, military, and economic glory, power, and prosperity. He was trying to confirm, "Teacher, your credentialing miracles make it clear that God has sent you. Therefore, I am interested in knowing the message you bring from him. I hope it is a message about man's right relationship to God and to his realm."

What Jesus heard in Nicodemus's salutation was, "Teacher from God, what message from God do you bring us?"

Jesus took Nicodemus seriously. He knew he was talking with a sincere man who not only had become disillusioned with the flimsy

THE NEW BIRTH RESTORES THE NAME-EXALTING IMAGE

answers of his religion and his theological contemporaries but whose heart the Holy Spirit was enlightening. He did not correct his inquirer's understanding of his credentials, but by his silence accepted them. He grasped the opportunity offered him to spend serious time with a sincere but ignorant leader on so monumental a subject. Jesus took the opportunity to announce to Nicodemus and the world God's means of setting mankind right with himself—of restoring humanity and the system that surrounds and supports people, the only means by which he could properly vindicate his own Name. Jesus the Creator was inaugurating the second birth, the supernatural re-creation of the dead image of God in mankind.

Only God can restore his image in mankind

So without waiting to hear Nicodemus express what he already knew was in his heart, Jesus replied, "God's message to you, to your colleagues, and to all men through me is this: I assert to you the truth: you are spiritually dead. Helpless. Only as God creates in your heart new life through new birth will you be able even to recognize, let alone participate in my kingdom, my good rule" (paraphrase of John 3:3). The *must* was not an *imperative*, not something Nicodemus must do for himself, but *essential*. No one who is dead to God can make themselves alive to God. No sightless person can give themselves sight.

Nicodemus did not correct Jesus. He did not say, "No, Jesus, that is not what I wanted to know." His silence on that matter indicated that Jesus correctly understood his heart.

But Nicodemus *was* surprised at Jesus' connection of the kingdom of God with what seemed to him to be a weird idea, a second birth. To him, the kingdom was political, economic, religious formality, and military. The only birth he knew was physical. What kind of birth provided an ability to recognize God and his kingdom? This teacher's way of talking about religion perplexed him. He blurted, "How can someone be born when they are old? Surely they cannot enter a second time into their mother's womb to be reborn!" (v. 4).

Jesus had taken him to the only place from which a spiritually dead person could begin to see and appreciate God for who he is, that of one whose image of God could be restored only by a new birth that included restoring spiritual sight.

Nicodemus was hearing the Author of all truth and all life proclaim a central truth of all existence, one that all human history has been illustrating and demonstrating: the children of Adam are so helplessly dead that without a new beginning—a new birth, a new creation, a restoration of life, a spiritual resurrection, including having our spiritual sight restored—are we capable of even seeing God's true kingdom. Our spiritual eyes are as dead as our hearts.

Nicodemus knew himself to be truly Jewish, circumcised, orthodox, honest, legally unblemished, and of the highest rank, a respected member of the Jewish Supreme Council. He possessed every humanly identified personal and official claim to membership in God's Jewish kingdom that his contemporaries recognized. In his Jewish culture, being born into the right clan would have been the single most important predictor of success in life. That's why Jesus' words stung him. Jesus stunned him by saying that life in God's realm is *not* determined by our genealogy, by birth to our physical parents, or by our attainments, or any associated trappings.

It was beginning to dawn on Nicodemus that this new teacher, whom he knew *came from God,* was telling him that he lacked even the first condition of Kingdom citizenship, the faculty to recognize that kingdom. To possess that faculty, he required a new birth, one from above.

Who could perform this second birth?

Who could restore the dead image of God in mankind through the new birth? Only the God whose name is Creator is capable of

THE NEW BIRTH RESTORES THE NAME-EXALTING IMAGE

re-creating and restoring creation. God, who established his Name by creating good soil out of nothing, and very good humankind out of that soil, can restore his Name through the second birth of members of the human race. Only the One who himself lives, and who gives life, can restore life to the dead. Only the One who gives the first birth can give the second birth. That is why "the birth *from above*" is a synonym for the new birth.

> No corpse ever resurrected itself;
> no baby ever birthed itself.

Jesus repeated, "Very truly I tell you, no one can enter the kingdom of God unless they are born of water and the Spirit" (v.5). And he said, "the wind blows where it will."

Other parts of the Story make clear, continuing the vocabulary of birth, that the Holy Spirit's rebirthing work within the spiritually dead person involves two phases. Since Jesus gave us the birth metaphor, let's use its implications to understand its steps.

Conception

Just as God was the immediate Source of human life in Creation, he is the immediate Source of the new life in the second birth. Whether in the original Creation or in the re-creation of the new birth, the initiative and the power always are God's, and only his. God always initiates relationship. The Spirit *gives* life to the one dead in sin, including freedom from the bondage of sin and Satan, and the ability and desire to freely receive Christ.

The New Testament identifies the truth of the Gospel to be the *means*, the seed, the Spirit uses in his re-birthing work: "He chose to give us birth through the word of truth, that we might be a kind of first fruits of all he created" (James 1:18; plus John 17:8 and 14). The Holy Spirit first sows the seed of God's Word in the mind, heart, and conscience (James 1:18). There he germinates it into spiritual life (John 7:38-39; 1 Peter 1:23-25; 2:2; 3:23).

Gestation

Spiritual gestation includes the Spirit's influences on the person through his powerful words that bring them to the point of the repenting faith we call "conversion." These influences include the words that convince the sinner of their need, of their desperate condition of spiritual death (1 Thessalonians 1:4-5). "Our gospel came to you not simply with words but also with power, with the Holy Spirit and deep conviction" (1 Thessalonians 1:5). The Spirit expresses and implants the Word of Truth in the heart, gradually informing and convincing the person of their lostness and of their failure to have fulfilled their purpose in having been given life in the first place—to exalt the Name. He convinces the sinner of their deserved condemnation (John 16:8-11), making them willing to repent (John 16:8). The person realizes the seriousness of being dead in sin, an enemy of God, and therefore a stench in God's nostrils instead of a pleasure to him. This intense guilt, shame, and sorrow, of heavy condemnation, is not only for specific moral sins and failings, but for the prideful heart that has generated them. For insulting God by arrogantly having failed to know him, love him, worship him, treasure him, or serve him and his interests. For having rebelled against him, attempting to dethrone him by assuming superiority over him in moral judgment, knowledge, and motive. This conviction realizes the terrible present and eternal consequences of that enmity with God that has failed to live up to and exalt the Name. This is the "godly sorrow" that works the repentance of the subsequent conversion (2 Corinthians 7:10). Commonly, the Spirit may bring this conception and conviction through the person's reading the Story; through a believer's witness; through someone preaching the Story; or, rarely, even by a vision independent of human means, as he did Cornelius of Caesarea (Acts 10). The Spirit includes

THE NEW BIRTH RESTORES THE NAME-EXALTING IMAGE

the words that give one enough information about Jesus Christ to realize his divine nature and his loving self-sacrifice. He informs them of who Jesus Christ is and what he has done to reconcile them with God. "Just as Moses lifted up the snake in the wilderness, so the Son of Man must be lifted up, that everyone who believes may have eternal life in him" (John 3:14-15). Earlier Jesus had told his disciples, "And I, if I am lifted up from the earth, will draw all men to Myself." The evangelist's role is to lift up Jesus. The Spirit may be counted on to use Jesus' story in the message of the evangelist to do his life-giving work in the heart of the hearer. (See also John 14:25-26; 16:12-15). Awareness that God is both ultimately right and supremely good is the effect of the Spirit's enlightening work, and the beginning of conversion.

Delivery

The Story includes the stories of several deliveries—new birthings, conversions. A few, such as the Ethiopian government official (Acts 8:26-40), the apostle Paul (Acts 9:1-19), and the business woman Lydia (Acts 16:11-15), experienced the new birth in near-instant conversions or after only relatively short acquaintances with the truth about Jesus. More experience longer gestation periods, only gradually arriving at faith, little by little realizing the reality of who Jesus is and what he did. At times the Spirit gives new life in "people movements" (Acts 2:31:31-47). The operation is up to him. But in conversion, all who are the subjects of God's saving grace alike renounce their old objects of faith as they transfer their faith to Christ alone.

Only the Holy Spirit knows how to create new spiritual life. Only he can transform anyone into the same image "with ever-increasing glory" (2 Corinthians 3:18).

Just as the Holy Spirit uses his powerful, effective Word about Jesus to conceive and develop new spiritual life in the person, with the same Word he brings the new babe to delivery. That does not suggest coercion. It does indicate resurrection of spiritual freedom that can recognize and act on the truth in Christ. The Spirit's work creates a spirit—a new nature, a new heart—that therefore *does* trust God, and wants to. Just as we can hear and feel the wind, we can recognize the results of the second birth.

Jesus only briefly mentioned to Nicodemus the delivery phase of the Spirit's rebirthing work. Since only God can accomplish the rebirthing, Jesus had no need to describe to Nicodemus the process by which the Spirit makes it happen. He works in the part of human makeup to which we have no creative access. That part is a new central being, a new heart capable of recognizing and receiving Jesus. It shows in a new set of desires to hunger for him and for the fame of his Name (Ephesians 2:10). This new creation is reconciled to God (2 Corinthians 5:17–19, 21) by being united with Christ who always is united with the Father (John 17:20–23).

That union with Christ is what frees the sinner from the guilt and bonds of sin, darkness, and death, because Jesus died for all (1 John 2:2). His full payment is credited to the sinner's account (Romans 6:3–10; 8:1–2).

> We'll say more about conversion and its repenting faith later. But here it needs to be said plainly that probably even the most fully informed person, including Saul of Tarsus, did not know and understand all this about the new birth at the moment when the Holy Spirit gave it to them. Since God gives even some young children the new birth, it is clear that only later, "growing in grace and knowledge" (2 Peter 1:2; 3:18), they will grasp more and more of what it means to be born again and be found in union with Christ. This will be true of every one born from above.

How would God perform the new birth delivery?

Jesus explained to Nicodemus no more about the mystery of *how* the Holy Spirit gives or performs that new birth than he did about his original creation of the cosmos, the world, and man. Nicodemus wasn't ready to re-learn that all life, physical and spiritual, depends on God, for all life comes only from him.

Jesus had his messengers Peter, Paul, John, and James teach more about the reborn person's experience of it, including in conversion. In a bit, we will explore some of their combined teaching about regenerating new birth and the resulting life.

What Jesus did tell Nicodemus is what is important to the Story at this point: the new birth is not the work of humans but of the Holy Spirit (John 3:5–8). The Spirit performs it in the spiritual part of a person. It is only as a response to the Spirit's implantation of new life in the heart that the person can "receive him"—can so fully believe in the name of Jesus, the only Son of God (John 3:15–18 with 1:12) that they commit and submit their whole life and eternity to Jesus Christ as Savior and Lord (Colossians 2:6).

Again, Jesus' thought was so huge that at first its enormity eluded Nicodemus. He did not comprehend the difference between a *second* beginning, like that of their first, and a *different* beginning, one of the spirit, implanted by the Holy Spirit.

Jesus informed his ignorance: "I affirm with double emphasis, unless anyone is born of water and the Spirit, he cannot enter the kingdom of God. That which is born of the flesh is flesh, and that which is born of the Spirit is spirit. Don't marvel that I said to you, 'You all must be born again.'"

Jesus' point was and is that a natural person is blind to God and his good rule, deaf to God's expressions of the laws of his kingdom, insensitive to God's presence everywhere in his realm, and therefore at sea about his purpose in life and the moral issues surrounding that life. That is, they are dead to God. Lost people must be born again because in their first birth all have been born in sin, as King David made clear (Psalm 51:5). Nicodemus should have known about this. The natural person lives as a practical atheist, as though God does not exist. They are either ignorant of or in deliberate denial of God; they also are in constant rebellion against God and his legitimate rule of what he owns by creative right. To Jesus, a natural person's performance-based religion is futile, for he knows that God prizes the sincerity of the pure heart, the inner person that truly knows, trusts, and wants to exalt God instead of only themself. Without such a heart, the natural person is blind and deaf to God's presence. The natural person is alien to God and to the existence of his good realm.

> But a natural man does not accept the things of the Spirit of God,
> for they are foolishness to him;
> and he cannot understand them,
> because they are spiritually discerned.
> —Paul, 1 Corinthians 2:14

Natural people are the center of their own life. They are unaware that they were born to play a role in God's Story, the Story that makes it clear that God is the Source, center, and end of all things. The natural person is born ignorant that they were intended to be a prince or princess of the Most High King. They grow up under the rule of the usurper to God's throne. Jesus' analysis of anyone's independent ability to achieve a place in his kingdom was, "With man this is impossible, but with God all things are possible" (Matthew 19:17–26). To become aware of God, to know God as the true Father King and to recognize God as active in their human realm, the naturally born person needs to start life over, to begin again with new spiritual senses that recognize God. Only the birth from above imparts that sensitivity to God, the awareness of King God to a degree not naturally possible.

Matthew emphasized Jesus' pivotal issue, human unwillingness to recognize and bow to him as their King, Emmanuel—God

THE NEW BIRTH RESTORES THE NAME-EXALTING IMAGE

with them. Jesus made the point with his parable about a landowner who rented his prized vineyard to greedy tenants. They capped their cocky rebellion by killing the owner's son when he came to collect his rightful share of the crop. Jesus closed that story with, "He will bring those wretches to a wretched end, … and he will rent the vineyard to other tenants, who will give him his share of the crop at harvest time" (Matthew 21:41). Instead of joyfully crowning Jesus as their rightful King, the leaders and people betrayed him (26:69–78), lied about him (26:59), repeatedly rejected him (27:37, 42–42; 24:46), and killed him (27:32–44). How could those who could not recognize Jesus as King recognize his realm? Jesus yearned for the people, spiritually dead as they were, to believe that he was God with them, among them, the living God who could restore their true and full life (John 11:25–26). Their inability and refusal to believe proved how dead and blind they were. Death's stench reeks from the spiritual corpses of natural man.

Why would God give the new birth that would restore his image in man?

Why not just throw the whole mess of wicked, dead humankind into an incinerator? God's first motive is his love for his own Name. The angel world knew what God knew, that his Name rides partly on man's reflection of himself and that his pleasure is in man's fulfilling his assigned role, properly reflecting his image (Romans 8:38; Ephesians 3:8–10; 6:12; Colossians 1:16; 2:15; Hebrews 2:1; 1 Peter 3:22). In other words, in Christ and his reborn children, God is re-creating mankind in his likeness. Just shrugging his shoulders at the rebels would have admitted failure of his special plan. It's all about the Name.

> In Christ and his reborn children,
> God is re-creating mankind in his likeness.

His second motive is love for those that bear his image, no matter how ruined. God *loved* the world this way ... (John 3:16).

What is God's *ultimate* reason for restoring helplessly dead mankind to himself?

After our entire history of individual and corporate misrepresentations of the Name that have resulted in death, God is restoring his image in humankind so that "we might be for the praise of his glory" (Ephesians 1:12). Here also, then, is the most basic motive for coming back to God, and therefore the primary purpose for evangelism. God is restoring people so that "through the church, the manifold wisdom of God should be made known to the rulers and authorities in the heavenly realms" (Ephesians 3:10-12). He is restoring man's purity and blameless righteousness "to the glory and praise of God" (Philippians 1:11). The new birth's restoration of God's living image in mankind restores God's Name as supreme. It's all about the Name.

God is accomplishing this restoration and reconciliation through, and only through, uniting sinners with his Son, Jesus Christ, the Source of the restored image (2 Corinthians 5:17-19). As Jesus taught his disciples, and Paul reemphasized, by the new birth the Spirit "baptizes" one forever into union with Christ both in the timeless mind and will of God, and in the person's real time and experience as well (John 14:1-17:26; Romans 6:3-4; Galatians 3:27). God can be pleased with mankind again, because through that union, he sees Christ in us and us in Christ.

Rebirth into union with God in Christ

The birth from above restores the original relationship of God with man because, by virtue of being united with the life of Christ, the reborn life is as united with the Father as is the life of the Son. In another New Testament term, the new life is the spiritual life of

THE NEW BIRTH RESTORES THE NAME-EXALTING IMAGE

Christ "indwelling the heart" (Romans 6:11; 8:1, 10; Philippians 1:11; Colossians 2:13). Jesus is the Mediator, the Connector (1 Timothy 2:5). In that reunion or reconciliation, and only by the living energy of Christ in him, the new person cheerfully, gratefully, intentionally, and joyfully lives out God's values, purposes, and commands with the object of restoring God's Name among men and women (John 14:13, 14; 15:8–10; Romans 8:1; Philippians 1:9–11, 21; 2:1–11; etc.).

Since union with Christ is such a huge and central part of the Story, it requires a chapter of special consideration. So we need to press the pause button on Jesus' conversation with Nicodemus and bring into focus mankind's reconciliation and reunion with God through what the rest of the New Testament describes as "union with Christ."

Chapter 20

Christ reunites mankind with God in himself

What union with God in Christ *means*:

The massiveness of what new birth into union with Christ is and means both fires and exhausts the imagination. Reuniting himself with people in Christ is God's means of restoring his life and image in spiritually dead man. It is his only means of vindicating his Name from Satan's false accusations. The finest minds do not fully comprehend everything about this union. Yet from Jesus' perspective it is so real and intimate that when those who are united with him suffer, he suffers (Colossians 1:24). When Jesus first confronted one of his believers' first persecutors, the Pharisee Saul, on the road to Damascus, he challenged him, "Saul, Saul, why are you persecuting *me*?" (Acts 9:4 ESV). Later, after Jesus renamed him "Paul," he wrote, "God has chosen to make known among the Gentiles the glorious riches of this mystery, which is *Christ in you*, the hope of glory" (Colossians 1:27), and "The law of the Spirit, of *life in Christ Jesus*, has freed us from the law of sin and death" (Romans 8:1).

> The law of the Spirit,
> which is the law of life in Christ Jesus,
> has freed us from the law of sin and death"
> —Paul, Romans 8:1

Some theologians refer to union with Christ also as "identification with Christ." This identification is the spiritual connection with Jesus Christ that the Holy Spirit establishes in the new birth. To be in this union is to be "in Christ" (Ephesians repeatedly; Philippians 1:1; 3:8-9; Colossians 2:9-15; etc.). It is by, because of, and *only* because of that connection that every aspect of Jesus' saving Person and work is both attributed to and conveyed to those who have been born again by the Holy Spirit's work.

While Jesus announced to Nicodemus the necessity and fact of the new birth into that union, he later unpacked more of its meaning to the disciples as he prepared them for his death and return to heaven (John 14-17). Still later, Paul, Peter, and John assumed the new birth as the basis for their further teaching about how believers live out life in union with Christ.

Various New Testament figures of speech illustrate the meaning of this union-identification. Jesus used physical likenesses to describe the spiritual realities. In one, the "vine and the branches" (John 15:1-6), he described the union as connection with him, the source of spiritual life. The fruit results from Jesus' living energy—the vine's life-giving sap—moving into the believer—the life-receiving branch. The branch is *in* the vine, so that the life of the vine can flow *in* the branch. The believer's spiritual life and usefulness continue as he "abides in the vine." Jesus summarized, "Without me you can do nothing."

Another metaphor is the relationship of a human head with its body (Ephesians 1:22-23; 4:12-16). This depicts the living union of the directing Christ and the dependently obedient Church. The believer cannot live without the life and direction of his head, the

Lord Jesus. This is part of what it means to be a disciple, a "follower of Christ."

Another figure is marriage (Ephesians 5:23–32). Christ has betrothed himself to the Church, his Bride (2 Corinthians 11:2). Legally, first century betrothal was as binding as marriage, awaiting only its consummation in living together. Paul likened the spiritual intimacy of Christ with his Church to the marital relationship (Ephesians 5:23–32). It implies joyous anticipation, trustful dependency, exclusivity, and permanence. The admittedly mysterious metaphor depicts a spiritual unity as intimately fulfilling and creative as the "one body" physical union of a husband and wife in marriage. Christ has committed himself to his Bride forever.

Still another figure for new birth is baptism in water (Acts 2:23; 6:4; 8:12; 10:48; Romans 6:3; Galatians 3:27; Colossians 2:12). Water baptism is both a real and a metaphorical experience. Submission to water baptism is the act by which the follower of Christ symbolizes their *immersion* into union with Christ. The figure pictures the believer as *surrounded* by Christ, indicating that everything about his new life is involved with, and depends on, Jesus Christ. This hints again at Jesus' words "Without me you can do nothing." Being immersed in Christ certainly suggests that life in union with him is much more completely saturating, much more all-encompassing, than merely adding a religious dimension to life.

Other New Testament expressions for the relationship include "into Christ" (Romans 6:3–4; Galatians 3:27); "in him" (Ephesians 1:4); "in the Beloved" (Ephesians 1:6); and references such as "with Christ" (1 Corinthians 1:9; Colossians 3:1, 3) and "through Christ" (Romans 6:23; Ephesians 1:5, 7; Colossians 1:20). Still more Story synonyms for God's restored union with his believers, some metaphorical, include at least: *connected with, attached to, participating with, partakers of, united with, one with, yoked with, indwelt by, inhabited by, Christ lives in you, walk with, walk in, placed into, adopted into, abide in, grafted into, in covenant with, clothed with, in fellowship with, and espoused to.* All speak of the believer's *incorporation into* Christ and his Church. Those so united with Christ are described as *sons* or *children of God, brothers* (siblings) *with, joint-heirs with, citizens of his kingdom,* and *sheep of his pasture.* All these terms express real, vital connection or union of one kind or another. Each of them indicates oneness of identity, heart, purpose, goal, object, values, character, behavior, mission, work, and celebratory rest. Just the number of synonyms indicates the importance of the union.

Galatians 3:27 reads, "For as many of you as were baptized into Christ have put on Christ." Writing about this experience that also is a metaphor, John Calvin wrote, "Paul teaches that in baptism we 'put on Christ.' ... Faith does not overthrow reality and the effect. The only way we are conjoined to Christ is by raising our minds above the world [into the spiritual realm]. Accordingly, the bond of our union with Christ is faith, which raises us upwards and casts its anchor in heaven, so that instead of subjecting Christ to the figments of our reason, we seek [and see] him above in his glory."[6]

In this union, God considers ("reckons," credits) the reborn to be identified with (united with) the Person and work of Christ, in both directions. Christ assumes all the liabilities of the sinners with whom he unites himself. And he shares with them all the assets of his character qualities and all his virtuous work, including his own intimate relationship with the Father. "In him the whole fulness of deity dwells bodily, and you have been *filled in him* ... having been *buried with him* in baptism, in which you were also *raised with him* through faith in the powerful working God, who raised him from the dead. And you, who were dead in your trespasses and the uncircumcision of your flesh, God *made alive together with him....*" (Colossians 2:9–15 ESV, emphasis added).

This is but one example of the vastness of what being united with Christ means. To paraphrase what Jesus said to his disciples in the Upper Room (John 14:6), "I am the Way back to the Father; I am the Truth about the Father; I am the model Life of the Son with the

Father. No one comes to the Father *but by me.*" Since Jesus' name *is* that Truth, faith in that name—that he is truth—is the only gate through which any one can step to know God as he is, or to begin to be confident in knowing and doing his will, of living and dying with reliable purpose. The Son always is in union with the Father. When the Holy Spirit unites people with Christ through the new birth, he reunites them with the Father by virtue of that fact. Essentially, they rely on their union with Christ for their relationship with God. This explains " … there is no other Name … by which we must be saved." Only those are reconciled with the Father who are in union with the Christ who always is in perfect union with the Father. Thus, God is restoring his Name as Father.

The Holy Spirit is the Person of the Trinity who through the Word enlightens, convicts, convinces, gives new life in the new birth, and gives the faith that receives the Christ who is "the Life," forming the union as he immerses the person in Christ (Matthew 3:11; Romans 6:3; etc.). "God … made you alive together with him …" (Colossians 2:13). The Holy Spirit thus baptizes him into Christ's body, the Church (1 Corinthians 12:13), for to be joined with Christ is to be joined also with the rest of his body, the Church.

The recipient experiences and demonstrates the union initially as they turn away from their previous god to place their faith in Jesus Christ, receiving him. That faith believes what God has said about himself and about Jesus, trusts who Jesus is and what he did to be sufficient for full reconciliation with God, and forever commits himself to his kingship.

Just as a couple seals their marriage by the giving and receiving of rings, in water baptism the new believer confirms the sincerity of their new faith in Christ by taking his name (Matthew 28:19-20), and is sealed in that faith by the Spirit's indwelling. Paul described the relationship as "baptism into Christ" (Galatians 3:27), expressed bodily by submitting to water baptism (Colossians 2:12).

Peter used another startling expression for this union, one that is pertinent to the new birth. He wrote that God has called us to "his own glory and excellence, by which he has granted to us his precious and very great promises, so that through them you may *become partakers of the divine nature*, having escaped from the corruption that is in the world because of sinful desire" (2 Peter 1:3b–4, ESV, emphasis added). Peter was referring not only to the new birth but to God's work in Christ and in the believer that emancipates sinners from the necessity of succumbing to their sinful desires so they may *participate in the nature of God*! Jesus' death not only justified God's forgiveness of our sinful guilt, but his resurrection gave us power over temptation through the Holy Spirit's indwelling. Peter did not mean that believers *become* gods but that they become *like* God in righteous living. He restores us in his likeness so that we once again reflect part of his holy nature. He gives us Christ-like new values, Christ-like new attitudes, and Christ-like new ethics. Part of Jesus' redeeming work restores our new nature's capacity to obey God freely. This is the "new self" Paul described (Ephesians 4:24). Only God's empowering grace could restore anyone so as to enable them to exhibit some of his characteristic moral holiness.

It is all too easy to maintain the pre-new birth mind-set that considers Jesus to be entirely independent from us but influencing us. Union with Christ contradicts that. After the new birth, in every situation, the believer is living in union with Christ, and he is living in and through us. That was what Paul meant by, "To me, to live is Christ!" (Philippians 1:21)

Another approach to understanding union with Christ sees the two ways in which he is united with his believers:

God united himself with mankind in the incarnation of Christ

First, Jesus Christ—in whom lives all the fullness of God in bodily form (Colossians 2:9)—*in his incarnation joined himself with all humanity.* As the Son of Man, fully human while still fully God, while "laying aside" some of his divine rights (Philippians 2:6–7), on mankind's behalf and in his place fulfilled God's law as well as both God's and man's parts of the ancient covenants. And in that union with mankind, Christ assumed responsibility for the deadly *consequences* of the full depths of our sinful nature and acts, all our inner corruptions that produce our external moral lapses and our failures to live up to the image of God in us. In some mysterious but very real way Jesus Christ took on his innocent shoulders the guilt of humanity's sin. For our sake God "made him who had no sin to be sin for us, so that in him we might become the righteousness of God" (2 Corinthians 5:21). Those consequences of *our* guilt, depravity, and degradation ended in Jesus dying the most ignominious and agonizing death available to a human.

Paul expressed the same reality to the Galatians this way: "Christ redeemed us from the curse of the law by becoming a curse for us—for it is written, 'Cursed is everyone who is hanged on a tree'—so that in Christ Jesus the blessing of Abraham might come to the Gentiles, so that we might receive the promised Spirit through faith" (Galatians 3:13–14 ESV). Just one of the great realities expressed in this sentence is the exchange that Christ accomplished in his spiritual union with us and ours with him: he assumed the curse we deserved while giving us eternal relationship with himself.

Only Christ lived up to God's standards. Only he demonstrated the pure righteousness of which we sinners naturally are destitute. Only Christ incurred no guilt of his own. Christ, and he in us, pleases God *for* us. He kept the law for us and now keeps it through us. He paid the penalty for our law breaking. Only the union with him that God performs confers credit for his righteousness to us. Our deliverance from the domain of darkness and transference into the kingdom of his beloved Son (Colossians 1:13) that are involved hint at God's ancient miraculous and spectacular deliverance of his people from Egyptian slavery. Only God could have done that. Only the God who is the eternal Son of Man could keep the law for all, and then pay man's penalty for failing to keep it.

It is Christ in us
who pleases God for us.

This monumentally important aspect of the union has to do with Jesus uniting himself with us. It is the base that makes possible the second aspect.

God unites people with himself in Jesus Christ through the new birth

The Story's second use of *union* involves how through the new birth God graciously reunites people with himself in Christ.

In that reuniting connection, and in exchange for our guilt, God confers on his adopted child credit for every virtue of Christ and every good thing he did to bring us back to himself. "We implore you on behalf of Christ, be reconciled to God. For our sake he made him to be sin who knew no sin, so that in him we might become the righteousness of God" (2 Corinthians 5:20b–21 ESV).

My hope is in the Lord who gave himself for me,
And paid the price of all my sin at Calvary.
No merit of my own his anger to suppress.
My only hope is found in Jesus' righteousness.
—Norman J. Clayton, 1903–1992

Jesus did and does all this for us by uniting himself with us in incarnation and uniting us with himself by the new birth. In the corruption of spiritual death we have nothing to offer God that can fully please him and fulfill our side of his covenants with humankind.

Only the pure God-man could and would do so. Only our union with him connects us with God. Our only appropriate response is the repenting faith that recognizes and receives Jesus as our substitute and lays down our life in total surrender to him (Ephesians 5:2). The Holy Spirit alone gives us the ability, desire, and faith to do so. Union with God in Christ Jesus is all of God, and thus gives credit and glory only to his Name.

While the Holy Spirit generates the life that restores sinners *to* and *in* the image of God, Jesus Christ *is* himself the living *perfect* image of *God* enfleshed. "He [Christ] is the radiance of the glory of God and the exact imprint of his nature, and he upholds the universe by the word of his power" (Hebrews 1:3 ESV). "[The Son] is the image of the invisible God" (Colossians 1:15 ESV). Those whom God unites with Christ receive *him* in order to be able to reflect that image of God. Jesus also becomes the believer's pattern, example, and model. Paul wrote to the Roman believers, "Clothe yourselves with the Lord Jesus Christ" (Romans 13:14). Our union with Christ gives us a new suit of clothing, *his* righteousness, to replace our grave clothes of rotten self-righteousness. Paul wrote, "… all of us who have been baptized into Christ Jesus were baptized into his death. We were buried therefore with him by baptism into death, in order that, just as Christ was raised from the dead by the glory of the Father, we too might walk in newness of life." Living like Christ lived is implicit in the new birth (Romans 6:3–4 ESV). The way God planned and provided to restore his living image in spiritually dead humankind was to give them life enough to receive Christ, the complete and perfect God, not only as their substitute sufferer for sin but as their indwelling new life, their spring of righteous life. God restores his Name by reuniting spiritually dead people with himself in Christ, thus restoring in man the spiritual life that sees and exalts God. Those who see that restored life exalt God's Name. Jesus says, "Whoever believes in me, as Scripture has said, rivers of living water will flow from within them" (John 7:38).

> Jesus is the name above all names.
> That name sums up all of God
> and all of what it means to be united with God.
> —Philippians 2:9–11

Both Christ's union with man and the Spirit's uniting us with him are involved in God's work to reconcile, reunite, and reconnect man with himself, restoring his image in them.

What union with God in Christ *does*:

Paul described the reborn's reunited relationship with God as the work of God that places the believer in a new position, "in Christ" (Ephesians 1:3). He went on in just that one letter to the Ephesian church to use the concept or the words 105 times. Along with much of the rest of the New Testament, the letter's purpose, theme, and subject is teaching the rebirthed what it means to be *in Christ* and live out that identity.

God unites, connects, and identifies the believer with Christ:

- in his death (Romans 6:1–11), thus providing forgiveness (Colossians 1:14; 2:13), reconciliation with God (John 14:6), and justification (Romans 5:17b, 18b). Jesus' self-sacrifice, his one act of righteousness, resulted in justification to all men.
- in his burial (Romans 6:4), thus ending mankind's bondage to sin;
- in his resurrection (Colossians 3:1), thus granting new spiritual life and eventual resurrection after death;
- in his ascension (Ephesians 2:6), thus assuring them of heaven;

- in his reign (2 Timothy 2:12), thus assuring them eternally satisfying usefulness to the Name;
- in his victory over sin (Galatians 2:19-20; 6:14, Colossians 2:15) and sin's world (Colossians 2:20), thus assuring them current resistance to temptation and future sinlessness;
- in his person (1 Corinthians 1:30), thus providing both credit for his wisdom, righteousness, redemption, and set apartness for God, and the reality of those virtues;
- and in his glory (Romans 8:17; Colossians 2:4), thus assuring the believer's final future glorification.

The glory of God's great Name radiates throughout the world's darkness through the union of the living Christ with his believers, and theirs with him.

Rebirth into union with Christ restores relationship with God

Union describes a relationship of mutual identity, oneness, and harmony. That original relationship of man with God that Adam lost in Eden is what Christ restores in the new birth. By uniting us with himself, the Second Person, Jesus reconciles us rebels with God (2 Corinthians 5:18-20).

Perhaps the most striking and comprehensive single statement of this union is that of Ephesians 1:9-10: God "made known to us the mystery of his will according to his good pleasure, which he purposed in Christ, to be put into effect when the times reach their fulfillment—to bring unity to all things in heaven and on earth under Christ." It is *in Christ* that everything humanity's sin killed, fragmented, and separated from God and from each other is being and will be reunited, reconnected, restored, and reconciled with God and with one another. That *restored* unity and harmony are the result of the union with Christ.

Jesus said more about a believer's union with himself than he said directly about even the new birth that produces it. For examples, see Matthew 10:40; Mark 9:37; John 6:53–57; 15:5–7; and 17:20–23.

> Jesus said more about a believer's union with himself than he said about the new birth that produces it.

While Jesus introduced Nicodemus to the new birth, he amplified to his disciples its effect—this new relationship of union—during his last supper with them in Jerusalem's upper room. Saying to them that soon afterward he would die and rise again, he encouraged them with, "You will realize that I am in my Father, and you are in me, and I am in you" (John 14:19–20).

Union with Christ is a relationship so real and intimate that Paul described it as Christ "living in you" (Romans 8:9–10; 2 Corinthians 6:16; 13:5; Galatians 2:20; Ephesians 2:22; Colossians 1:27). Obviously, this "indwelling" does not mean that the physical Jesus occupies the believer's physical body, but that the Spirit of Jesus lives in vital union with the new spirit of the believer (Romans 8:11). The union is spiritual in nature. It restores to one the heart that sees the supremacy of God's Name in Jesus, and begins to live for its fame.

Another expression of the union of the believer with God in Christ is its primary evidence and effect: the Holy Spirit transforms and infuses the heart with Christ's life. He fills the heart with a new objective, both immediate and eternal, the love for God that both knows him now and wants to know him increasingly forever—for *his* sake. Not just to know *about* him, but to *know him*. Not just as an academic subject about which to teach and preach but to *know God* personally because the newborn loves him. Jesus prayed, "Father, … glorify your Son, that your Son may glorify you. For you granted him authority over all people that he might give eternal life to all those you have given him. Now this is eternal life: that they know you, the only true God, and Jesus Christ, whom you have sent" (John 17:1–3). That "knowing" is by intimate experience.

Paul expressed the depth of such knowing this way: "Whatever were gains to me I now consider loss for the sake of Christ. What is more, I consider everything a loss because of the surpassing worth of knowing Christ Jesus my Lord, for whose sake I have lost all things. I consider them garbage, that I may gain Christ and be found in him, not having a righteousness of my own that comes from the law, but that which is through faith in Christ—the righteousness that comes from God on the basis of faith. I want to know Christ—yes, to know the power of his resurrection and participation in his sufferings, becoming like him in his death, and so, somehow, attaining to the resurrection from the dead" (Philippians 3:7–11).

Such a new heart clearly is the opposite of the old, selfish heart. The old heart determined to disbelieve and disobey God. The new heart—Jesus' heart—loves to please God through submissive obedience to his will. "Father, may your will be done on earth as it is in heaven" (Matthew 6:10). Part of Jesus' meaning was that he would so change hearts through union with his own giving nature and his love for the Father, that as restored people in his kingdom's restored heaven and earth they would find their greatest and endless fulfillment in joining the Son's eternal praise to the Name. There the brilliance of the multiplied goodnesses of Gods' righteousness, and the responding praise of his restored people join those of the angels to so permeate and saturate everything and every heart that no separate temple is either commodious enough or needed in which to worship him. So Jesus' invitation is, "Come into union with Me in whose worship alone is to be found the *abundant* life, the mountain peak shalom of *giving* worship."

The vastness of this requires expansion:

Every person hungers for the righteousness that was lost in Adam's fall. That righteousness is but one element of the image of God lost in the Fall. It includes the element of truly godly love—the capacity to love as God loves. God restores that lost righteousness by uniting the new born with the righteous Christ. Thus, the reborn's love for

God, the love that gives him such pleasure, is the love of Jesus Christ welling up in them. Union with Christ is not a quid pro quo transaction, but the gift that enables Jesus to love and praise the Father through and with his restored brothers and sisters (Hebrews 2:11-13). The normal expression of Christ becomes the love of the one with whom he unites himself.

The love that a half gospel promotes only delights in *being loved*, enjoying the love that God shows toward them. That he does so is its own marvel. But God's love, the love that overflows from Jesus, is love that *gives ... everything*. And it is with the *giving* love, this truly Christlike, God-like love, that he fills the heart and drive of those with whom he unites himself in the new birth. Mary Magdalene expressed the love that grows from the new birth. She bathed Jesus' feet with tears of repentance, and with the costly ointment of gratitude. Jesus declared of her, "Her many sins have been forgiven, for [knowing this] she loved much. But he who has been forgiven little loves little" (Luke 7:47).

This is the love about which Jesus had so much to say, the love that is to be the Church's primary demonstration of godliness, "By this all people will know that you are my disciples, if you have love one to another" (John 13:35 ESV). "We love him because he first loved us." Even a cursory reading of Ephesians 1 and 3:1-13 will bring all this together. Later, in the same letter, Paul prayed, "For this reason I bow my knees before the Father ... that according to the riches of his glory he may grant you to be strengthened with power through his Spirit in your inner being, so that Christ may dwell in your hearts through faith—that you, being rooted and grounded in love, may have strength to comprehend with all the saints what is the breadth and length and height and depth, and to know the love of Christ that surpasses knowledge, that you may be filled with all the fullness of God" (Ephesians 3:14-19 ESV). His urgency about *agape*, the love that gives, expresses the same (1 Corinthians 13).

True nobility, that of a prince, caring enough to give sacrificially, is part of the righteousness that the living Christ shares with the heart of the one united with him.

The effect of such new love for God is to share in Christ's intent to exalt the glory of his Name. Paul's introduction to his letter to the Roman church includes, "Through [Jesus Christ our Lord] we received grace and apostleship to call the Gentiles to the obedience that comes from faith for his name's sake. And you also are among those Gentiles who are called to belong to Jesus Christ" (Romans 1:5–6).

> Christ is the Lord!
> O praise his name forever!

What a relationship this is! The Holy Spirit gives Jesus' followers the same kind of oneness with him that he eternally enjoys with the Father! That oneness includes the Son's faith in the Father, now both attributed to and conveyed to the one born again. We'll develop both aspects of faith a bit later.

And what a Gospel is this! The multi-grain, whole-grain Gospel rises far above the gimmee gospel that offers only a ticket out of hell. The Story's Good News puts the attention back where it was in the beginning, on the Glory of the Name—the Name that created a good earth inhabited by very good creative givers who lived in the productive shalom of peace with each other because they supremely loved the God whose Name is Love. His heaven is for the restored, those with the new nature of Christ, forever fully occupied with the supreme joy of knowing, adoring, praising, thanking, and serving God in all his radiance.

Union with Christ restores God's image in a person by both crediting and conveying Christ's character qualities.

Union with Christ not only *credits* his saving work to the believer (Romans 6:1–11) but *conveys* his living virtues to him (1 Corinthians 1:30; Galatians 4:19; Colossians 2:9;). He both *attributes* and *imparts* his righteousness to the rebirthed. God's reuniting work in Christ makes the reborn person become one with him in both his death for sin and to sin and his resurrection to new life (Romans 6:3–7). God is pleased with Christ for us and in us!

Preaching only a few man-centered benefits of salvation overlooks this essential part of the Story. Those benefits are the K2 and Lhotse surrounding the Everest of restoring the Name. For to restore his name among men and angels, God must restore man to his original goodness, part of God's image, that reflected God's Name.

In the new birth, God counteracts the death of his likeness with which Satan gripped humankind in Adam's fall. The Holy Spirit restores the sin-killed life of the human spirit. Jesus, attributing his authority to the Father, said, "Very truly I tell you, whoever hears my word and believes him who sent me has eternal life and will not be judged, but has crossed over from death to life" (John 5:24). He said to some Pharisees, "I give them [my believers] eternal life, and they shall never perish; no one will snatch them out of my hand" (John 10:28). And on the eve of his betrayal, Jesus thanked the Father that "you have given him [meaning himself, speaking in the third person] authority over all flesh, to give eternal life to all whom you have given him. And this is eternal life, that they know you, the only true God, and Jesus Christ whom you have sent" (John 17:2–3 ESV). Eternal life has as much to do with present life quality, meaning, and energy for true usefulness as it does with future time and timelessness with God.

That new living spirit in Christ is "created after the likeness of God in [the] true righteousness and holiness" with which the reborn are "clothed" (Ephesians 4:24). All of these virtues are the qualities of Christ, the second Adam, that he attributes to them and shares with them. So Christ gets the credit for them. In this second creation God does what spiritually dead people cannot do for themselves: he restores his image in them. Is anything too hard for God? It's all about restoring the Name.

So, for the person reborn into union with Christ, everything is new. Union with Christ restores the Edenic relationship between God and man. That union restores the spiritual life that the first Adam forfeited. And that union restores the believer's likeness to God that Adam's fall ruined. The Holy Spirit does all of this by connecting Christ with the sinful person and the sinner with Christ.

What Adam's fall killed, including his likeness to God, Christ—God's fully alive image in man—restores by his union with us and ours with him. Both the process and the result exalt the Name.

God in Christ took on our nature and by new birth restores to us the likeness of his nature. That new nature is one of knowledge, values, attitudes, motives, desires, will, behavior, works, suffering, and joy.

The restored likeness restores spiritual life, the mind of God, righteousness, true holiness, liberated creativity, love for fulfilling God's mandates, full generosity, and motivating energy to put others first. Although those whom God restores remain human creatures, he gives them incredible rights and powers to join others and Christ in exalting the Name.

More *effects, results, and evidences* of God's granting union with Christ through the new birth

Conversion

In terms of a person's time and experience, the first evidence of the new birth into union with Christ is the conversion we mentioned earlier. Conversion begins in conviction, the sequence of realizations of sinfulness of which the Holy Spirit makes the person conscious. Conviction may be more intense for some who recognize their greater accumulation of guilts, rationalizations, and erroneous judgments of God, the hardness of their rebellion.

Next is meaningful, dawning awareness of who Jesus is and what he has done to make possible reconciliation with God. This light shines on how God has sacrificed himself in Christ's human death to provide the forgiveness that expresses his unconditional love. It involves the change of heart that desires to see and know him as he truly is, to believe the truth about him, to bow to the wonder of his awesome reality, power, goodness, wisdom, and to be willing to receive him in every dimension of his person, as Sacrifice, Lord, Healer, Strength, etc.

Conversion continues with repentance, the act of turning away from all competing spiritual dependencies now recognized to be degraded and degrading fakes (Acts 11:18; Romans 2:4; 2 Timothy 2:25). True union of heart with Christ is exclusive. It renounces all other gods (1 Thessalonians 1:9–10).

Finally, conversion persuades the sinner to believe in Christ, to receive him. The new born, as an empty cup, receives their new precious Treasure, Christ, by believing and relying exclusively on him. They open their whole being to God in a prayer that mixes sorrowing repentance with grateful trust in Jesus' sacrificial death and resurrection (Romans 10:9–10). They cry to God, "Yes! Thank you!" They receive Christ with all that he is and does to bring them back into fellowship with the Father (John 1:12; 3:16). The new birth has planted in their heart the willingness to see, know, please, and serve God's desires.

In conversion,
the newborn opens their whole being to God in a prayer
that mixes sorrowing repentance
with grateful trust in Jesus' sacrificial death and resurrection

---

John 1:12–13 reads, "But to all who did receive him (Jesus), who believed in his name, he gave the right to become children of God, who were born, not of blood nor of the will of man, but of God." If verse 12 is read carelessly in isolation from verse 13, receiving Christ and becoming God's child sound like cause-and-effect in time. That is, the new birth sounds like the *result* and *effect* of believing.

However, notice that a comma, not a period, follows the phrase "the children of God." Verses 12 and 13 are one sentence. In that sequence, the modifying clause that follows the comma—"who were born, not of blood nor of the will of man, but of God"—*explains* the previous fact, rather than being the effect of a cause. A sound paraphrase is: "They who are (re)born by the will of God are the children of God. They receive Christ."

We will deal again with receiving Christ as part of our discussion of the faith factor.

The conversion experience recognizes, confirms, demonstrates, and exercises the new life the Holy Spirit gives. The rebirthed person knows they have been born again because they know that the Holy Spirit has turned their heart *away from* their false objects of spiritual dependency *to* trust only Jesus Christ.

The inward experience of conversion is expressed and demonstrated outwardly in obeying Jesus' command to submit to water baptism (Matthew 28:19). In baptism, the reborn person demonstrates repentance and renunciation of their previous gods by allowing themself to be buried in water as Jesus was buried in the tomb (Romans 6:1–14; Galatians 3:27). By allowing themself to be raised from the water, they demonstrate that they now live by the resurrection life of Christ. They joyfully take Christ's name (Acts 8:16), acknowledging and proclaiming their multi-dimensional oneness or union with Christ, who united himself with us. Submission to baptism is the action that symbolizes, actualizes, and demonstrates the submitting faith, belief that Jesus died and rose in union with us so that in repenting faith we recognize and confirm reunion with God. Therefore, to refuse water baptism raises a major question about the reality of one's profession of new birth and union with Christ. Refusal of public identification with Christ is of the same class of behaviors as a new bride's refusal of her groom's ring and his name.

Princely qualities

Just as a newborn soon becomes aware of those around them, and of themselves, so the newly reborn person becomes aware of their new self and others in a new set of relationships. Just as a newborn first bonds with its mother, the reborn first focuses on the One who spiritually has begotten them, God. Soon they bond with others in the spiritual family, the Church of Jesus Christ, others who also have been born again, the King's children.

The new birth's signs of life include also resemblances to the King that are to be expected of his princes and princesses. This is the restored image that expresses itself in noble living. Jesus described these characteristics in the Beatitudes of Matthew 5. They are: utter humility that mourns sinfulness; total dependence on God for forgiveness; redeemed life and all that it includes; contented and even eager submission to God's sovereign rule, laws, and provision; emotional healing that enables one to share God's love to relieve the distress of others; genuine longing for complete righteousness; purity of heart that equips one to see and treasure God supremely; the sense and ability to join God in restoring harmony among people and the sin-disturbed elements of life; and the supreme love and loyalty to God that enable one to experience joy even in suffering with him.

The fruit of the Spirit

The "fruit of the Spirit" (Galatian 5:22–23) suggests more of what the Holy Spirit restores in the rebirthed character. The fruit includes discernment that recognizes worthy objects of the true love that replaces self-centered lust; joy in those right objects; peaceful, contented patience while God is working out his Story; accurate perception of what others need in kindness, gentleness, and goodness; and understanding of the scope of God's plans that provide faithful, enduring self-control while he does so.

In the effects of the new birth, God displays to all the world how *he* can change rebellious sinners into a new people, those who trust and obey him as their God. They become like Christ in humility, grace, generosity, righteousness, justice, peace, and usefulness.

Knowing God by name

Satan had strategized mankind's fall by blinding the first Adam to the knowledge of God, who is known by his names. The Holy Spirit's second birth through union with the second Adam restores the knowledge of God through restoring understanding and respect for his names, starting with Creator, King, Shepherd who sacrifices himself, and Lamb of God.

Prayer in the Name

The prayer that receives Christ becomes the first in an eternity of communications with God. Hearing him speak through his Word, and responding to him in prayer becomes a constant delight. Reopened friendship—conversation—with God is at the heart of the abundant life Jesus came to restore.

Union with Christ is so real that the Father loves to do what the believer asks "in Jesus' name." The reborn heart sees prayer as Jesus expressed it, as focused on God's Name and kingdom interests. That is, God promised that when the believer's heart is so full of Christ's heart values, when they are in such harmony with Jesus' concerns that the Holy Spirit can lead them to ask for what Jesus wants, he will say *yes* every time. Both the petition and its answer become the means of joining with the Son to exalt the Father. That is what Jesus meant when he promised his disciples, "I will do whatever you ask in my name, so that the Father may be glorified in the Son" (John 14:13). Paraphrase: "I will do whatever you ask in my name that joins the Son to exalt the Father."

> All true prayer begins in heaven
> and results in glory to the Name.

Responsible Sonship

The new birth provides a sense of responsible being, of being a responsible and accountable entity. Both Adam and Eve had denied this element of the image by shifting blame. This restored recognition of responsibility permits a believer to confess sin, to say the same thing about it that God does, agreeing with him as to sin's source, effects, culpability, and consequences (1 John 1:9).

Jesus Christ identified himself with us so that the Father may identify us as one with him. He shares his divine Sonship with us, having adopted us as his spiritual *siblings,* so that God considers us to be his joint heirs (Romans 8:15, 17; Galatians 4:5; Ephesians 1:5; 3:6). Union means that one can know that they matter to the triune God. The reborn heart sees prayer as Jesus expressed it, not only as focused on God's Name and kingdom interests, but also as petition and its answer to be the means of assisting the Son to exalt the Father (John 14:13–14), and that he understands them. We also *know* each other (Matthew 11:27; 7:23; John 17:3; Philippians 3:10; Colossians 1:10; 2 Peter 1:3).

Our first priority is to grasp the fact that God, not man, creates this union. We only *receive* union, by receiving Christ. Faith does not create or initiate either the new birth or union with Christ. Faith says only, "Thank you, God!" Paul wrote to "God's holy people in Colossae, the faithful brothers and sisters in Christ," that he was "giving joyful thanks to the Father, who has qualified you to share in the inheritance of his holy people in the kingdom of light. For he has rescued us from the dominion of darkness and brought us into the kingdom of the Son he loves, in whom we have redemption, the forgiveness of sins" (Colossians 1:2, 12–14).

Before the throne of God above,
I have a strong, a perfect plea:
A great High Priest, Whose name is love,
Who ever lives and pleads for me.

My name is graven on His hands,
My name is written on His heart;
I know that while in heav'n He stands
No tongue can bid me thence depart.

When Satan tempts me to despair,
And tells me of the guilt within, I look
Upward, above, and see Him there,
Who made an end of all my sin.

Because the sinless Savior died,
My sinful soul is counted free;
For God, the Just, is satisfied
To look on Him and pardon me.

Behold Him there! The Risen Lamb!
My perfect, spotless righteousness,
The great unchangeable I AM,
The King of glory and of grace!

One with Himself, I cannot die,
My soul is purchased by His blood;
My life is hid with Christ on high,
With Christ, my Savior, and my God.

—Charitie Lees Bancroft, 1863

Chapter 21

The faith factor, and its Source

The Source of Saving Faith

Saving faith in God, particularly in his goodness and rightness, the faith that Adam denied and that Jesus lived to the full, is Christ's faith attributed to the believer and imparted to them by his union/indwelling, a basic gift and effect of the new birth. Watch how this works out:

The seemingly finest, most nobly moral sinner could never earn acceptability with God, and does not want to, for they are dead. But Jesus, the Second Person, always is acceptable to the Father. When the Holy Spirit joins a sinner to Christ by the new birth, the Father accepts them on the basis of Christ's acceptability. "But when the goodness and loving kindness of God our Savior appeared, he saved us, not because of works done by us in righteousness, but according to his own mercy, by the washing of regeneration and renewal of the Holy Spirit, whom he poured out on us richly through Jesus Christ our Savior, that being justified by his grace we might become heirs according to the hope of eternal life" (Titus 3:4–7 ESV).

Two effects of union with Christ—attribution and experience—have to do not only with forgiveness but also with faith. In justification, God *attributes* both Christ's death and his faith to the believer's account; in regeneration God *imparts* his faith to the believer. The Holy Spirit *implants* Christ's faith in the believer, faith to receive Christ, and faith to believe that both aspects of the union are so. The three Persons get *all* the credit for their joint work in justifying lost man. Only the union with Christ that the Holy Spirit accomplishes reconciles anyone that is restored to God. Not one of the restored will usurp—or want—any of the credit, for they will know that God has done all of it. "*God* saves!" It's all about the Name. Abraham's faith—that was credited to him for righteousness—was no meritorious work of his own, but faith *in God* to do what only he could do. That is not to say that God was not *pleased* with Abraham's faith, but that his faith did not earn merit with God.

Galatians 2:20 is Paul's great declaration of this truth. He mentions two aspects of the union.

The two aspects of union with Christ

The first is "I have been crucified with Christ": *i.e.,* "Through faith I have come into fellowship with Christ's death on the cross, so that what happened to Christ has happened to me also." In this effect of union with Christ's death, Paul found not only forgiveness but also power to combat in himself the corrupt desires, dispositions, and decisions of the old nature that misrepresent God's good Name.

The second is "Christ lives in me." In this effect of union with Christ's resurrection, Paul found power to live and serve: "The life I now live in the body, I live by faith in the Son of God, who loved me and gave himself for me."

Don't miss the clause "*I live by faith in the Son of God.*" Just as it was Paul's union with Christ's death that broke sin's power over him, it was the power of Christ's living faith that energized him to lift up God's name with such powerful motives, desires, dispositions, and decisions as to evangelize much of the Gentile world.

> Living in union with Christ Jesus
> means *living by faith in the Son of God*

Habakkuk predicted this amazing reality (2:4): "The righteous person will live by his faithfulness." Paul quoted this as part of the good news he proclaimed, in affirmation that the believer lives by faith—*his* faith, Jesus' faith (Romans 1:17). Paul's experience is that of every believer.

Dr. John Lange's appropriate paraphrase of Galatians 2:20 is, "The very life that I live is Christ Himself, and therefore Christ and I are in this matter altogether one thing."[7] Dr. Lange went on to quote John Brown: "*Christ's* relations to God are *my* relations. His views are my views; His feeling my feelings."[8]

God the Spirit gives to the believer the great gift of the indwelling Christ, and with him his faith that is able to receive him and live in him and by him. This faith is but one gift of Christ's resurrection life that the Holy Spirit gives to the one he places in Christ, making the believer *in him* "the righteousness of God" (2 Corinthians 5:21).

The believer's faith relies on the power of the indwelling Christ to overcome the temptations and corruptions of our old life and live his believing, healing, productive life in union with our spirit, so as to energize us with the motives and abilities of his vibrant resurrection life.

While a sinner can do nothing to possess this faith except say to God, "Yes" and "Thank you," as they receive it, in so receiving it they become responsible to exercise it, guard it, cultivate it, and grow in it.

> Even the believer's faith in God and his goodness
> is really Jesus' faith
> attributed and imparted to the believer.

The Object of Saving Faith

As we said when previously discussing conversion, faith in God's being, his essential goodness, and his Word, focused on Christ's character, his Word, and his work is the first evidence and demonstration of oneness with him.

Obviously, the person whom the Holy Spirit unites with Jesus Christ has a responsive role to play. After all, God is creating a new *relationship* with the new person. The New Testament writers variously describe that role as "believe on Jesus," "have faith," "receive Jesus," and "believe on his name." (Today's common phrase, "accept Christ," appears nowhere in the Story.) All four phrases speak about the same essential thing, *the faith in God* that Eve and Adam renounced and forfeited in Eden when they chose to trust Satan's word instead of God's. And all four focus that faith on the second Person, the Son of God, the living Word of God, with whom the Holy Spirit—saving faith's *source*—forms the faith union. The last of those terms, "believe on his name," reveals another facet of how saving faith itself is all about the Name.

Connection with Jesus—union with him—is the reason the only true *object* of saving faith is Jesus Christ. Being a child of God depends on being united with Jesus: "to all who did receive him, to those who believed in his name, he gave the right to become children of God" (John 1:12). Only receiving Christ confirms the union with the One whose Name makes all the difference between staying dead and living eternally.

This faith, this "believing in" Jesus, is not your everyday faith in the ability of an elevator to raise you to upper floors, or in the accuracy of the weather forecast. Placing faith in Jesus once and for all is literal abandonment to him, submission to him. That is far more significant than believing that an elevator is safe. Such faith's object is Jesus Christ himself, his saving-restoring acts, and his Word (John 6:69; 11:29; 20:31). He is the One who must be believed. This is "believing in" or "believing on" the Son (John 3:16, 18, 36; 1 John 3:23; 5:10, 13; etc.). He and his work are *trusted* and *fully relied on* as the *only* and *sufficient* means of reconciliation with God. Jesus is both the *provider* of saving faith and the *object* of it. Such trust is the essential element in the *nature* of saving faith. In disbelief of God, Adam and Eve cut themselves off from him; the Spirit's gift of faith reconnects and reunites the new-birthed with God and his life.

Therefore, true faith *thanks* God for what he has done and said in and through Jesus Christ, and for who Jesus is. This faith repents from the ingratitude, the victim spirit that thinks it deserves whatever it wants, the sinful attitude into which Satan tricked Eve in the garden. Paul wrote to Philemon, "… that the participation of your faith may become effectual by the acknowledging of every good thing that is in you in Christ Jesus" (Philemon 1:6).

And such true faith renounces all competing gods, all competing ultimate dependencies, all other ways of life. Particularly, faith renounces Satan and all his lies and ways. Therefore, to refuse to receive life in union with Christ—to refuse to believe on his name—is to confirm oneself in eternal death. Yet, most continue to believe Satan's lie, "Out of so many religious paths that lead to God, pick the one that you like best."

Faith is only as good as its object. No thinking person would rely on magic to make them right with God. No wise person would rely on me to make them right with God. Only One is worthy of such faith. Any so-called "faith" that does not gratefully center and fix solely on Jesus Christ in his pure righteousness and sacrificial work is false and useless. False objects of faith include faith itself, faith in any decision—even a religious decision—, faith in any system of theology, and faith in any church or religious institution. None of those can restore anyone to God. For none of them focuses *outside* the self, on God. Only Jesus can do that. Only union with Christ receives those blessings. It's all about the Name.

Faith's real and only value is its object.

Such faith *in Jesus Christ* pleases God because it is Christ's faith expressed through the believer. Our trusting Jesus gives God pleasure (1 Thessalonians 4:1; Hebrews 11:5). Both the believing itself and the correct object of that faith are important to God.

God wrapped up in Jesus Christ all his blessings for mankind, and therefore in our trusting his name. And all God's curses rest on those who trust and follow any other dependency. Notice the powerful words of the first Psalm (my paraphrase):

"*Blessed* is the one whom God *graces* to avoid walking in the counsel of the wicked, to avoid standing wistfully looking at the way of sinners, and to avoid sitting down at home with scoffers; God blesses them by giving them delight in the law of the LORD, so that day and night he meditates on God's ways.

"He is like a tree planted by streams of water, that yields its fruit in God's time; its leaf does not wither; in all that he does, he prospers.

"The wicked are not so. They are like chaff that the wind blows away.

"Therefore, the wicked will not be able to remain on their feet in the judgment, nor sinners to find a place at home in the congregation of the righteous; for the Lord charts the way of the righteous, but the way of the wicked will perish."

How marvelously *good* God is to grace sinners with such blessings in Christ!

Faith's role and nature: *the new birth and the responsibility to believe*

Further, perhaps the most significant and plainly stated issue is that God holds the individual responsible to confirm reception of the new birth by exercising the faith he has given to them. God warns

THE FAITH FACTOR, AND ITS SOURCE

that the one who refuses to believe on Christ—refuses to receive him—confirms the sentence of condemnation on themselves. "Whoever believes in [Christ Jesus] is not condemned, but whoever does not believe is condemned already, because he has not believed in the name of the only Son of God.... Whoever believes in the Son has eternal life; whoever does not obey the Son shall not see life, but the wrath of God remains on him" (John 3:18, 36 ESV).

The sinner does not cooperate with God in creating new inner life united with Christ, but they are required to lift up empty hands to "receive" it (John 3:16) by "believing on Jesus Christ"—i.e., "believing on his name" (John 1:12; 3:18; 20:3; 1 John 3:23). Earlier we discussed this truth of John 1:12. This is what "having faith" means (Mark 11:22; Acts 20:21; Romans 4:11; Hebrews 10:39). As we said, faith believes and trusts the Story's truth about Jesus, so as to receive him in all that he has done to restore us. All four terms imply beginning to live on the basis of the truth, acting on the fact that God has given new life through union with the crucified and resurrected Christ. Months later, Jesus established two acts by which his believers publicly exhibit, declare, and demonstrate that faith-union: *reception* of water baptism (Matthew 28:19-20) and regular *reception* of the bread and cup with other believers at his table (Luke 22:14-22; 1 Corinthians 11:22-26).

When one, by the convincing work of the Holy Spirit through the Word of God, becomes awed by the graces of God's nature and work—by the awesomeness of his Name—and thus convinced of the sinfulness of how they have been treating him, and realizes that Jesus is all the above, their newly given faith *receives* Christ as their God and Savior.

> The first responsibility of the object of God's saving work is to *receive it* as a gift from God.

John's message from Jesus is this: the new birth is something *God* chooses to do for his own vindication, pleasure, and exaltation. When one *realizes* all this, they show the signs of the new life God already has formed in them. This realization is as much a part of the new life as the breath of life itself. The new birth is not something one dead in sins does or even desires for themselves, so the Story contains no references to anyone desiring the new birth or asking, "God, please give me the new birth. I want to be born again."

Look at it this way. In God's view, faith is not a merit-earning *qualification* for restoration to his graces, something we live up to in order to deserve salvation. Faith is the Holy Spirit's *gift* of the God-ordained *means of receiving* his *gift* of union with Christ who *is* the Savior-Restorer. Faith is the activation code that comes with a new gift card whose logo is "Union with Christ." The card is preloaded with the bottomless value of Jesus Christ's virtues and work, all the worth of his superlative moral character and miracle working power. The card has no expiration date. The recipient has only to sign the card and activate it, thereby receiving its credits as available to *them*. Then each time they swipe or tap the card, they exercise faith that *Jesus'* virtues and powers are operating in their behalf.

Faith is the activation code
that comes with the new gift card
of union with Christ.
Each swipe or tap of the card
is another act of faith.

The gift of union with Christ is received, confirmed, and realized by the gift of faith. That faith is the exercise of receiving Christ as Savior and Lord. It has no merit of its own. Its exercise is to receive Christ and his merit. Christ is the only legitimate object of saving faith. If that faith is the Holy Spirit's gift, it will focus on the right object, Jesus Christ. Which leads us to the facts on which true faith fixes.

Faith and facts

When Jesus spoke of faith, he included spiritual understanding. Understanding information. Facts. Truth. Faith not only believes in Christ, but it grasps the meaning of who he is, what he has done, and what he is doing. This is the *content* of saving faith. Jesus chided the disciples for their lack of faith when they did not understand that in warning them against the "yeast" of the Pharisees he meant their false teaching that permeates and influences all of life (Matthew 16:7–12). Later, Jesus said they could derive true faith from understanding God's ways, will, and means and from agreement with his purposes (Matthew 21:18–22). Still later, he complimented the Roman centurion for his faith that was rooted in his understanding of Jesus' authority (Luke 7:9). Other examples of Jesus' use of "faith" to describe the spiritual understanding that is faith's content—the truth that must be believed—were recorded by Luke (8:48; 9:41). When Jesus said "faith," he included the truth to believe as well as the believing attitude and belief's action, the receiving of Christ. Such faith involves the intellect as well as the heart. The necessary knowledge includes *awareness* of God, of his reality (Hebrews 11:6), his presence, his good intentions (Romans 8:28–30), his gracious purposes, plans, and works, including his becoming man in Christ (John 1:1–14; 12:41, 44–45; 14:6–13), his sacrificial, atoning death on the cross, the vindicating resurrection (Romans 10:9–10), all in the context that God certainly will vindicate and exalt his Name as the righteous Creator and Restorer of a good creation (Revelation chapters 21 and 22).

In that new life, God heals the sinner's blindness. The Spirit gives them the faculty of spiritual sight. With new eyes that use the gift of faith (Matthew 16:16–17; Luke 8:10; 10:22; Acts 11:21; Romans 12:3; 1 Corinthians 2:14; Ephesians 2:8–9; Philippians 1:29; 2 Peter 1:1), they recognize God's radiant goodness in Jesus and his awesome authority as they never before have realized it. Jesus "opened their minds to understand the Scriptures" (Luke 24:45); "The Lord opened her heart to pay attention to what was said by Paul" (Acts 16:14). The new life makes the person acutely aware of having insulted God all their life by distrusting him and resisting his rule. The new birth unlocks them from the dark chains of distrustful, self-centered arrogance, freeing them to believe and receive the humbling truth of God. It changes their attitude toward God from one of rebellious distrust to one of submissive trust. That trust enables the person to confess to God the idolatrous rebellion about which they had been blind. They submit their heart, mind, life, and eternal destiny to Jesus Christ as their King. They humbly recognize the majestic glory and grace represented by the Name. Such faith, seeing the glory of Jesus' perfections and sacrifice, cries out, "I love him!" It *receives* Jesus Christ.

> God's gift of saving faith
> believes the Story's truth about Jesus Christ
> so as to receive him as Savior and Lord.

Most of all, they recognize that Jesus is who he asserted himself to be—not only the pure and perfect God, the Son, but the One who sacrificed himself on Calvary's cross to atone for all men's sins and sinful nature. They realize the meaning of Jesus' Name, *Savior, Restorer*. The faith component of this newborn image of God humbly but gladly and gratefully believes what the Bible says about Jesus, receiving him, welcoming him as Savior and Sovereign King (John 1:12; 3:16, 36; 5:24; Romans 10:9–10). Isn't all this far more than "getting a ticket out of Hell," or forgiveness, important as those are?

But that faith is not complicated. It is very simple. Jesus described such trust as that of "a little child" (Matthew 18:4 with 19:13–14). A small child's trust in their (relatively) good father is unselfish and transparent. The child who is raised by a good, safe, strong, loving father naturally trusts their father. Even worships him.

The essential matter about faith, whether it is the simple faith of the child or the more fully informed and developed faith of the more mature, is that it is fixed on Jesus Christ, trusting *him* to save and restore.

All this is natural to the reborn, the one blessed with new life by the Holy Spirit. Such saving faith is the first sign of new life bestowed in the birth from above.

All this is wrapped up in "receiving" Christ, the only legitimate object of true, saving faith. The Holy Spirit includes in the new birth the gift of spiritual eyes to recognize the truth that is in Christ Jesus and the willingness to trust him. We spoke of the union with Christ by which God attributes all Christ's virtues and saving work to the account of the one united to him. Those virtues include Jesus' implicit and absolute faith in the Father, his belief in him. In the new birth, God credits or attributes to the repenting believer the faith of Jesus. Saving faith receives the gift paid for by Another. By union with Christ, the Spirit also imparts or communicates to the reborn the faith to receive him. Once given that faith, the newborn's role and responsibility is to confirm and seal that faith by exercising and developing it (Romans 1:17; Galatians 3:11; Hebrews 10:38).

Those references say that with his Word the Holy Spirit *creates in the subject* the ability to believe or receive Christ, along with recognition of Jesus Christ and his work as the only worthy object of that faith. That is our reason for saying that the Holy Spirit *gives* saving faith. He is its source, the One who generates it in the new birth. In terms of time and human experience, the Spirit's work is a process, a period of gestation. In terms of his timelessness, the elements of his creative working are simultaneous. The combined work of Jesus Christ and the Holy Spirit bring about the new birth that includes the ability and desire to believe on him.

To describe the faith factor another way, to receive Christ is to acknowledge, own, and enjoy the union with him that the Holy Spirit accomplishes. Such faith lifts a grateful "Thank You!" to God for oneness with him in Christ. It expresses humble gratitude for the honor of knowing him, along with all his goodness, all they are and will become in Christ, all he has done in Christ, and all he is doing in Christ. Faith thanks God for the deeply desired forgiveness that Jesus earned for him. It trusts him to keep his promises to live his life through one.

Thus, when it seems to the one in Christ, wracked with pain, that they can go on living no longer, they will find that he is going on *for* them. When temptation becomes too strong to resist, the one who has received Christ will find him able to say no on their behalf. When the Christian worker finds God's assignment to be too far beyond their wisdom or strength to fulfill, they find Christ's strength to be sufficient. To be united with Christ is to be able to look to him, with all the sincere worship and confidence that are God's gift, and say "*My* Lord and *my* God!"

> And now for me he stands before the Father's throne.
> He shows his wounded hands, and names me as his own.
> His grace has planned it all; 'tis mine but to believe,
> and recognize his work of love, and Christ receive.
> —Norman J. Clayton, 1903–1992

Because the Story uses the marriage union to illustrate the relationship of Christ united to his Church, I like to use that picture to illustrate what it means for a person to receive Christ. At any wedding, the groom first asserts and affirms the sincerity of his lifelong love for, and commitment to, the highest welfare of the woman who stands at his side. Only when she is satisfied that he means what he says, and is capable of fulfilling his vows and taking responsibility for doing so, is it her turn to respond with her similar vow of lifelong and exclusive commitment. In making that marriage vow, she "receives" the man as her husband. She receives his *name* and all that it stands for.

Chapter 22

Union with Christ develops the image

To recap, union with Christ is the essential reconciled relationship with God that he restores in one whom he places "in Christ" (2 Corinthians 5:17; Ephesians 1:1, 3; Philippians 1:1). God restores his image in humankind in and by Jesus Christ. Through the new birth, those who by responding faith are confirmed in union with Christ have the divine image restored in them. It is *because* of union with Christ, and only because of it, that everything else is so for the believer.

The everything else includes God's works of election, predestination, setting apart, calling, reconciliation, justification, forgiveness, regeneration, restoration to his likeness in holiness, righteousness, wisdom, and even glorification, all the faculties lost in Adam's fall. I merely relist these in a sort of *logical* sequence of meanings, not an attempted *time* sequence. For the elements are *timeless* to God, while we time-bound beings struggle to conceive of them in either logical or consecutive arrangements that God has not further defined for us. Those elements are immediately and simultaneously true with respect to a person's union with Christ. The elements are Christs' virtues, received in and with him. It is Christ who is received, and union with him is the gift the Spirit forms. Christ is life, and the fountain of new life. He brings with him *his* forgiving, justifying, sanctifying, image restoring, assuring, glorifying work.

Assurance

How, then, can one know they are united with Christ? How can one be sure they have been born again? What are some *evidences* of one's faith union with Jesus Christ? What are the signs of new life in Christ? They can know by the fact that the central object of their faith is the Story's Jesus Christ. They have recognized Jesus as the Savior-Restorer sent from God, and bowed to him as King. They are trusting only *Jesus Christ* to save them, and he knows that. They know that if Jesus doesn't keep his word to give them what they need to give proper glory to God, no other way exists. They love God in Christ, expressing that love in joyful obedience to his will. Such love is infallible evidence of the new birth. That love obediently trusts in God's ultimate and eternal goodness, justice, and rightness—in his Name.

> It is by his doing that you are in Christ Jesus,
> who has become for us wisdom from God—
> that is, our righteousness,
> holiness and redemption.
> —1 Corinthians 1:30

The new birth anticipates growth

So, in the reborn, the restored image of God is both actual (immediate) and potential (as a seed germinates and as a baby grows). *Now* believers bear God's restored image; *then* we shall bear it completely (1 Corinthians 15:45–49). *Now* we bear it by attribution and in real but growing experience; *then* in completed perfection. Paul acknowledged the gradual development of the restored image in his letters to churches. He wrote to the church in Corinth, "We all, with unveiled face beholding the glory of the Lord, are being transformed into the same image from one degree of glory to another. For this comes from the Lord who is the Spirit" (2 Corinthians 3:18 ESV). And he wrote to the church at Ephesus, Jesus "gave the apostles, the prophets, the evangelists, the shepherds and teachers, to equip the saints for the work of ministry, for building up the body of Christ, until we all attain to the unity of the faith and of the knowledge of the Son of God, to mature manhood, to the measure of the stature of the fullness of Christ" (Ephesians 4:11–13 ESV).

Notice the communal nature of that growth along with other believers. Union with Christ is relational, also uniting each believer with all others in the community of restored and restoring image bearers.

Peter wrote in a similar vein, "So put away all malice and all deceit and hypocrisy and envy and all slander. Like newborn infants, long for the pure spiritual milk, that by it you may grow up into salvation—if indeed you have tasted that the Lord is good" (1 Peter 2:1–3 ESV). In his second letter he added, "His divine power has granted to us all things that pertain to life and godliness, through the knowledge of him who called us to his own glory and excellence, by which he has granted to us his precious and very great promises, so that through them you may become partakers of the divine nature, having escaped from the corruption that is in the world because of sinful desire. For this very reason, make every effort to supplement your faith with virtue, and virtue with knowledge, and knowledge with self-control, and self-control with steadfastness, and steadfastness with godliness, and godliness with brotherly affection, and brotherly affection with love" (2 Peter 1:3–7 ESV).

According to John, that likeness to God, begun in the new birth and growing more complete through the remainder of the believer's life, will show itself mature at Christ's reappearance: "Dear friends, now we are children of God, and what we will be has not yet been made known. But we know that when Christ appears, we shall be like him, for we shall see him as he is" (1 John 3:2). See also Romans 8:28; Philippians 1:6; and 1 Peter 1:22—2:3.

> The restored image of God in Christ,
> begun in the new birth,
> grows for the rest of the believer's life
> until fully mature at Christ's appearance.

But even that maturity is only relative. In addition to these wondrous realities, those in Christ will find the next life to be overflowing with new and endless realizations of God's *infinite* goodness, glory, power, wisdom, grace, etc. How could one who fully reflects God's likeness, so that they are filled with joyful thanksgiving for the privilege of being in his presence for eternity, ever feel bored as they get to know God better and better and better *forever*? No end exists to any of God's glories, let alone to their composite brilliance. The Name is infinite.

Contemplating the scope of what God gives to the one he unites with Christ leaves one speechless! And we have much more to learn and comprehend about it. No wonder Paul describes the Christian life as all new (2 Corinthians 5:17; Colossians 1:13). Every benefit and blessing the believer enjoys has to do with, and is the direct result of, God's uniting them with Christ. The list starts with spiritual life itself (John 14:6; 19:30–31; Romans 8:1). Only life's Creator could restore that long-lost spiritual life, the essence of which is to *know* God (John 17:3). So Jesus gets the credit for all of it. This is the evidence for the assertion "*God* saves." We receive the benefits of God's saving work in Jesus Christ only by our God-given union with him.

Just as the Lake Michigan car ferry purser accepted my check only because I was Marshall Reed's son-in-law, all the above benefits come to the reborn when they confirm new birth by receiving Jesus Christ.

UNION WITH CHRIST DEVELOPS THE IMAGE

Only the sacrifice of Another saves sinners. That other is the Lord, Jesus Christ the Righteous One. I repeat, the marvelous truth is that God credits to those whom the Spirit unites with Christ all of Jesus' virtues, all his righteousness, wisdom, etc., while he takes responsibility for all their guilt and failures.

The expanse and depth of this union with God in Christ leaves room for no other so-called salvation. No room for self-effort or trust in any other source. Since Jesus Christ is both our Creator and our Restorer (Colossians 1:15–23), no reason exists to worship angels—other creatures of his (Colossians 1:16). Nor can special rites, dietary laws, or secret knowledge accomplish our restoration, since Jesus has already accomplished it (Colossians 1:21–23). The one who is united with Jesus has *God*. He has seen God in Christ as God sees them in Christ, knows God in Christ as God knows them in Christ, and trusts and loves God in Christ as God loves them in Christ. Jesus Christ is the only One who can restore peace between an estranged sinner and God. He is history's only mediator between humanity and God (1 Timothy 2:5; Hebrew 12:14). Only the One who is both God and man can bring pure God and dead people together. No wonder Peter exclaimed, "Salvation is found in no one else, for there is no other name under heaven given to mankind by which we must be saved" (Acts 4:12).

"Receiving Christ" is and means this: God is pleased when the helpless sinner confesses, "God, from now on, I am relying on your pleasure in Christ Jesus, in your satisfaction in all that he is and has done, and in the fact that you are putting on my account all that he is and has done. Thank you for uniting me with him."

Only one right answer may be given to the hypothetical question, "Why should I let you into my heaven?" that God might address to one standing at heaven's gate hoping for entrance. The only right answer: "I have no right. Only Jesus has a right to heaven. He shares his right with me."

> Jesus Christ is made to me all I need, all I need.
> He alone is all my plea. He is all I need.
> Wisdom, righteousness, and power,
> Holiness forevermore.
> My redemption true and sure:
> He is all I need.
> —Charles P. Jones (1865–1949)

What union with Christ does not mean

To avoid possible misunderstanding, we mention these limitations, several matters that union with Christ does *not* mean:

Union with Christ does not make a believer God

While the identification of a believer with Christ results in God's attributing (reckoning) certain aspects of the person and work of Christ to them, this does not extend to possession of the non-communicable attributes of the second Person. Neither all mankind as God's image-bearers nor the new person in Christ, shares, for example, Christ's essential timelessness, his absolute self-sufficiency, his omniscience, omnipotence, or omnipresence. Nor is the personal distinction between Christ and the believer erased.

Union is not an ecstatic mystical experience

The Story does not describe union with Christ in mystical terms. Mysticism here means ecstatic religious experiences that are incapable of expression in words, a supposed union that involves continuity of being between man and God. No Scripture validates the idea that in Christ man's spirit fuses with God's in such a way as to make them one personality. The union does not contradict or change God's essential difference from his creature. Instead, this union expresses the result of Christ's work that reconciles the sinner with God, along with the work of the Holy Spirit that through the new birth restores the living image of God. In this connection the virtues of Christ attributed and imparted to the believer by God as consequence of the relationship continue eternally to depend on Christ. The relationship with God involves the believer's use of their normal faculties, energized by the Holy Spirit, to fulfill all the aspects of relationship with God, to worship and serve God both in themself and as reflected in others.

The legal indicators of union with Christ do not require further mystical or physical union. The marriage metaphor—the Church being Christ's Bride—indicates union of the spirits, a union that is not mystical in nature but covenantal. Even our brotherhood with Christ, derived from joint sonship with the Father, is adoptive, and therefore only legal. The metaphorical expressions do not require or suggest mystical connection. No biblically indicated quality or dimension of the united relationship with God goes beyond legal, relational, volitional, spiritual, or emotional qualities or considerations. Since the sinner receives and maintains the relationship by the faith God's Spirit gives, the essential nature of the union also is that of faith; it is a covenant relationship. *Sola Scriptura; sola gratia; sola fide.*

Union is not spiritual evolution

This is a good place to introduce an important implication of Jesus' remark, "That which is born of the flesh is flesh, and that which is born of the spirit is spirit." Edwyn C. Hoskyns writes, "Jesus made crystal clear that 'there is no evolution from flesh into spirit!' The spiritual aspect of the kingdom of God demands that entrance into that kingdom requires a spiritual *birth*. There are two levels of existence; the one is the sphere of [self-centered] flesh, the 'old nature,' and the other of [God-centered] spirit. On each level, like produces like. One can pass from the lower order, the realm of the flesh, into the higher order, the realm of the spirit, only by being born again. Jesus is emphasizing that spirit regeneration is indispensable to our relating to God Who is Spirit (John 4:24)."[9]

It is into the relationship of union with Christ that the Holy Spirit rebirths and immerses one (Acts 8:16; Romans 6:3–4; 1 Corinthians 1:13; 12:13; Galatians 3:27). "Therefore, if anyone is in Christ, the new creation has come" (2 Corinthians 5:17). That comprehensive statement, which includes both union with Christ and new creation, is the "Resume" button that takes us back to the new birth, the event by which the Holy Spirit unites the chosen recipient with Christ.

Therefore, if anyone is in Christ,
the new creation has come.
—2 Corinthians 5:17

By emphasizing to Nicodemus the necessity of the new birth, Jesus made a major point: just as no one but God can create life out of nothing, no spiritually dead person can restore spiritual life to themself or restore in themself the missing elements of God's image. No part of the Story records God requiring any spiritually dead person to perform any act that deserves, earns or purchases the gift of new birth. Instead, Jesus said, "The wind blows where it pleases. You hear its sound, but you cannot tell where it comes from or where it is going. So it is with everyone born of the Spirit" (John 3:8). And in a prayer Jesus said, "No one knows the Son except the Father, and no one knows the Father except the Son and those to whom the Son chooses to reveal him" (Matthew 11:27). It is only God's new creation that gives anyone the spiritual faculty that can hear and respond to his multiple loving invitations to come to him. The sinner's *only* part is to respond by receiving the gift of Jesus Christ by faith. What a gift of grace it is to be united with Christ by the new birth, and to enjoy his indwelling ability to exalt the Name.

UNION WITH CHRIST DEVELOPS THE IMAGE

For centuries, the God who respects the freedom he has given to humans more than we respect God's innate sovereign freedom, had demonstrated and proved the necessity for the new birth as he allowed people their freedom to rebel against himself, to destroy and degrade everything they touched in their chronic misuse of that freedom. God demonstrated his own restoring, self-giving, redeeming heart in the repeated political, economic, and spiritual rescues and revivals he had given his special people, Israel. And in the non-Jews he welcomed from time to time.

> God respects man's freedom
> more than man respects God's freedom

And during all those centuries God demonstrated his patience. "But when the set time had fully come, God sent his Son, born of a woman, born under the law, to redeem those under the law, that we might receive adoption to sonship. Because you are his sons, God sent the Spirit of his Son into our hearts, the Spirit who calls out, '*Abba*, Father'" (Galatians 4:4–6).

Jesus' very assertion that everybody must be born again in order even to have capacity to see God's kingdom also indicates that every natural person has something missing in their personality, something that only the new birth can supply. We know that something to be the qualities of God's image—including spiritual perception—described by his names.

Jesus knew he needed to unmask the religious system of the day, represented in Nicodemus's seeking-God's-favor-by-performance-based legalism. At its heart it was nothing but another symptom of the dead humanistic self-idolatry seeded by God's enemy in Adam. It was the religious nth degree of that which Satan had offered Adam in the garden, the reverse knowledge of good and evil—essential self-centeredness instead of God-centeredness. Its poison had killed man's connecting likeness to God. Jesus knew he had to topple from its iconic pedestal the resulting humanism, represented by its self-exalting expression in Pharisaism. For God, the only thing that will do is a new life core, a new heart, a new creation, a new personality that centers on God and others. Such a life core, being impossible for any human to generate, God himself must create, by new birth—the birth from above.

> Only God can create the new heart
> that is capable of pleasing him.

Jesus was saying to Nicodemus, and through him to all of us, "I did not come to give you a prescription you can take to make yourself well. I have no therapy *you* can follow to restore your relationship with God. You are *dead* to God. Helpless. You can do *nothing* to restore spiritual life, the image of God, or right relationship with God. If you are to be rescued, *God* himself must start over with you, creating in you new spiritual life, a new heart. You must be born again."

He was saying that the kingdom of God—the rule of God, the order of God, embodied in himself—must, and would, consist of a new race of humans fully capable of pleasing God only by being a race united with and indwelt by Jesus Christ himself. His life born in them would restore the image, creating the new man. Later on, by saying, "Without me, you can do nothing," Jesus flatly asserted independent human inability to create such a new person

In their letters to Christian churches, neither Peter, Paul, nor James is reported to have gone back over what Jesus told Nicodemus. In the energy of the Holy Spirit, they taught their reborn readers how to live the new life they had been given. An example is Colossians 2:6–15.

The essential and stupendous message, the Everest among the other majestic peaks of this part of the Story, is that *the God who created mankind in the first place solved the deadly consequences of man's rebellion by uniting sinners with Christ Jesus in a new creation that includes the rebirth of the image of God in man!* He took the initiative. He is responsible for creating a new humanity in Christ. Salvation is of *God*! This is God's way of justifying his original creation of a good humankind. It's all about the Name.

Dying on the cross, the cross we deserved, Jesus did the work that broke Satan's power, freeing his captives to receive him. "Since therefore the children share in flesh and blood, he himself [Jesus] likewise partook of the same things, that through death he might destroy the one who has the power of death, that is, the devil, and deliver all those who through fear of death were subject to lifelong slavery" (Hebrews 2:14-15 ESV). "And you, who were dead in your trespasses and the uncircumcision of your flesh, God made alive together with him, having forgiven us all our trespasses, by canceling the record of debt that stood against us with its legal demands. This he set aside, nailing it to the cross. He disarmed the rulers and authorities and put them to open shame by triumphing over them" (Colossians 2:13-15 ESV). The new birth includes the gift of freedom from Satanic bondage to sin, thus providing the new freedom to repent and receive Christ. With that freedom the Spirit gives the attitude that wants to express itself by receiving Christ and living in him. The center of life in Christ becomes exalting the glory of God. So repenting faith is of no earned merit to the recipient; instead, it is part of the gift of new spiritual life.

Day to Day in Christ

Those loaded down by the challenges and miseries of daily life may ask: Of what practical daily use is this union with God in Christ through the new birth? What does union with Christ mean to those burdened by world, local and personal poverty, crime, marriage conflict and disappointment, rebellious children, opioid misuse, terrorism, the weaknesses of the old nature, disease and loss, or unfulfilled aspirations? What is the relevance of the Name? In light of all the above, I almost blush to ask the question. After beginning to grasp the marvel of union with God in Christ, even phrasing the subject this way seems sacrilegious. But the question has an answer: union with Christ, in whom the whole of God dwells bodily, provides to the reborn his *life* to live as triumphantly as Jesus did with and above all these pressures. "Let us run with perseverance the race marked out for us, fixing our eyes on Jesus, who for the joy set before him endured the cross, scorning its shame" (Hebrews 12:1–2).

Only the new heart's indwelling Christ has power to overcome the characteristics of one's old nature: self-centeredness, lustfulness, faithless disobedience, and covetousness. The new person in Christ demonstrates thankful, grateful contentment, for it finds God in his goodness to be enough. Coming to Christ, the renewed heart finds abundant life abiding in him.

With their newly enlightened mind and spirit, the reborn conducts their life in the light of God's truth that gradually corrects the habitual errors accumulated in their personal, family, and genealogical memory bank. They find Christ able to live up to their lifelong aspirations for missing goodness and wisdom, capacities capable of development and enlargement.

> Only union with Christ makes one capable
> of right aspirations,
> and of reaching them.

Their new heart discerns their stewardship and need to develop those qualities they now realize belong not to themself but are being held in trust for their King—their time, their good proclivities and capabilities, their talents and spiritual gifts, their financial resources, and their accumulated awareness of truth.

To say it in mechanical terms, the new birth installs in the old body a person with an entirely reversed set of values, capacities, and attitudes, one who recognizes God as desirable King and who passionately desires to share the King's desirably good qualities in every way.

That reversal turns the person away from their plunge toward outer darkness back toward the God in whom they find their new life. No wonder Jesus describes them as "born again."

In *The Message*'s paraphrase of Matthew 18:3, note Jesus' use of words similar to what he said to Nicodemus about the nature of the reborn person: "Unless you return to square one and start over like children, you're not even going to get a look at the kingdom, let alone get in."

If this new birth initiates a new *life*, then this life truly is from God. For as we already know, he is the only source of life, the only Creator of human or spirit life of any kind, for he is the only being that exists in the essential sense of non-created life. In his "I am the life," Jesus implied, "I am the living one. I AM." His rebirthing work implants in the old body a new kind of life, one not previously there. As we've said elsewhere, if the old nature is a set of deadly *desires*, then the new nature, this new life, consists of a new set of energizing desires and attitudes, aspirations to give God glory by serving him and others in his name and for his purposes. Such new desires reflect a new awareness of who God really is, and why he is so worthy of our adoring, worshipful service. Only this new heart makes one capable of fulfilling the greatest of all commands: the first one, to love God with the whole being. To make his Name great.

Only a new heart
makes anyone able to keep the greatest of all commands,
to love God

The new heart, then, is truly revolutionary in character. It reverses the whole direction and value system of the individual in whom God plants it. God is not salvaging the old man, but replacing it with a new man. To rescue humanity, he is creating within the corporate body of old mankind a new mankind in Christ—yes, individually, one by one, but ultimately a whole new human race that reflects the Name.

The foregoing extensive discussion about Jesus' conversation with Nicodemus about the new birth, connected as it is with union with Christ, is one of the most significant truths Jesus taught as he corrected the lies in which Satan had bound mankind for so many centuries. That is why we have spent so much time recounting and explaining it.

But Nicodemus did not yet know all this. He was not prepared to grasp it. Jesus' announced the means of restoring man's image of God through the inception and development of the new birth, which seemed to Nicodemus to be a new concept. Yet perhaps it stirred his thoughts of Scriptures he long had held in mystery. The prophets Jeremiah and Ezekiel had predicted that one day God would give Israel a new heart. And the basis and cost for the new birth were prefigured in the Old Testament's sacrificial system, on which Jesus focused Nicodemus's attention with the reminder, "Just as Moses lifted up the snake in the wilderness, so the Son of Man must be lifted up, that everyone who believes may have eternal life in him" (John 3:14–15).

When Jesus told Nicodemus, "You must be born again," he knew that God's name rode on his ability to restore mankind to that original goodness, that pure reflection of his likeness, that Adam and Eve had enjoyed before Satan's seduction. God is restoring his good Name through restoring his Church in the likeness of Christ (Romans 8:28–30; Ephesians 2:10).

The Story does not leave us clueless about how Nicodemus immediately or eventually responded to Jesus' announcement of the new birth. The last word we hear of him, he was helping Joseph of Arimathea remove Jesus' dead body from his cross and burying him in his friend's tomb. Yes, the *Pharisee* had become willing to identify himself publicly with the condemned, despised Jesus in his polluting death.

For those still skeptical about Jesus' claim to the Name and its restoring ability, he had more evidence.

Chapter 23

The King's ultimate credentials

The model prayer and the Name

Before his conversation with Nicodemus, we heard Jesus in his mountaintop sermon describing his true kingdom's characteristics.

In that discourse's directions about prayer, Jesus gave his disciples a model for all their praying. In that model he listed as the first and primary petition his followers are to offer, "Our Father in heaven, hallowed be your name" (Matthew 6:9). Jesus' primary concern was restoring respectful reverence for his Father's name among all people everywhere. Everything he was, said, and did earnestly worked to that great end. It's all about the Name.

From Jesus' viewpoint, every request the model prayer expresses aims toward the restoration of God's name. That includes the petitions about his universal rule and his will. It involved the forgiveness of all that has hindered those objectives and the prevention of all future such hindrances. Even the fourth petition—for God's provision of the disciples' daily needs—is not *selfishly* personal but assumes that since the disciple's very life is devoted to the purposes of fulfilling the other five God-centered petitions, it requires and depends on God's provision in order to do so. Expressed sincerely, every element of the prayer realigns the believer individually and corporately in the work of God that restores his Name.

In another part of the same sermon, Jesus described his loving hopes for his Bride, the Church, as its members live out the new life he described: "You are the light of the world. A town built on a hill cannot be hidden.... Let your light shine before others, that they may see your good deeds and glorify your Father in heaven" (Matthew 5:14–16). His Father's name always was Jesus' top priority.

Jesus' own life restored God's image in mankind. This chapter could include multiple events and encounters in Jesus' earthly life that demonstrated him to be the restored perfect man, the superb man, the one and only man of all time who maintained perfect obedience to the Father and his eternal laws. Other events and words showed how Jesus was restoring mankind in God's image through making atonement and redemption for sinners. Jesus' sayings and conduct consistently fulfilled and vindicated God's law. And as we're about to see, his ultimate triumph consisted in the way he vindicated the goodness of God's name.

Christ's healing touch

In his turning-point dialogue with Jewish leaders recorded in John 5:26, Jesus identified himself as the Source of Life: "For as the Father has life in himself, so he has granted the Son also to have life in himself." This, undergirded by John 3:6–8, is one of the clearest statements in human language that God has used to express the idea of divine triunity, the essence of what we try to express as his one-being-in-three-persons nature. The Father, the Son, and the Holy Spirit share in being the source of all other life. Jesus spoke with the voice of God to restore life to dead limbs, dead bodies (Mark 5:41; Luke 7:14; John 11:43), and dead spirits (John 6:53). This is the work that is the most God-exalting, for he *is* the life that is the source of all other life.

THE KING'S ULTIMATE CREDENTIALS

Jesus shared his life with many sick, disabled, dying, and dead people whom he met. He demonstrated regal lordship over every kind of congenital and acquired disease, even those caused by evil spirits. He healed blindness, paralysis, chronic hemorrhaging, and epilepsy. He raised dead bodies back to life. With just a touch, or only a word, in person and by long-distance, he mastered every arena of human and spiritual degeneration.

Every wonder work, every life-restoring healing, identified Jesus as the Creator, the self-existing I AM, the *good* God. Every miracle exposed pretended good as evil in effect. Every healing overcame the effects of sin with the true good that vindicates and exalts the Name.

Jesus used those credentials to give courage to the man who first introduced him to the world, John the Baptizer. John was in King Herod's prison, expecting nothing but beheading for pointing out Herod's wickedness. He began to have unwelcome and depressing doubts about his degree of usefulness in life. *Did I understand correctly that I was to introduce Messiah to the world? Or was I deceiving myself? Is Jesus really that coming One?*

So he sent a couple of his followers to inquire of Jesus, "Are you the one who is to come? Or should we expect someone else?"

Jesus sent the men back to John with this brief word: "Go back and report to John what you have seen and heard: The blind have sight restored, the lame walk again, those who have leprosy have clean skin restored, the deaf hear again, the paralyzed move freely again, the demonized have their right minds restored, the dead have life restored, and the good news is proclaimed to the poor" (Luke 7:18, 22). Jesus was the Restorer.

Jesus knew that John would understand what he meant. *John, you were right to introduce me as the Lamb of God. You are graced to see the evidences of what God sent you to predict and introduce, the Messiah you expected. The healer. The life-giver. I am he. So don't lose that perspective and heart now that you are suffering what I am now undergoing and soon will suffer to the ultimate degree.*

Jesus combined the highest wisdom with the highest power in his reply: he appealed to his works, by which John could not fail to recognize him as Messiah.

Jesus' reassuring message to John contained also intimation of the Bible's main plot line, the ultimate vindication of God's name. How? The undeniable fact was that Jesus, the God-Man, was publicly and repeatedly demonstrating power over Satan's continuing lie that God was both evil and impotent. Jesus was doing what Satan never could or would do, *restoring the sin-damaged image of God in man.* The Creator of the originally very good image was at work on earth vindicating his good name by *restoring that image through new birth that united people with Christ.*

Especially during the latter months of his work on earth, Jesus made it more and more clear that he would not complete his earthly work during those years. After his death and resurrection, he would go back to heaven for a while. He did not specify the length of time he would remain away. Then he would come again to earth in the kind of royal kingship that would be expected of the Ruler of the universe. In dynamic power and glory he would expose and end all of Satan's lying schemes and restore the righteousness and justice of productive peace.

One of the wonders of that coming personal reign of Christ will be his purifying and healing touch that brings original health and peace back to the ecology. He will remove the enemy, Satan, the author of death, from power. His imprisonment of Satan will free the world from all his deadly influence (see Isaiah 11 and 12; 65:17–25; Hebrews 8:11). One of the last scenes the Bible predicts is that of the restored people of God in his presence, each with the name of their Redeemer, the Lamb, inscribed on their foreheads (Revelation 22:4).

God is as committed to the joy of his Bride as he is to that of his beloved Israel. The mutual joy of God in Christ's Church and of that Church in God are expressed in the Westminster Catechism's answer to the question "What is man's purpose?": "Man's purpose is to glorify God and to enjoy him forever." Our joy in knowing God is the fulfillment of one reason for our creation. We know God by his names.

> "Bless the Lord, O my soul, and all that is within me,
> Bless his holy Name!"
> —Moses, Psalm 103:1

Jesus restored God's Name. Jesus knew and said that *Shepherd* was one of God's names he was restoring to its preeminence. He declared, "I am the good shepherd. The good shepherd lays down his life for the sheep.... I lay down my life for the sheep.... The reason my Father loves me is that I lay down my life—only to take it up again.... I give [my sheep] eternal life, and they shall never perish; no one can snatch them out of my hand. My Father, who has given them to me, is greater than all; no one can snatch them out of my Father's hand. I and the Father are one" (excerpted from John 10:11–30).

Jesus revealed himself as the Lamb of God

Jesus was not only God the Good Shepherd, and Chief Shepherd (1 Peter 5:4), at the same time he was also the Shepherd's Lamb. His official introducer, John the Baptist, had twice used that name: "Look, the Lamb of God, who takes away the sin of the world" (John 1:29, 35). The Lamb was nothing less than the sacrifice that made atonement for all sin (Romans 3:25). Jesus knew that in crucifixion he would give his life blood as the atoning sacrifice for the sins of the whole world (Matthew 26:2; 27:19; Luke 23:14; 1 John 2:2; 4:10).

That sacrifice had to be perfect. Without flaw. The physically flawless lamb represented the undefiled moral perfection of its divine/human counterpart, Jesus. In all his life, no one found a defect. Of any kind. No shortfall of righteousness. He maintained full and complete, joyfully positive influence on all his relationships. He committed no sin of any kind or degree. This was true not only in his every word and conduct but in every thought, imagination, and motive. Jesus resisted every temptation, maintaining the moral purity that was but one expression of his infinite holiness (Matthew 4:1–10; Luke 23:47; 1 Corinthians 5:21; Hebrews 7:26–27; 1 John 3:5). Jesus did not join sinners in sinning but only in experiencing sin's consequences, and that for our sake. As John twice announced, God's perfect Lamb came to take away our sin. He spent 33 years proving his preparation for that sinless role, living up to that name.

Besides giving hints in the form of such metaphors, Jesus plainly and repeatedly predicted not only his approaching death but the means by which he would die, crucifixion (Matthew 12:8; 16:21; 20:17–19; 21:33–39; 26:1–2, 23–24; John 3:14–16), and his death's intended effect, atoning for the sin of the world (Luke 19:10; Ephesians 1:7–14; 1 Peter 3:18).

Jesus' crucifixion had a much higher ultimate purpose than most people normally recognize or teach. Yes, he did die to make atonement for the sins of the world. But he expressed his even higher purpose when some Greeks tried to interview him. He said,

"'The hour has come for the Son of Man to be glorified. Very truly I tell you, unless a kernel of wheat falls to the ground and dies, it remains only a single seed. But if it dies, it produces many seeds.... Now my heart is troubled, and what shall I say? "Father, save me from this hour"? No, it was for this very reason I came to this hour. Father, glorify your name!' Then a voice came from heaven, 'I have glorified it, and will glorify it again.' The crowd that was there and heard it said it had thundered; others said an angel has spoken to him. Jesus said, 'This voice was for your benefit, not mine. Now is the time for judgment on this world; now the prince of this world will be driven out. And I, when I am lifted up from the earth, will draw all people to myself.' He said this to show the kind of death he was going to die" (John 12:23–36).

THE KING'S ULTIMATE CREDENTIALS

> Jesus' ultimate purpose for suffering crucifixion was to exalt the glory of his Father's name!

In his humanity, Jesus found this sacrifice to be no easier than you or I would have found it. On the night of his betrayal, he prayed, "My Father, if it is possible, may this cup be taken from me. Yet not as I will, but as you will" (Matthew 26:39). Jesus was implying, *Father, if there is any other way to restore your name, I will take it.* There was no other way. Everything good about God's name could be contained, expressed, and demonstrated only in self-sacrifice. Jesus was the sacrificial Lamb of God.

Jesus' final report about his highest calling: the glory of the Name

Just before that betrayal and voluntary death, in a lengthy prayer recorded only by John, Jesus more clearly expressed his higher purpose for dying: to glorify his Father's Name. It was near the end of his last supper with his remaining eleven disciples that Jesus "looked toward heaven and prayed: 'Father, … glorify your Son, that your Son may glorify you.… I have brought you glory on earth by finishing the work you gave me to do. And now, Father, glorify me in your presence with the glory I had with you before the world began'" (John 17:1, 4–5).

Portions of that sublime final report include: "I have made [your name] known to them" (v. 26); "protect [your believers] by the power of your name" (v. 11); and "I want those you have given me to be with me where I am, and to see my glory, the glory you have given me because you loved me before the creation of the world" (v. 24). Jesus' entire life on earth was all about the Name, so that God would be known the way he wants to be known.

In every word he said, in every act he chose, and in all he was, while on earth Jesus maintained perfect unity with the Father. Everything he said was in and for the Name of the Father. Every action he took was in the authority of the Father, and for the Father's honor.

Even more remarkable, Jesus promised that his resurrection would follow that death (Matthew 19:28-30; John 10:17-18; see also John 10:10; 11:25-26). Even though Jesus left it to his messengers later to explain the details of how his sacrifice accomplished the restoration of man's broken relationship with God (Paul's Romans, Galatians, etc. and Peter's and John's letters to the churches), he clearly declared the saving, restoring nature of his sacrifice at which he had earlier hinted (John 3:14, 16). And his own resurrection proved that he had accomplished it. For that reason, ever since Jesus left his tomb, his doubters and enemies have been trying to disprove his resurrection. The Holy Spirit anticipated that campaign by repeatedly documenting Jesus' resurrection, so many times and with so many witnesses that this chapter has not enough room to list them all.

In his identification with humanity in Jesus Christ, *God sacrificed himself* in order to restore rebel mankind. Nothing else could more fully vindicate God's goodness and thus restore his Name among people and before angels. In self-sacrifice Jesus opened the way to restore us to God, to give us rebels the heart to repent of our failure to respect the Name. And he set in motion his plan for his ambassadors to restore the Name throughout the earth (Matthew 28:19-20).

Jesus' Kingship recognized

Thus, one day, Jesus asked his disciples, "Who do you say that I am?" That was another way of asking, "What is my name?" I'll paraphrase from Matthew 16:13-20 the rest of that historic conversation.

Peter, in his usual impulsive way, blurted out, "You are the Messiah, the Son of the living God."

We can only try to imagine what Peter's reply must have meant to Jesus. Perhaps, "He got it!"

Jesus replied, "You are blessed, Simon! For you did not learn this

THE KING'S ULTIMATE CREDENTIALS

from other people. But my Father who is in heaven revealed it to you."

Jesus went on, "Now that you know my real Name, I am going to tell you *your* name, who you are. You are Peter, a small, unstable rock. And on *this* rock I am going to build my church, and the gates of Hell shall not prevent me from doing so."

Because Peter always would be an impulsive, easily moveable rock for whom Jesus planned a huge task, many Bible students believe that the rock—"*this* rock"—on which Jesus said he would build his church is himself, the ever-reliable Son of the living God, the second person of the triune Godhead. He is the energy behind the work of every truly successful person.

In other words, Jesus seems to have been saying, "Small rock, I am going to build my victorious Church on the immoveable, irresistible rock of who you just confessed me to be—God. And you, although a small, independently unreliable stone, get to have part in it as you trust me to do through you what only I am capable of doing." It's all about the Name.

The Story's turn. The King suffers instead of the subjects

Every real story has a "turn," the event by which the increasing plot tension is broken and at least hints that the hero will overcome the villain.

In this Story's turn, Jesus the Christ, the second Person of the triune godhead, the Jesus who had proved himself to be the Servant-King over all, offered the summit of that service in his self-sacrifice that atoned for the world's sins and sinfulness. This was service that only God could render. At the same time it was both seeming defeat and actual victory.

All four evangelists recounted details of the next three day's events that exalted the Name. The details that had been predicted by the prophets and that Jesus had repeatedly predicted to the twelve were all fulfilled in detail. Jesus' final Passover supper with his friends, the multi-dimensioned symbol of his impending sacrifice. His farewell teaching, example, and encouragements to them, thinking not of himself but of them. "Don't let your hearts be troubled. Trust me as you trust our Father." His exposure of the betrayer lurking among them. His last hymn with them. His final report prayer to his Father. In Gethsemane, his last excruciating struggle with human resistance to pain, then willing submission to its necessity. All exalting the Name. Judas's betrayal kiss. The arrest. The turned backs of his friends. The illegal nighttime mock hearing before the religious rulers, looking for indictable charges to cover their hatred. The Pharisee's sly suggestion that one person could die to prevent many from suffering Roman reaction to the uproar *they* were causing. The futile procession of paid liars to accuse him. The deceived deceiving. Accusing the pure Name. Representing us. Peter's cowardly denial of ever having known Jesus. The official trial by the religious council. More innocent quotes twisted into incriminations. The trial's predetermined verdict. Pilate's inquiry and its outcome: "Innocent of all charges!" Jesus' mute appearance before the merely curious Herod. The second mock trial before Pilate. The twisted accusation that Jesus had tried to usurp political rule. To foment rebellion and revolution. Pilate's second verdict of innocence, unknowingly exalting the Name. His offer to sacrifice Barabbas instead of Jesus being refused. The last appearance before the helpless Pilate. The sentence of death for which the leaders had been screaming themselves hoarse: "Caesar is our *only* king!" The scourging. Each vicious lash ripping skin from the flesh of Jesus' back and shoulders. And flesh and tendon from the bone. The kind that tore life's last quivers from some of its victims. All of this accepted voluntarily. Representing us. For only others, especially the Name. The mock coronation at the hands of the Roman soldiers. The purple robe thrown roughly around the raw shoulders. The crown—of thorns that spoke of the woe of thorns brought on man and earth by Adam's fall. The cringing Pilate's final cave-in. The final Pharisaic shout, "*Caesar* is our only king!" The procession to Skull Hill. The

THE KING'S ULTIMATE CREDENTIALS

crushing weight of the death instrument's crossbeam. The women's compassion. Jesus' refusal of anesthetic. The agony of being spiked to the wood, quickly passed over by the reporters with the respectful words "They crucified him." All this only for others, for the Name. The sign nailed above his head stating his crime: "King of the Jews." God shrouding the scene in darkness. Jesus' six compassionate remarks, all directed at the comfort, forgiveness, and care of others. All squeezed out between gasps for breath due to the excruciating weight of his body against the spikes. The incalculable weight of the world's cumulative guilt. The insults and blasphemies hurled at him. The sense of abandonment by even the Father. And never a word of self-defense. Of blame. Or of accusation. All exalting the Name. The last word, not of a victim or a loser's tragic defeat, but of the triumphant Winner: "It is finished!" What a Name! Only now could he give up his last breath, commending his spirit to the Father. Jesus had vindicated God's Name. Defeated Satan. The Giver gave all. But not for himself. For others. For God's Name. For us. For all the others in the world.

Then the earthquake. Rock split. Long-sealed graves cracked open as their occupants rose to life. The temple curtain preventing access to the Most Holy Place rent from top to bottom. The centurion's awestruck, "Surely this was the Son of God!" The Name was vindicated.

Then the death-confirming spear thrust. The removal of the corpse from the cross. The partial preparation for burial. The entombment. The huge stone slab rolled into place to secure the tomb. The guard set. The disciples' despair over their sent One, for whom they had waited so long, ... their leader, ... their miracle-worker ... dead! Along with their hope. Their minds asked, *What about the Name?*

They did not understand. Jesus, the Second Person, had sacrificed himself in place of those who deserved such crucifixion. In doing so, he once for all exposed and refuted Satan's self-serving accusation that God is not good. He routed the enemy (Colossians 2:15). Jesus won the crucial battle for the Name. God is *good*!

The final, most convincing evidence of pure goodness

The tomb held him only "three days and three nights." As he had predicted. Sunday broke with another earthquake. A radiant angel rolled back the stone slab, stunning the guards senseless. When Jesus' women friends arrived to complete the burial procedures, they found the body absent. Instead, two men in dazzling clothing. Their words: "Jesus is alive." "As promised." It's all about the Name.

The first to see him was Mary Magdalene. Yes, a woman first! He had banished seven demons from her. Mary and the two women with her notified the male disciples. First his closest friends, Peter and John. They *ran* to the tomb, finding it as the women had said.

In the next five weeks and three days, Jesus personally and repeatedly appeared to the remaining eleven disciples. All of them. Even Thomas, who required seeing him with his own eyes. Repeatedly. Even eating with them. A fish breakfast. He forgave their cowardice. Restored their hope. Received their *worship*. As Lord and God. They knew the Name. He spent several hours the first Sunday taking a walk with two less intimate disciples. Later, his brother James. A crowd of more than five hundred who knew him well enough to vouch that they had seen alive the One they knew had died. Still later, his violent enemy, Saul, whom he renamed Paul.

Jesus' victorious death fulfilled the defeat God had predicted to Satan in Eden: "I will put enmity between you and the woman, and between your offspring and hers; he will crush your head, and you will strike his heel" (Genesis 3:15). By allowing Satan to strike Jesus' heel with human death, God at the same time was crushing his head, as he proved on the next Sunday morning when he left his tomb, alive. Jesus had promised what no other man ever could when he predicted: "I will lay down my life. And I will take it back again." And he did it—what no other man has ever done, or could do. The One in whom unsupported life exists, the I AM, the Creator of all other (dependent) life, gave up life for others, and then reclaimed it. Mystery of

THE KING'S ULTIMATE CREDENTIALS

mysteries. Paradox of paradoxes. But so. True. The rock of our hope.

On the afternoon of Jesus' resurrection, during that walk of several hours, he began to open the eyes and minds of his disciples to understand how *everything* in the Old Testament pointed to his coming to make God visibly known (Luke 24:13–27). It's *all* about the Name.

Paul further described this in Philippians 2:6–11. In the sacrificial condescension and humiliation of his incarnation, Jesus earned the highest name by which God can be known (Philippians 2:9–11). The redeeming work of the Lord Jesus Christ involves the ultimate divine purpose by which he will "bring everything under his control" (Philippians 3:21). Some day, whether willingly or unwillingly; whether out of grateful, awe-filled adoration, or out of guilty fear, all creation will bow the knee to the Lordship of Christ. "Then the end will come, when he hands over the kingdom to God the Father after he has destroyed all dominion, authority and power. For he must reign until he has put all his enemies under his feet" (1 Corinthians 15:24-25). It's all about the Name.

In suffering that death and resurrection, Jesus restored life to humankind. He was fulfilling his repeated promise, "Whoever believes in the Son has eternal life" (John 3:36); "The one who believes in me will live, even though he dies" (John 11:25); "I am … the life" (John 14:6); and "I have come that they may have life, and have it to the full" (John 10:10). This *full* life is that of the resurrected Christ, the restored image of God. It is the *God*-centered life that exalts the Name.

Jesus lived up to that Name. He vindicated that Name. He restored that Name.

This was the combination of events God's prophets had been predicting throughout Israel's history, the events that changed everything, the primary events for which Jesus had come. The Story had turned. Christ, the ideal Man, the perfect image of God, fulfilled God's law of love, goodness, and righteousness. He lived up to the King's name. That act of sacrifice, and that resurrection, forever vindicated and restored God's Name. No richer gift can be imagined than that the universe's Creator, the ultimate King, would sacrifice his own life in order to restore his rebellious creatures to their original image of himself. This gift was ultimate proof of God's pure goodness. In that gift, God once and forever vindicated his good Name. The Lamb would be praised forever.

> The glory of God shone from the cross and the open tomb.

Hanging from the spikes on his cross, the Shepherd King proved the sincerity of his devoted caring for all people by offering himself as their substitute sacrifice, "the Lamb of God come to bear the sin of the world" (John 1:29, 36; 3:16; Philippians 2:5-11; etc.). In submitting to crucifixion in the place of sinful mankind, Jesus gave undeniable proof that God is good, sacrificing himself for the benefit of his creatures. On Mount Calvary, and in Jesus' empty grave, God defeated all his enemies by once for all proving the honor of his Name. Even with both hands nailed to the cross, Jesus had crushed Satan's head beneath his spiked feet. Everything since has been part of the mop-up operation.

Jesus emphasized the terrible consequences that those who reject his good, gracious rule would bring on themselves (Matthew 7:23; 23:13-39; 24:45-51; 25:29-46). Even more, he emphasized the blessings he had in store for those who believed, trusted, and submitted to his good rule (Matthew 5:3-10; John 3:17-21, 36). Israel, nationally, *did* reject Jesus as their king, and in so doing pruned themselves off the tree of God's people. By their own choice they rejected him and forfeited his kingdom's blessings, along with himself. Their hardheartedness did not stop Jesus from establishing his realm in the Gentile world, among those chosen to be children of light, grafted into the people of God in place of Israel, (Matthew 27:24-25; John 19:11-15; Romans 9-11).

When Israel crucified Christ instead of crowning him, they forfeited the honor of their high calling to introduce their King to the world. So God said, "Okay, have it your way for another couple of thousand years. While you pout I'll send other messengers to the Gentiles. I'm pruning you off my vine for a while. I'll get back to you when you have learned the hard way to appreciate the grace of my calling."

The King departed

Jesus had let his disciples know that after his death and resurrection he would return to heaven for a while. Following his appearances to those many witnesses, forty days after his resurrection Jesus said his final goodbye and rose bodily out of sight into heaven (Luke 24:50; Acts 9:1–9). Attending angels urged the awestruck disciples to prepare themselves to receive the promised Holy Spirit. He would empower them to do what Jesus had commissioned and trained them to do (Acts 1:10–11).

During Christ's physical absence from earth, both his Jewish people and the Gentile world are learning the terrifying consequences of having rejected him as their King.

Each time Jesus revealed another of his divine names, someone soon attempted to refute, reject, or oppose it. About these multiplied and overwhelming evidences of his divine kingship, and when even pagan Pilate declared to the chief priests "He is your king!" They replied, "We have no king but Caesar!" (John 19:14–15). Every reader of these words will declare either, "Jesus is *my* King!" or "I have no king but _____!"

Describing these credentials underlying Jesus' title of King does not intend to imply that this was the only name of deity Jesus carried, deserved, validated, or restored. It is only one example of the many names of God that he properly bore, the ways in which he gave evidence that he was Shepherd King God in human flesh. As John wrote to the readers of his account of Jesus' life, "Jesus performed many other signs in the presence of his disciples, which are not recorded in this book. But these are written that you may believe that Jesus is the Messiah, the Son of God, and that by believing you may have life in his name" (John 20:30-31).

Among his objectives, Jesus came to vindicate and fulfill God's law, rescue sinners, restore the lost, redeem the captives, restore justice and righteousness, heal man's broken relationship with his Creator, bring spiritually dead man back to God and his likeness, and defeat Satan and correct his lies. All of it depended on, and contributed to, restoring the Name.

As Luke suggested in his introduction to the book of Acts, that story continues. It continues because Jesus' last words to his disciples were, "As you go into all the world, make *disciples* of all nations, baptizing them into the Name of the Father, the Son, and the Holy Spirit, teaching them to observe everything I have commanded you. And as you do so, you will find me to be with you, even to the ends of the earth" (Matthew 29:19-20, my paraphrase).

Yes, Jesus knew and explained precisely and comprehensively why he had become a man. He was here to begin to restore God's trustworthy Name among men. And he did. It's all about the Name.

Summary: The brilliance of Christ's glorious Name

All the resplendence of God's ruling glory resides in the second Person, Jesus Christ. God's full glory radiated from Jesus' face, his lifestyle, his words, and his work (John 1:1-14; 17:5, 24; 2 Corinthians 4:6; Colossians 2:9; Hebrews 1:3). In fact, Jesus embodied all the "radiance of God's glory" (Hebrews 1:3). In the Son's incarnation, Jesus fulfilled all that God originally intended man to be, a flawless reflection of all the glories of God. Now the Holy Spirit is restoring people in that likeness by uniting them with Jesus, the Christ (Romans 8:28-31; Hebrews 1:3). Jesus came as the last Adam, bearing what the first Adam had forfeited, the image of God. He became the Head of a new

THE KING'S ULTIMATE CREDENTIALS

race of people, those rebirthed with new natures, the restored image of God like that of the Christ with whom the Spirit has united them. Jesus is the Name.

God's glory shines in and through the eternal Son, King Jesus, and his Good News, and therefore through his names. John's Gospel begins with this reference to Jesus: "In him was life, and that life was the light of all mankind" (John 1:4). After Saul, on his way to chain Christians in prison, was literally blinded by a brilliant vision of the Jesus he hated, he wrote, "The god of this age has blinded the minds of unbelievers, so that they cannot see the light of the gospel that displays the glory of Christ, who is the image of God.... For God, who said, 'Let light shine out of darkness,' made his light shine in our hearts to give us the light of the knowledge of God's glory displayed in the face of Christ" (2 Corinthians 4:4–6). The brilliance of Jesus' face broke through the sin-blinded heart of Saul of Tarsus as he rode toward Damascus to harass Christians (Acts 9:3). With every breath of his life from that day on, he worked to exalt that Name.

Revelation 21:23–25 also describes the glory of God in terms of the light that saturates his city.

One paraphrase of the New Testament, *The Message*, sums up this truth in its rendering of John 1:14 and 18: "The Word became flesh and blood, and moved into the neighborhood. We saw the glory with our own eyes, the one-of-a-kind glory, like Father, like Son, generous inside and out, true from start to finish.... No one has ever seen God, not so much as a glimpse. This one-of-a-kind God-Expression, who exists at the very heart of the Father, has made him plain as day."

God, or any of his creatures, may be known by his descriptive names. In incarnation, Jesus revealed God's names as Emmanuel (meaning God with us), King of his kingdom, King of righteousness, King of Glory, enfleshed Truth, Ruler of Nations, and Restorer of life and health. These are but a few. All of the names of God join in Jesus at the Everest of the cross.

Thus, the restored people of God properly sing songs of the Savior's names, such as "We Sing the Boundless Praise," "The Name of Jesus Is So Sweet," "The Precious Name of Jesus," "There's Something about That Name," and "Join All the Glorious Names."

> Join all the glorious names of wisdom, love, and power
> That ever mortals knew, that angels ever bore:
> All are too poor to speak His worth, too poor to set my Savior forth.
>
> Great Prophet of my God, my tongue would bless thy name:
> By Thee the joyful news of our salvation came,
> The joyful new of sins forgiv'n, of hell subdued and peace with heav'n.
>
> Jesus, my great High Priest, offered His blood, and died;
> My guilty conscience seeks no sacrifice beside:
> His pow'rful blood did once atone and now it pleads before the throne.
>
> Thou art my Counselor, my Pattern, and my Guide,
> And thou my Shepherd art; Oh, keep me near Thy side:
> Nor let my feet e'er turn astray to wander in the crooked way.
>
> My Savior and my Lord, My Conquer'r and my King,
> Thy scepter and Thy sword, Thy reigning grace I sing.
> Thine is the pow'r. Behold I sit in willing bonds beneath Thy feet.
>
> —Isaac Watts

Chapter 24

Jesus' ambassadors build the church of his Name

Through his promised Holy Spirit, Jesus began to keep his commitment to build his kingdom. The immediate microcosm and expression of that realm is the Church that Jesus promised to build, and with which he would connect his Name. Luke told the story of that body's founding in the second portion of his Gospel, also known as the Acts of the Apostles. More accurately, the book might be titled the Acts of the Holy Spirit, for as the first part of Luke's Gospel told the story of what "Jesus *began* to do" while he was on earth in the flesh, this second part describes what Jesus *continued* to do through his Holy Spirit, the third Person of the godhead. Jesus sent him to earth to continue his work of restoring God's name by developing the Church, his body and his Bride, the people of his name in the world.

So, after reviewing just enough of the ending of Jesus' story to connect the two accounts, Luke continued God's Story of his name by first describing the descent of the Holy Spirit from heaven to initiate the church (Acts 2). Then he told the stories of a number of believers who were filled with the Holy Spirit for the task of laying the foundation of that Church. He introduced or amplified the spiritual biographies of those who would write letters ("epistles") to the churches that would guide the church of his name through the age, preparing and preserving it for the promised return of the King. Those letters became the bulk of the New Testament. He described the early victories and astounding growth of the Church, along with some of its positive influences on its surrounding societies.

Luke, writing as candidly about the Church as those who penned the Old Testament accounts of Israel, also described some of its early failures to represent God's name well. His history of the Church's first years includes details of events orchestrated by Satan to defeat the Holy Spirit's work.

For example, when a prominent couple in the Jerusalem church attempted to exalt their own name instead of God's by puffing the story of their "sacrificial" gift to help needy fellow members, the Holy Spirit instantly ended their lives (Acts 5:1-11). The Spirit was emphasizing what Jesus repeatedly taught his first disciples, warning that only humility and transparent honesty that sought to exalt only one Name would preserve the fellowship.

Then half-hearted believers began to disrupt the churches by requiring converts to keep the pet Jewish but already obsolete Old Testament ceremonial laws. The Holy Spirit stepped in by stimulating an interchurch council that denounced the legalistic attempt, thereby freeing the Church to spread Christ's Name into Gentile lands and hearts (e.g., acts 15:1-35).

In two dimensions God's messenger, Paul, linked God's name with man's. He scolded disobedient disciples in Rome: "God's name is blasphemed among the Gentiles because of you" (Romans 2:24). In a happier word, he told the Thessalonian believers that the stalwart way in which they were suffering positively affected their Savior's Name among observers. In the context of encouraging them in their suffering (2 Thessalonians 1:5-10), he wrote, "We pray this so that the name of our Lord Jesus may be glorified in you, and you in him, according to the grace of our God and the Lord Jesus Christ" (v. 12). Believers add honor and luster to Christ's name when they suffer well, not with bitter recriminations and violence but with hope and even joy for the honor of suffering for his sake and Name.

Satan has been doing everything he can to denigrate the name of the Church's Founder and Energizer. His divisively deadly efforts have continued through the centuries, and, if anything, with increasing cleverness and harassing hatred as the King's return draws nearer. At times Satan has corrupted the Church's members and leaders to such a degree that it became all but useless, allowing all society to fall into dark times. During the Dark Ages he tricked others into arming even children to conduct literal warfare, creating perhaps history's first child soldiers. He influenced leaders to transform church discipline into corruptions that preserved personal power by killing true reformers, claiming God's authority for doing so. Satan has stimulated hate-filled persecution against followers of Christ in every century, persecution even at the hands of others in the Church itself. One effect Satan did not anticipate has been to create heroic martyrs—men, women, and children who in some cases have calmly, and even joyfully, accepted violent death rather than deny the Name that saved them. Satan has done everything he could to cast doubt on Jesus' promises to preserve the citizens of his realm and to return victoriously as the true Shepherd King of the world.

But "the one who is in you is greater than the one who is in the world" (1 John 4:4). In spite of Satan's divisive work through the church age, the Holy Spirit has strengthened and revived the Church time after time, during wave after wave. We are living in the age that still hears the echoes of one of the most vigorous church-planting efforts world missions has ever seen. Missionaries and nationals are translating the Story into the world's heart tongues. And we are seeing signs of a new wave of evangelism, shallow as it may yet be, growing out of nations that only recently were mission fields. While God is preserving his Church, is that body truly "hallowing" the Name?

Chapter 25

Jesus' Messengers Build on the Name

After Jesus, the Christ, left earth to return to his glory in heaven, the Gospel writers recorded enough of Jesus' miraculous works and profoundly simple teachings that revealed in him all the qualities and characteristics of the invisible Father and the Spirit. As we have seen, Jesus was the living, breathing, eating, drinking Son of God, deity in flesh, the living Word of God (John 1:14, 18; 5:37; 6:46; 1 Timothy 6:16, 17; 1 John 4:12; etc.).

Those writers documented Jesus' assertions of bearing godhood in all its names, and their proofs: "I am …": "the good shepherd" (John 10:11, 14); "the light of the world" (John 8:12); "the bread of life" (John 6:35, 48, 51, 58); "the water of life" (John 4:14; Revelation 21:6); "the Son of Man" (Matthew 16:27; 24:30; Mark 2:28; 14:21); "the Son of God" (Mark 1:1; 5:7 Luke 22:66–71; John 20:31); "the Messiah" (John 4:25–26); "the way, the truth, and the life" (John 14:6); "the king of Israel" (John 1:49; 12:13; 18:36–37); and even "the Father" (John 14: 8–11). Those who had heard Jesus in person recognized that in all these names he claimed to be God (John 8:52–59). To those among them who determined to avoid the truth, those claims were the kind of blasphemy that deserved stoning. But by the time of his resurrection everyone who heard Jesus knew that he claimed to be God.

Those like the apostle Paul, whom God called to explain the mysteries of the Restorer's life and some of those involving his teaching, wrote that Jesus, the second Person of the godhead, as the God-Man, was also the second Adam (Romans 5:12-21). In his own peerless life, and by spiritually rebirthing humans, Jesus was restoring God's Name and image in humankind by establishing a new spiritual family with a new citizenship in the Father's family and kingdom. To these he chose to be his children, God gave new hearts through the birth from above (John 3:3-8). Such hearts were made capable of recognizing the depths of their spiritual helplessness. Such were made able to joyfully receive Jesus into the Lordship of their lives. Such hearts "believed on the name of the Lord" (Acts 2:21; 19:5; Romans 10:13) and were baptized in and into his name (Acts 2:38, 41).

The explanatory biographical accounts of Jesus' life on earth, and the letters of these special messengers, the men sent by Jesus to make known these things, make up most of the pages of the New Testament. Those letters, inspired by the Holy Spirit as they are, keep Jesus' promise to send the third Person of the Trinity to be with the Church forever (John 14:16); to teach his followers all things and remind them of everything he had said to them" (John 14:26); to "prove the world to be in the wrong about sin and righteousness and judgment" (John 16:8); and to guide his people into all truth (John 16:13).

Near the close of his life, Paul gave this witness: "I was shown mercy so that in me, the worst of sinners, Christ Jesus might display his immense patience as an example for those who would believe in him and receive eternal life. Now to the King eternal, immortal, invisible, the only God, be honor and glory for ever and ever. Amen" (1 Timothy 1:16-17).

Another example is the narrative of how God humiliated pagan efforts to imitate his messengers' authentic work of freeing people from demonic possession. At that stage of Paul's evangelistic journeys, God's power showed through his miracles, including the way he relieved many from possession by demons. When seven pagan exorcists tried to copy Paul's ability from God to cast out demons, and ended up instead fleeing naked from the violent fury of the single evil spirit, "the name of the Lord Jesus was held in high honor," and "the word of the Lord spread widely and grew in power" (Acts 19:17, 20). It's all about his name.

The predictions about the King's return have not been fulfilled—yet. Some of the predictions God made to his special people of Israel as subjects and heralds of his kingship have yet to be fulfilled (Romans 9–11).

God made one of those earlier promises during a key crisis in Israel's earlier history. In discipline for their perpetual disobedience, God had released the brutal Babylonian King Nebuchadnezzar to lay siege to Jerusalem, planning to deport most of its surviving populace to his capital. The deportation would last seventy years. Yet God had just told his prophet Jeremiah to buy a particular parcel of Judean land in his hometown of Anathoth, to be secured by deed to his descendants, for, he said, "My people again shall buy houses and fields and vineyards in this land." The city registrar, Baruch, sealed the deed in a nearly indestructible clay jar (Jeremiah 32).

Then Jeremiah prayed, "Lord God, you have made the heavens and the earth by your great power and by your outstretched arm! Nothing is too hard for you.... You have shown signs and wonders in the land of Egypt, and to this day in Israel and among all mankind, and have made a name for yourself, as at this day. You brought your people out of Egypt ... and you gave them this land that you had sworn to their fathers to give them, a land flowing with milk and honey.... But they did not obey your voice or walk in your law.... Therefore you have made all this disaster come upon them.... Yet, you, O Lord God, have said to me, 'Buy the field for money and get witnesses—though the city is given into the hands of the Chaldeans.'" Jeremiah was asking God to explain his reason for this peculiar order in the face of the enemy's pending invasion, occupation, and deportation of the populace to Babylon.

God replied, "[You are right.] I am the LORD, the God of all flesh. Nothing is too hard for me.... Watch me. I will gather my people from all the countries to which I drove them in my anger and my wrath, and in great indignation. I will bring them back to this place, and I will make them dwell in safety. They shall be my people, and I will be their God. I will give them one heart and one way, that they may revere me forever, for their own good and the good of the children after them. I will make with them an everlasting covenant, that I will not turn away from doing good to them. And I will put fear of me in their hearts, that they may not turn from me. I will rejoice in doing them good, and I will plant them in this land in faithfulness, with all my heart and all my soul.... Fields shall be bought in this land ... for I will restore their fortunes, declares the LORD."

God already has kept two stages of that promise. Seventy years later, he returned some of the deportees to Judea, where they settled down and prospered. We may assume that Jeremiah's grandchildren occupied the deeded parcel. However, more than four hundred years later, when the further degraded nation refused to recognize Jesus as their long-awaited Messiah, God let the Roman army destroy Jerusalem again, dispersing the remaining Jews around the world.

And nearly two thousand years later, in 1948, God put it in the hearts of the fledgling United Nations to grant a portion of Palestine back to Israel so they could begin to regather in their land. They are prospering there today. However, God has yet to open their national heart to recognize that he kept his word and sent their promised Messiah to reestablish his Name. But God will restore, revive, and resurrect Israel to fulfill its role among his people in his Story. His name rides on that promise: "I will bring Judah and Israel back from captivity and will rebuild them as they were before. I will cleanse them from all the sin they have committed against me and will forgive all their sins of rebellion against me. Then this city will bring me renown, joy, praise and honor before all nations on earth that hear of all the good things I do for it; and they will be in awe and will tremble at the abundant prosperity and peace I provide for it" (Jeremiah 33:7-9).

In order to teach us just how difficult a thing only God can do, he is letting mankind get ourselves into such an impossible mess that at last we will recognize ourselves to be incapable of getting out of it. After the anti-Christ is exposed as incapable of keeping his demogogical promises to bring universal peace and prosperity, mankind will be at the end of history's rope—realizing our spiritual and moral helplessness, our deadness. Only then will the only *living* God—the One who will have defeated all Israel's enemies while restoring them to their promised land, who has restored child-bearing ability to the barren, who in Jesus has restored his own life—completely restore his rule on earth and in the heavens and consign Satan to his place in the Lake of Fire with all who have allowed themselves to be blinded by his lies. For that God, the only living God, nothing is too hard.

Until that time, in every era of that continuing story, some of Jesus' chosen representatives have accepted their commission to represent the Name and build his Church. But in many instances we are doing only a relatively poor job of building. And all too often of tearing down our own mistakes. Church history includes a litany of theological errors, mistakes, moral failures, poor attitudes, cover-ups, false starts, and diversions of purpose. These failures include inadequate representations of the Gospel, part "gospels," and misleading "gospels," all leading people away from the truth that is in Christ alone. Satan continues attacking relentlessly. The cosmic war that began in Eden rages unabated (see Ephesians 6:12). That battle continues, perhaps even more malevolently. But Jesus Christ will restore, revive, and preserve his betrothed bride, his Church. He promised. His name rides on keeping that promise.

God has not delegated to his creatures the role of telling him when he must keep his promises. Yet all God's promises to his children remain in force. And the fulfillment of his promises to the world remain as certain (see Matthew 24:27-35; 2 Thessalonians 1:8-12). It's all about the name.

Until that moment comes, God constantly continues to demonstrate himself to be worthy of the total trust that produces obedient faith. That is God's message in his *providential care of all people*. For example, "Your Father in heaven ... causes his sun to rise on the evil and the good, and sends rain on the righteous and the unrighteous" (Matthew 5:45).

That also is God's message through the nation he chose to be his special people. Moses' successor, Joshua, had prayed, "Pardon your servant, Lord. What can I say, now that Israel has been routed by its enemies? The Canaanites and the other people of the country will hear about this and they will surround us and wipe out our name from the earth. What then will you do for your own great name?" (Joshua 7:8-9).

God's name is most at stake, because if he is not all that he says he is (eternal, sovereign, good, right, just, full of good will to all, loving, kind, wise, all-powerful, all-knowing, etc.), if he is not everywhere present, Creator of all good, etc., then no human has a god worth trusting, loving, and serving. Mankind's ultimate meaning is wrapped up in his Creator, the God of the Story, all of which is expressed in the glory of his Name. The rightfully sanguine God shares his goodness with his whole universe! It's all about the Name.

The whole New Testament part of the story shouts the glory of the Name. Beginning with the angel's announcement to the confused Joseph that his betrothed virgin Mary's Son was to be named Jesus, the Savior-Restorer, and Emmanuel, God with us (Matthew 1:21, 23) through the rest of the gospels, the history of the early Church, the rest of the New Testament, and up to this day, all has been done to exalt and restore the glory of the Name.

> Therefore God exalted him to the highest place
> and gave him the name that is above every name,
> that at the name of Jesus every knee should bow,
> in heaven and on earth and under the earth,
> and every tongue acknowledge that Jesus Christ is Lord,
> to the glory of God the Father.
> —Philippians 2:9–11

John 1:12 declares that those who believe "in his name" are the children of God. They participate in the restoration of the supremacy of his trustworthy Name.

Matthew recorded in chapter 6 of his Gospel what Jesus proclaimed as the first prayer God loves to hear from anyone. His words in verse 9 may be expanded as, "May your name be hallowed, revered, and respected everywhere by all." That is the work of his Church today—to make his Name known. Only such reverence fulfills the first, greatest law of life: "Love the LORD your God with all your heart and with all your soul and with all your strength" (Deuteronomy 6:5; see also Matthew 22:37).

Stage 5

THE RESTORED NAME EXALTED ETERNALLY

Jesus promised to come back to earth at a future date known only to the Father. First he will call his Bride, the Church, to meet him in the air (1 Thessalonians 4:14–17). Later, in as dramatic a fashion as he left, he will return to Jerusalem to inaugurate his thousand-year personal rule of righteousness and peace (Mark 13:26; 14:62; Romans 8:21; 2 Thessalonians 1:6–10; Revelation 19:11–20:6). Paul refers to "the day he comes to be glorified in his holy people and to be marveled at among all those who have believed" (2 Thessalonians 1:10). God's *primary* purpose for that day is to give believers opportunity to express our adoration of Jesus. That is the first object of his coming—to restore the first right thing, the worship of God in Christ, forever. True faith expects to praise God's Name in Jesus' exaltation. He has predestined us for that joy just as much as he has promised to conform us to the likeness of Christ, the restored image of God (Romans 8:29; Ephesians 1:5–6). It's all about the Name.

Yes, restored, born-again people will enjoy their glory, too, but mainly and first as their restoration enhances Christ's name (2 Thessalonians 1:10; 1 John: 2–3; Jude 24–25).

The resolution of Satan's long conflict with God already is determined. Episodes and events of it have been overt and covert throughout the Story. The Story's final chapters, projected in the New Testament's predictive history, "The Revelation to John"—still to be lived out but perhaps beginning in our time and that of our immediate descendants—foretell the last failed efforts of the enemy to pull down God's name (Revelation 12:1–13:18; with 15:1–18:5; 19:17–20:3; 7–10), as well as God's full restoration of it.

Chapter 12:7–17 describes what will be Satan's last direct attack on God in heaven. That conflict ends with God literally throwing Satan "down to the earth" with all his angels for the final time. In that judgment Satan will forever lose his opportunity to accuse Christian believers directly to God's face. And he finally will lose his freedom to accuse God of anything.

Chapter 13 predicts how Satan's agents—the evil beast, the dragon, and all who bow to him—will blaspheme God's name in their attempt to rule God's world (vv. 2–9 and 11–17).

God will allow and orchestrate one of those closing events, the great tribulation over all the earth. Often predicted throughout the Story, chapter 16 describes this seven-year period as the most unmitigated and relentless terror the earth has ever known. God will use the suffering of those years for several purposes. One will be to remind everyone of the consequences of following Satan, deliberately or blindly. In Revelation 2:10–11 and 3:10–11 God hints at his reason for allowing some of his followers to suffer the horrors of that time. While Satan will use that worst suffering of all history to try to wipe the Jews and the name of Christ from the face of the earth, *God* will use it to demonstrate his faithfulness to those willing to suffer martyrdom for the sake of his Name. These two passages encourage such suffering saints not to lose their hope in God's eventual vindication: "I will ... keep you from the hour of trial that is to come on the whole world to test the inhabitants of the earth."

The tribulation's testing also will give the world one more

opportunity to turn *to* God for the relief from the devil's raging malice that only he can give. Instead, the world will continue to turn *away* from God, blaming him for the evil. Just as the Pharisees of Jesus' days on earth blasphemed the Holy Spirit by giving Satan credit for some of Jesus' miracles, during this coming tribulation hardened sinners will blaspheme God's name by blaming him for Satan's evil. As readers of this book know, nothing will be new about such false blaming. Thus, while in the Garden of Eden Satan began his campaign to ruin God's name, during that coming crisis he will make one more attempt to get people to blame God instead of properly taking responsibility themselves for the historic suffering with which he will besiege the world during the tribulation.

Chapter 17 portrays God permitting Satan and his agents their last gasp on earth, blustering only in futility against the Lamb of God.

Among the tasks Jesus took on when he became human was resolving the Story's primary conflict, that of destroying the power of Satan (Acts 26:18; Romans 16:20). Revelation 19:11—20:3, 7–10 writes Christ's final victories and Satan's permanent obituary. Finally, the King, recognized as eternal Judge, will sentence and banish Satan, open his final court for unbelieving humanity, banish death and Hell along with them to the Lake of Fire, and establish the new heaven and new earth with a new Jerusalem as its capital (Revelation 20:7—21:4). Jesus said, "Truly I tell you, at the renewal of all things, when the Son of Man sits on his glorious throne, you who have followed me will also sit on twelve thrones, judging the twelve tribes of Israel" (Matthew 19:28). These events are just as certain to occur as were Jesus' crucifixion and resurrection (1 Thessalonians 4:14). His Name rides on the fulfillment of these promises.

Clauses from Revelation 19, 21, and 22 portray the part to be played by Christ and his names in those last great confrontations: "I saw heaven standing open and there before me was a white horse, whose rider is called Faithful and True (19:11).... He has a name written on him that no one knows but he himself (19:12).... His name is the Word of God (19:13) ... On his robe and on his thigh he has this name written: KING OF KINGS AND LORD OF LORDS (19:16).... [His servants] will see his face, and his name will be on their foreheads (22:4) ... I am the Alpha and the Omega, the First and the Last, the Beginning and the End (22:13).... I, Jesus, have sent my angel to give you this testimony for the churches. I am the Root and the Offspring of David, and the bright Morning Star" (22:16).

With Satan and his influence forever banished to the escape proof Lake of Fire along with that of the still rebellious evil spirits and human followers, and with redeemed humankind restored to its role as the accurate reflectors of God's glory and multipliers of his Name, all restored creation will unite in harmonious and eternal praise to the glory of the Name (Romans 8:21; Revelation 20–22). In the new heavens and new earth, we will be able to use our joyful freedom without the danger of rebellion. The scars in Jesus' hands, feet, and side will remind us of what that freedom cost him.

The culminating end, the dénouement, of the Bible's main story—the account of Satan's enmity against God, as played out on earth's stage with mankind as the foil, falling to Satan's false accusations against God—closes with God restoring his Name by fully restoring humans to that pure likeness to himself in which he had created them (Hebrews 11:40; 12:2, 22b–23). Christ's personal and eternal reign will restore all things right, forever (Isaiah 32:1). Christ, the incarnate eternal Son, will have finished preparing his Bride, the Church, as part of that restored mankind, the people of God (Ephesians 5:22–32, etc.). In doing so, God will have turned Satan's destructive effort into nothing less than preparation for the absolute purity of the new earth and heavens that never will be denied the joy of knowing the full goodness of God's righteousness!

In a great anthem of praise, heavenly voices, joined by those of the twenty-four elders of Revelation 11, will recognize the delivery of the kingdoms of this world back to Jesus Christ's immediate rule as King of all. That magnificent music will mark the most stupendous inauguration of a new government in history. The centerpiece of the hymn is the glorious Name, that of Jesus Christ, whose reign never will end: "The kingdom of the world has become the kingdom of our Lord and of his Christ, and he will reign for ever and ever.... We give thanks to you, Lord God Almighty, who is and was, because you have taken your great power and have begun to reign...." The Holy Spirit used Zechariah, among others, to predict this event: "The Lord will be king over the whole earth. On that day there will be one Lord, and his name the only name" (Zechariah 14:9).

> My gracious Master and my God,
> assist me to proclaim,
> to spread through all the earth abroad
> the honors of Thy name.
> —Charles Wesley

This is the great "regeneration" or "restoration" about which Jesus and his messengers spoke, when all things are put under his feet (1 Corinthians 15:27). This is the ultimate answer to the prayer Jesus patterned: "May your kingdom come on earth as it is in heaven" (see Matthew 5:10). His Name's restoration is God's reason for restoring humankind and all things under his rule, "in order that in the coming ages he might show the incomparable riches of his grace, expressed in his kindness to us in Christ Jesus" (Ephesians 2:7).

In that restored kingdom, God finally and completely will restore fallen mankind to his original nature and purpose, knowing and loving God as his Supreme Treasure (Philippians 3:8). Restored man's primary and perpetually joyful occupation in heaven will be seeing and praising Christ's glory, lifting up the restored Name (Malachi 5:2b–3; John 17:24).

This was man's chief loss in the fall, the knowing of God by his names, for truly to know him well enough to call him by name is to love him. And to love him is to want to know him better. We know him through his names. Those who really *know* Jesus know *God*. The added marvel is that those who know God in Christ will spend all eternity getting to know the Infinite One, the great I AM, ever more fully. Endlessly. their future is filled with perpetual growth in joyfully knowing God. God will be known and loved for who he is. The ultimate good news is that God *is*, and he is *good*. It's all about the Name.

"Hallelujah! Hallelujah! Hallelujah!
For the Lord God omnipotent reigns!
King of Kings, and Lord of Lords!
And he shall reign forever and ever!
Hallelujah! Hallelujah! Hallelujah!"
—George Frederick Handel, 1741

SECTION 3

EPILOGUE, ACKNOWLEDGMENTS, END NOTES

Epilogue

Ultimately, what is at stake in the war that Satan began before God planted Eden's garden, the war that will last until the final judgment? The struggle is for ownership of God's system and God's glory, both of which are reflected in God's Name.

Even God's forgiving grace flows from this. If in frustration over our Satan-stimulated rebellion, God were to throw away all his creatures along with his creation, wouldn't Satan get the last laugh? If God does not *justly* forgive and restore man along with the rest of his created system, then God shows himself powerless. His promises are worthless. He is a failure. He cannot save anything or anyone. His Name is worthless. God saves people, first, in order to restore his Name.

Love sees the value of the one loved. The man who truly loves a woman not only is drawn to her but wants above all to benefit her interests and her welfare, no matter the cost to himself. He wants his friends to know his beloved, too. He wants to spread her fame, to make her known, to tell her story.

This places in its true perspective the meaning of God's number one command for man: "Love God with everything that you have" (Matthew 22:37–38). What is the highest gift of love one can give to God? That most valuable gift is to make him known, including especially to ones' family and best friends. So they, too, are blessed and benefitted by knowing him.

Jesus loves the Father. Most of all he wants to make God *known*. As he really is. Not as Satan has caricatured him. Not as fallen man has misrepresented him. So, in order to show us God, the second Person—the Son—joined us on earth in the only form we could recognize, a human one. Jesus' good works, his miracles, his timeless teachings, and every bit of his peerlessly sterling character all reveal and represent God in all the glory of his true goodness, rightness, justice, mercy, wisdom, self-control, and power. Jesus was, and is, all about the Name. To Jesus, the Good News is *God*. It's all about God and his good rule (Matthew 4:17; John 17).

On the afternoon of the day when Jesus rose from his grave, he joined two of his friends as they plodded seven miles to Emmaus. However, at first Jesus kept them from recognizing who he was. Jesus occupied the bulk of their several hour conversation with descriptions of the Story's references to himself. "Beginning with Moses and all the Prophets, he interpreted to them in all the Scriptures the things concerning himself" (Luke 24:27). He included the messages some passages only hinted at. He made it clear that the whole Story is about God in Christ. Any part we read confronts us with him.

Thus Paul wanted to *know* him in every dimension. He prayed that his friends would share that knowing (Ephesians 1:15-17). The Holy Spirit led the gospel writers to tell the story of *Jesus*, the real Jesus, and the Good News that Jesus was God *with us*. They wanted their readers to *know* God in Christ Jesus.

My growing awareness of that Story that contains the whole Gospel makes me more fully aware of my role to play in it: loving God by making him known, exalting his name, telling his Story. Hence this book. In the introduction I asserted that, good news as it is, God's great love that keeps sinners out of the Lake of Fire is only part of the Good News. Now we can see that bigger news that prepares them truly to appreciate and enjoy both earth and heaven, to fulfill their noble role here and there. The "kingdom of Heaven" about which Jesus said so much, the same Kingdom of God he commissioned his twelve disciples to preach, is found in the union with God in Christ that so enamors the heart with the wonder of the Name that it never tires of expressing its awe, of giving praise and thanks for the honor knowing him, and thus, of forever giving God the joy his Name deserves through an accurate reflection of his glory in their lives.

My highest good is God: knowing him, loving him *for his benefit and because his highest good desire is to be known, loved, and exalted … by his names.*

The prince of Old Testament prophets, Isaiah, predicting Jesus' incarnate ministry, summed all this up by writing, "How beautiful on the mountains are the feet of him who brings good news, who publishes peace, who brings good news of happiness, who publishes salvation (restoration), who says to Zion, "your God reigns!" (52:7, ESV)

Acknowledgments

No one does anything alone. Especially write a book.

My loyal and much loved wife of 62 years, Maxine Reed, has encouraged me every step of the way for the several years of the book's development. In fact, it was she, who on reading its very earliest draft years ago, said, "Fred, this *has* to be in print." Not only has she stood by my side, she has proof-read the digiscript at least thrice. A number of others endured pre-publication editions. Several friends and relatives, including Jack, Pat, Glen, Ken, Jerry, Randy, and Jared, have advised and encouraged me. My editor, Donna Huisjen, reduced the original digiscript to readable size. Family members contributed ideas and suggestions. Catherine Williams designed and produced the beautiful interior. Our son, Jeff, gave valuable help and designed the cover with the able assistance of Daniel Lane. My friend Joe kindly put me in touch with publishing resources. My sincere thanks to you all.

To the degree that this book properly tells truth, the Holy Spirit has taught, guided, inspired, and moved me. My Savior and his Story have been my energy. Without him, I can do nothing. It's all about the Name.

End notes

1. (p. 18) Cody C. Delistraty, quoted in the November 2014 *Reader's Digest*, p. 12.

2. (p. 37) Glen Davis, *The Daily Special … from the Orange Moon Cafe*, his daily online devotional.

3. (p. 70) Barbara Duguid, in an interview with Marvin Olasky before Patrick Henry College students, quoted in the October 27, 2018 *World Magazine*.

4. (p. 70) Ibid.

5. (p. 118) New Guinea Menya quote from "God Himself Must Fix Us" by Joseph Osborn, *Ethnos 360* magazine, October 2018, published and copyright by Ethnos 360.

6. (p. 227) John Calvin, quoted by Philip Schaff, *History of the Christian Church*, Volume 8, p. 313, AP&A three volume edition.

7. (p. 249) Dr. John Peter Lange, *Commentary on Galatians Through Colossians*, Grand Rapids, Zondervan's.

8. (p. 249) Ibid.

9. (p. 266) Sir Edwyn C. Hoskyns, *The Fourth Gospel*, ed F. N. Davey, London, EGN, Faber and Faber, 1947, quoted by John E. Best, *Exploring the Treasures of Your New Spirit*, 2012, Abundant Living Resources, Garland Texas.

Also available from JohnTenTen Press:

For One Who Seeks After God for the Sake of His Name
A booklet of nineteen prayers of adoration, affirmation, aspiration, appropriation, and action, that respond to God about and with the truths expressed in *Restoring the Glory of the NAME*.

By Fredric A. Carlson

Includes Dr. Victor Matthews' Daily Affirmation of Faith.

Editions are available for Husbands, Wives, and Singles.

$6.00 per copy plus Michigan sales tax and shipping;
$60.00 per dozen plus Michigan sales tax and shipping.

Profits from sales of this booklet are contributed to translating, publishing, and distributing Scriptures and literacy programs among the millions who still wait for God's Word in their heart languages.

Email order to: Orders@JohnTenTenPress.com.
Specify Husbands, Wives, or Singles edition.

www.ingramcontent.com/pod-product-compliance
Lightning Source LLC
Chambersburg PA
CBHW021053080526
44587CB00010B/235